2002 - 2003

The Best of The Amish Cook Volume 3

This was a time of transition for Lovina and family. There was the raw, fresh grief from the death of Lovina's mother, the original Amish Cook, Elizabeth Coblentz. Lovina dealt with the grief gracefully, picking up the pen and continuing the Amish Cook column. There was the estate of Elizabeth to finalize in an auction which took place in the spring of 2003.

The Amish Cook column has been written since 1991, starting with Lovina's mother, Elizabeth Coblentz. To read those columns, pick up The Best of The Amish Cook, Volume 1 and The Best of The Amish Cook, Volume 2!

Meanwhile, enjoy your journey following the first five years of The Amish Cook column as written by Lovina Eicher.

OCTOBER 2002

I am nervous and not sure how to begin this letter. It is very difficult for me to take over this column. I will never be able to write like my dear Mother did, but I will try my best. Mother is resting in peace now, but, oh, how we miss her! Life will never be the same without my parents. In less than two and a half years, we lost them both. I often think of what Mom would always say: "God makes no mistakes."

We must now go on with life and accept the changes that God sends to us. I will always cherish the good memories of my parents. I hope my husband Joe and I can raise our children the way they raised us. My sisters Verena and Susan came home with us the day after Mom's funeral and spent one and a half weeks here. It was nice to be together during this sad time. The home place seems so lonely now.

Church services were held here last Sunday, and we'll have them here again next time, the week after next. Mom was greatly missed at services Sunday. Mom always made the coffee for us girls whenever we had church at our houses.

I am 31 years old and am the sixth of eight children. Joe and I were married on July 15, 1993, and we have six children. Elizabeth is 8 and in second grade. Susan is 6 and in kindergarten. Verena is 4 and my little babysitter when the other two are in school. Benjamin is 3 years old, Loretta is 2, and baby Joseph was born this past summer. Benjamin and Loretta keep me on the go. They are so full of energy, but I am so thankful they are healthy.

My husband Joe has worked at a furniture factory in town for six years. I keep very busy just tending to the little ones and trying to keep up with the cleaning, cooking, ironing, laundry and all that goes with raising a family. There is a lot of work, but I wouldn't want it any other way.

My sister Liz and her husband Levi have church services at their house this Sunday. My sisters Verena, Susan, and Emma and I, and all of our children, spent the day there helping prepare. A huge laundry was done (including her curtains). Windows were cleaned and pumpkins were canned, which she had raised in her garden.
It was comforting to all to be together and talk about the many good memories we have of our parents. That's all we have left now.

OCTOBER 2002

Monday has arrived and the morning rush is over. My husband Joe went to work and my daughter Susan went off to school. She is in kindergarten this year. My daughter Elizabeth is home with the flu. Mornings sure have turned cooler. Wonder if we'll have a frost soon? We still have tomatoes, hot peppers, cabbage, and carrots out in the garden.

My sisters Susan and Verena spent the night here. They left awhile ago to go get our horse re-shod. Mom's horse is still recovering from West Nile virus. He's over 20 years old so I am surprised he has pulled through so far. Verena and Susan will use one of our horses or Jacob and Emma's horses for now.

Water is heating on the stove to do the laundry now. Laundry can really add up with six children. Verena and Susan will go past their home and bring their laundry here so we can just do everything together. Church services will be here again on Sunday so this will be a busy week.

This is now Tuesday evening and everyone has retired for the night. I just finished feeding baby Joseph. Hopefully he will sleep the whole night. Today has been another busy day. My sister, Emma, and her children, came to help with chores today and Verena and Susan were here today, also. Emma gave all three kerosene stoves a good, thorough cleaning. The pipelines could really get clogged up if they weren't cleaned out. I usually do mine twice a year. We washed out all the kerosene lights and put in fresh kerosene. We also did some housecleaning for church services to be held here this Sunday.

Mom usually cleaned my stoves and kerosene lights. These are jobs that take a lot of time. It has been three long weeks since dear mother passed away. We sure do miss her! Life just isn't the same. But let us remember the words she often said: "God makes no mistakes."

We are using our wood-stove these last few chilly mornings. Makes the house more comfortable. Thank you, readers, for all the encouraging cards that have been sent to the family.

Editor's Note: Lovina is still compiling and reviewing recipes, both her own collection and her mother's in preparation for sharing them in the column. Lovina will begin sharing her own recipes next week. Following is a family favorite spinach recipe, first shared in one of her mother's columns from 1994.

SWISS SPINACH BAKE
1 15.5 ounce can spinach (or equivalent of fresh, garden spinach)
4 beaten eggs
1 cup milk
1 cup shredded Swiss cheese
1 cup cubed bread
1/2 cup sliced green onions
1/4 cup grated Parmesan cheese

YIELD : 4 servings
PREP TIME : 15 minutes
BAKING : 30 minutes

Drain spinach and squeeze out excess liquid (substitute frozen chopped spinach, thawed , if desired). If using fresh spinach, wash thoroughly and tear leaves into bite-size pieces. Wilt spinach in a covered pan (adding no extra water). Combine the spinach with the beaten eggs, milk, cheese, bread crumbs, onions, and Parmesan cheese. Turn mixture into a greased 1 quart baking dish. Cover and bake at 375 degrees for 25 to 30 minutes or until done.

OCTOBER 2002

This was another cool autumn day. My sisters Verena and Susan are here today. We did a big laundry yesterday. It really dried nice outside on the line, although it was chilly work hanging it outside.

Church services were held here yesterday. There is an attached garage-type building next to our house where we hold services. We usually park our buggy in the garage. Having the services makes it easier to not have to move any furniture in the house. We can just set up our church benches in the garage. It was a chilly morning so we had to use a kerosene heater.

Lunch was served in the garage after church. Lunch consisted of bread, ham, cheese, pickles, red beets, tomatoes, hot peppers, peanut butter, hot pepper butter, rhubarb jam and butter. Coffee was also served and went very good on a cool day. We also served an evening supper for anyone that wanted to come back later in the day. Our menu was mashed potatoes, gravy, ham, green beans, cole slaw, cheese, tomatoes and hot peppers. Also, we had desserts called "strawberry delight" and "cherry delight." Cherry pie, cake, watermelon and Jello were served. We had plenty for everyone.

The floors were cleaned today and a lot of dishes were washed. We had a killing frost this morning so our garden is history for 2002. Before the frost, we dug up the carrots. My carrots did really good this year. Have some pretty good-sized ones. We also picked the hot peppers, tomatoes, and cabbage. Looks like I have another job waiting for me now: hot peppers to put into jars. I would also like to make green tomato pickles with my green tomatoes.
My oldest girls - Elizabeth and Susan - only had a half day of school today. They were glad to be home earlier. They can really help keep my younger ones contented and rock baby Joseph for me.

Our English walnuts are ready to be picked. They children enjoy cracking them open and eating them. We have two big trees in our backyard. They make such nice shade in the summer. Mom used to sit under these trees and crack open the nuts while the children brought them to her. Oh, what good memories we have of her. She was a very good mother! Not a day goes by that the children aren't asking about Grandma. She has her wish to be back with Dad. October 17th, 45 years ago, they were united in marriage.

You readers try this recipe for "strawberry delight", one of the desserts we served at our after-church meal.

STRAWBERRY DELIGHT
Crust:
1 1/ 2 cup crushed graham crackers (about 20 squares)

3 tablespoons sugar
5 tablespoons melted butter

Filling:
1 package (8 oz) cream cheese, softened
2 Tablespoons milk
2 Tablespoons sugar
1 tub (8 oz) non-dairy whipped topping
Glaze:
1 cup sugar
1/4 cup cornstarch

1 quart frozen or fresh strawberries, thawed and mostly drained. Mix crust ingredients in bowl; pat into 8" or 9" round pie pan or square baking dish. For filling, mix cream cheese, milk and sugar in bowl with wire whisk until smooth. Add whipped topping. Spread on crust. Chill. Meanwhile, stir together glaze topping ingredients in saucepan. Bring to a boil, stirring constantly until thickened. Remove from heat and let cool. Spread over filling when cool. Refrigerate until ready to serve.

OCTOBER 2002

This is Monday evening, and everyone is ready for bed. It has been a busy weekend. Saturday, my sisters Verena and Susan, and I, helped my sister Emma and her husband Jacob butcher chickens. And today, Verena, Susan, and I helped Emma process 24 quarts of chicken. We fried the chicken gizzards for lunch. Susan went out and was cleaning Emma's garden up, so it'll be ready to plow. Emma's garden really produced lots this year, even though it was so dry. We also did Emma's laundry. After washing all the dishes, we were all ready to call it a day.

This weekend was the second time for butchering chickens during the past month. On Labor Day we butchered 10 chickens and four roosters here. Mom had been here to show us how to clean and butcher them. I am glad she could show us yet. Mom had come the next day and helped me process 21 quarts of chicken. Joe grilled the four young roosters that evening. Our daughter, Elizabeth, brought home some little chickens from school last spring. Those four roosters were among them. She had fun feeding and watering them and watching them grow.

I remember when I was younger that Dad and Mom butchered chickens. I was the third youngest of us children and too young to help. I was always amazed at how the chickens could still jump around after their heads had been chopped off. We have 12 chickens left, and the children enjoy gathering the eggs. Joe and the children love homemade chicken noodle soup. The homegrown chickens make the best broth.

Sunday, at 5 a.m., it was quite a crowd that left for Michigan to visit my husband's father: myself, my husband Joe, and all of our children, plus Jacob, Emma and their children. It took us 3 1/2 hours to make the trip as we stopped and ate breakfast halfway up there. The children were excited to eat in a restaurant. (Editor's Note: The Amish are permitted to ride in automobiles driven by a non-Amish person for long trips; they don't own automobiles, however.) Joe's dad was very glad to see us. He had his 64th birthday on October 9th, so our children had all made cards for him. He is the only grandparent they have left. Joe's mom died 7 1/2 years ago at age 54. Our oldest child, Elizabeth, was only 10 months old.

Fish was on the menu for lunch as Joe's Dad has been fishing the day before. Later, we had snacks and visited Joe's sister, Carol and family, before heading back home. Joe's sister is building a new house. Looks like a lot of work, but will be nice when it's all done. Joe has three brothers and eight sisters. Six of his sisters and one brother live in Michigan, so we got to visit with most of them. The children were all asleep when we got home. It was a long day, but we all enjoyed it. Mother's presence was greatly missed. I think it did us all some good to leave and get away from everything for a day.

Brother Albert's are preparing for church services. They will be held at his place on Sunday. The leaves are now changing colors. Everywhere you look there are signs of autumn. The corn is being picked in the neighbor's field besides us. Our three tons of hard coal will come tomorrow. Before we know it, winter will be upon us. We won't burn coal until it gets colder, as our house gets too warm. We are burning wood now, and it feels good to have heat in the house.

NOVEMBER 2002

Some people may wonder what a typical day is like around here. Following is diary of this past Monday:

4:30 a.m. My husband Joe starts the woodstove and goes to do the chores. Mornings sure are chilly now. Feels good after it starts warming up in the house. I pack Joe's lunch and get him something for breakfast.

5:15 a.m. Joe is ready for work and is eating his breakfast.

5:30 a.m. Joe leaves for work, and I get daughters Elizabeth and Susan's clothes ready for school.

6 a.m. My sisters Verena and Susan are putting water on the stove to heat, to do a week's worth of laundry. They came home with us last night from our brother Albert's. Albert's had church services there yesterday. My family and some cousins were there for supper. Our dear mother was greatly missed!

6:30 a.m. Breakfast is ready. On the menu: Egg Dutch (omelette), bacon, cheese, homemade bread, and juice. All the children are awake now except baby Joseph. He usually wakes up to eat around 4 a.m. and goes back to sleep. He is three months old now and really starting to make sounds.

7 a.m. My daughters Elizabeth and Susan leave for school. My sisters Verena and Susan wash the dishes and sweep the floors, while I sort out the clothes and carry the water to wash.

9:30 a.m. Sister Susan has the wash lines all filled. We'll have to wait to hang out the rest until some of the clothes are dry. I usually wash twice a week and didn't get it done twice last week. Now, today, we have an extra huge wash. Meanwhile, Verena is mixing up a batch of chocolate chip cookies. Yum! My four-year-old daughter Verena is trying to help her. While they were baking the cookies, I rocked three-year-old Benjamin and two-year-old Loretta to sleep. Now they are both taking a nap.

11:30 a.m. Lunch is ready. We have a quick lunch of sandwiches. Sister Verena baked over 80 cookies, and they are delicious! I am sure they won't last too long around here. Benjamin and Loretta are refreshed after their naps.

1 p.m. Dishes are washed and put away. Sister Susan is picking marigolds for seed for next year. She's also putting all the weeds on a pile to burn, so the garden will be ready to plow. My sister Verena is mopping all the floors. My daughter Verena is taking a nap, and Benjamin and Loretta are playing outside. Such a nice day to be outdoors. We won't have many days like this left. I get in the clothes that are dry and hang out the rest. My sister Susan comes to help me before heading back out into the garden.

2:30 p.m. Sister Verena and I fold the clothes. There are so many little pieces to fold with six small children in this household. So many little socks to sort. Most of the laundry is dry. It really dried fast with the wind. It feels good to have everything clean again.

3:30 p.m. Girls are home from school and are sampling Verena's chocolate chip cookies.

5 p.m. My husband Joe is home from work. They are working 10 hours a day and also Saturdays during the forenoon sometimes.

5:30 p.m. Sisters Verena and Susan go home to get some clothes. I prepare a quick supper.

8 p.m. Dishes are washed. Everyone is tired and ready for bed. It has been another busy day.
Thanks again to all you readers for your kind words and encouraging cards. Here is Verena's chocolate chip cookie recipe:

VERENA'S CHOCOLATE CHIP COOKIES
4 1/2 cups flour
2 teaspoons soda
2 teaspoons salt
2 cups shortening
1 1/2 cups sugar
1 1/2 cups brown sugar
1 teaspoon water
2 teaspoons vanilla
4 eggs
12 ounces of chocolate chips
1 1/2 cup oatmeal

Preheat oven to 375. Sift flour, soda, and salt and set aside. In a separate bowl, stir shortening, sugars, water, and vanilla. Mix well. Beat in eggs and add set aside flour mixture. Then stir in chocolate chips and oatmeal. Drop by 1/2 teaspoon onto cookie sheet. Bake at 375 for 10to 12 minutes. Makes about 80 cookies.

NOVEMBER 2002

This is Sunday evening here at the Eichers. It's bedtime for the children. Morning comes too fast for the school-aged girls. They have completed their first semester of school. Time goes too fast.

We had an enjoyable evening. My husband Joe and I sang songs with the children. They enjoy that so much. Elizabeth, 8, and Susan, 6, do a very good job of singing. Three-year-old Benjamin even tries to yodel. It is so cute. Sweet, innocent children - what will they have to face while growing up in this troubled world? Prayers are badly needed for children around the world.

We had an enjoyable day today. Joe and I took the children driving around sight-seeing. We drove south from here around 8 miles. It brought back memories when we went past the farm where my Uncle Chris and Aunt Lizzie used to live on when I was growing up. So many changes. We started out around 9 a.m. and arrived back home at 3 p.m. We stopped in at a few places to give our horse a rest and so we could also warm up. We have to get used to driving in the cold again. Our buggies are open, with no roof. But we use an umbrella that holds off a lot of the cold wind. It was pretty chilly when we started out, but the sun came out and made it warmer.

We ended up eating lunch at my sister Emma's and Jacob's. They were surprised to see us drive in. Our horse "Diamond" was glad when we were home again. He is 8 1/2 years old. We raised him up from a colt. He is a good and safe family horse. We had him vaccinated for the West Nile virus. Sure would hate to lose him. A lot of horses died around here this summer from the virus. Mom's horse had the virus but pulled through OK. He's over 20 years old, so we were surprised he did. My sister, Liz, and her husband Levi lost their good horse from it. It was a safe horse that Liz could really drive, so they felt the loss.

The girls played with their dolls this afternoon when we got back, and Benjamin played with his toy horses. His little horses were always breaking through the fence. It's cute to listen to the children while they play. Such big imaginations.

The trees are showing their autumn splendors. We saw a lot of nice scenery today while driving around. God's wondrous work. The squirrels are busy gathering their nuts for the long winter ahead. We have a lot of trees around here, so there are a lot of leaves that have to be raked up. The girls enjoy doing it, and they also enjoy covering each other up with the leaves.   Joe started coal in the stove yesterday. Coal burns all night and makes a more even heat in the house. It's nice to wake up in the mornings and not have to start up the stove and have a cold house.

So it's been a long, enjoyable day. Joe has tucked all the children in their beds, and baby Joseph is almost asleep. It will feel good to retire for the day. Years fly by so fast, and it's nice to enjoy the children. Before we know it, they will all be grown up.

Sister Emma made these "no bake peanut butter cups" for her husband Jacob to treat the guys at work for his 30th birthday Nov. 1. Jacob works at the furniture factory with my husband Joe. These are delicious.

NO-BAKE PEANUT BUTTER CUPS
1 cup graham cracker crumbs
1 stick oleo, softened
2 cups powdered sugar
1 cup peanut butter
Topping:
1/2 cup sugar
2 tablespoons milk
2 tablespoons oleo
1 cup chocolate chips

Mix graham cracker crumbs, oleo, powdered sugar and butter together and press into an ungreased 9-by-13 pan. Then mix the topping ingredients, except for the chocolate chips, in a small saucepan. Bring to a boil over medium heat. Remove from heat and add chips. Stir until smooth. Spread over peanut butter mixture. Refrigerate or chill and cut into bars when set.

NOVEMBER 2002

A very beautiful fall day! How soon do you think the snow will be flying? Days like this sure make nice laundry days. Dread to think of hanging wash out this winter. Cold fingers! Brrrr! It is almost time for the school girls to come home. I left the di9shes to wash until they come home, so they can help me with them. Verena and Loretta are playing with their dolls. Benjamin and Joseph are taking a nap. I made vegetable soup for lunch. My sister Verena and a friend stopped in for awhile and ate lunch with the children and I. Our children love vegetable soup. They call it "Grandma's soup" as they just loved my mother's vegetable soup.

Yesterday, us six sisters - Leah, Liz, Emma, Verena, Susan, and I - spent the day at the homeplace. We went through Mom's drawers and closest. We divided her clothes between us girls. This was a very difficult day. So many memories and to know Mom will never wear her clothes again. We also emptied one of her wall cupboards and carried everything out onto tables in her shed. Mom had a lot of dishes.

We are slowly preparing for the day us eight children will get together to divide our parents belongings. I dread to think of that day, to see everything change. But it'll have to be done. Sometime. It brings a lot of tears to think they will never need their things again. But my parents are in a far better place. I would rather have them anyday than their belongings. I know we will have hard days ahead, but we need to turn to our "Heavenly Father" in times like these. God will not send us more than we can bear. I just took for granted that we would have them a lot longer.

Joe's grandmother is in the hospital. So I hope we can go give her a visit soon. I hope she can come home shortly and be feeling better again.

I'm still drying out buggy blankets from the heavy rains we were caught in on Sunday. I am so thankful we could come home and have all our buildings still standing. Quite a few barns were blown down and a lot other damages done north from here. Feel sorry for the people that have to rebuild. A person just never knows what will happen from day to day. It's a good thing we don't know our future.

This is now Thursday morning. My sisters Verena and Susan came for supper last night and spent the night here. Was glad to see them come. They have many lonely days with Mom not there with them. It's a nice but windy morning. Water is heating on the stove to do laundry. It shouldn't take long to dry with the wind. The farmers sure had nice weather to get all their crops in before winter arrives.

Here is my vegetable soup recipe that I served for lunch yesterday:

VEGETABLE SOUP
1 pound hamburger
1 onion, chopped
2 cups potatoes, diced
1 cup carrots, diced
1 pint corn
1 pint peas
1 quart tomato juice
1 1/2 teaspoons salt
1 teaspoon black pepper

Brown hamburger and onion in a skillet. Put hamburger and onion into a large pot and add potatoes, carrots, corn peas, tomato juice, and salt and pepper. Cook over medium heat until vegetables are soft.
Recipe Note: Sometimes I use a pint of beef chunks instead of hamburger. I also leave the onion whole and cook it with the rest of the vegetables.

NOVEMBER 2002

It is 5:35 a.m. My husband Joe just left for work. I'm holding Baby Joseph while I write this and he's almost asleep. It rained during the night. That should put more water in our cistern. We don't have a big cistern, so I am always glad for rain to fill it up. The rest of the children are still asleep. I'll let my school-age girls sleep for another hour, if they don't wake up before. We got to bed later than usual, so they probably will want to sleep later.

We went to sister Emma and Jacob's for supper last night. On our way home we stopped at brother Albert's awhile. They were still very busy cutting up beef. They were afraid it might warm up too much and wanted to get the meat processed or put on ice until today. A lot of hard work goes with processing meat. I'm sure they were all ready for bed by the time they were done.

I did laundry yesterday and everything dried nice. It was cold to hang it out, fingers got very cold! We had 22 degrees in the morning. Now this morning we had 46. Such a change in temperatures is not going to help the flu any. So far we are lucky not to get it. After doing the laundry, I cleaned out my bookcase and desk. Then sweeping the floors and washing the dishes more than filled up my day.

My kerosene lamps are all running low in kerosene, so those will have to be filled before tonight if we want to have light. I also hope to get some mending done today. I'm so behind in it. So many rips and tears to repair. My mother always repeated the old saying "a stitch in time saves nine." I have found out that holds true. My eight-year-old daughter Elizabeth keeps telling me her coat snaps are loose. She said she used to always ask Grandma to tighten them for her.

It is Sunday, Nov. 17th. It has been two months today since Dear Mother has passed away. At times I get such a longing to talk to her again. I do not want to be selfish, though, and wish her back into this troubled world of ours. God's ways are not our ways. Something we found that Mom had written in one of her journals sometime before she died was "God will make a way, when there seems to be no way." I often wonder what her thoughts were while writing those words.

I hope I can cut out and sew a new "cap" (head covering) for my daughter Loretta today. She has a bad habit of losing hers. We recently bought her new shoes and she decided to walk through the water puddles after a rain. Needless to say they were thoroughly soaked. A typical 2 year old, she's always into everything. I am thankful, though, that she is healthy. I'd rather see her into mischief than if she would be in bed sick.

The tornadoes north from here caused a lot of damage on Nov. 10. My cousin's buildings were really damaged. It sounds windy outside now.

A reader sent this recipe for homemade biscuits. I made them this morning for breakfast and they turned out good. Thank you to all the readers for the encouraging cards and notes!

CAKE BISCUITS
1 1/2 cups flour
3/4 teaspoon salt
1 teaspoon baking powder
2 eggs
1/2 cup sugar
1/2 cup margarine
1 teaspoon vanilla

Sift flour, salt, and baking powder together and set aside. In a separate bowl, beat eggs and sugar together with margarine until smooth. Add the vanilla. Combine all together. Blend and stir well. Into oiled pan
spoon batter by the spoonful. Bake in 375 degree oven until nicely browned. Brush margarine on top after removing from oven. Slice and serve like you would a cake. Has biscuit-like taste.

DECEMBER 2002

Tonight our minds are with Joe's cousin, Leander, and wife, Rosina, and their family. Their 13-year-old son, Phillip, was laid to rest today. He had a hunting accident on Saturday, which took his life. Phillip was their oldest child. This was such a shock for his Dad to find him and life had fled. God makes no mistakes, but we do question why. Someday we'll understand it all. May God comfort them through this time of trial.

Leander and Joe grew up together and were the same age. So this was quite a shock to us. We went to the funeral which was largely attended. We always wanted to go visit Leanders since they moved to their new place. Never in our minds did we think it would be this way. We took our three youngest children and my sister Verena along. Leander and Rosina live 1 1/2 hours from here, so we hired a driver to take us in van. We saw a few accidents on the way home. It was really snowing while we were at the graveyard for the burial. Was so glad once we were home as the roads were very slippery.

We saw Joe's Dad and his sisters, Esther and Loretta and children at the funeral. We also saw his sister Christine and family from Ovid, Michigan. We left our school-age girls, Elizabeth and Susan, and also Verena, off at sister Emma and Jacob's while we went to the funeral. We picked them up on our way home tonight. Was glad Emma could take care of them while we were gone. She has a daughter in school also, besides three other children. I'm sure she didn't have any free time today.

Saturday, Joe's Dad from Michigan gave us a big surprise by coming to spend the day with us. The children enjoyed the day with their Grandpa. Joe's sister, Maryann and family, dropped him off here while they attended a family gathering nearby. I fried chicken for the noon meal, along with potatoes, pork and beans, cole slaw, fruit, cookies, cinnamon rolls, homemade bread and jam. Joe's sister, Maryann, brought the rolls, bread, and jam. She also brought three dresses she sewed for my three oldest daughters. This was all very much appreciated. I am so behind with my sewing that sewed dresses like that mean so much to me.

I'm looking forward to Thursday and Friday. Joe will be off work and the girls home from school for Thanksgiving vacation. I hope all you readers had a happy and safe Thanksgiving. Are we thankful enough for all we have? These cold, windy winter days are perfect for a warm chili soup. Try this recipe!

SAVORY CHILI SOUP
2 pounds of ground sausage
1 cup of chopped onion
2 quarts of tomato juice
1 quarts of water
1 quart of cooked kidney beans
cup of sugar
teaspoon of chili powder
salt to taste
1/8 teaspoon of red pepper (optional)
4 rounded tablespoons of cornstarch, enough to thicken to satisfaction

Saute onion and hamburger until brown. Drain grease. Warm tomato juice, sugar, chili powder, salt, and water to the boiling point. Save some water to dissolve cornstarch. Add hamburger and cornstarch and stir until thickened. Add beans. Cook for 5-10 minutes.

DECEMBER 2002

We have entered the month of December already. It is hard to believe that Thanksgiving is over with for another year. I hope everyone is having a healthy and safe holiday season. We were supposed to go to Joe's Dad's in Michigan and have Thanksgiving with his family, but we didn't make it. It's a 2 1/2 to 3 hour drive from here, so it is not as easy to go as it would be if they were within reach of horse and buggy. We do plan to go for their Christmas gathering if we are all healthy and able to go; also, if the weather permits us to go. You never know during these winter months.

People are now busy shopping for Christmas. But let us remember the reason for the season. This will be a sad Christmas for my family, the first one without either of our parents. I treasure the special memories I have of them. May they rest in peace together now.

I fixed a turkey and all the trimmings on Sunday, since we didn't do anything on Thanksgiving. My sister Emma and husband Jacob and family came to enjoy the meal with us. We had plenty of food left. Turkey isn't one of our favorite meats. Jacob, Emma, Joe, and I spent the afternoon playing "Life on the Farm." This is a very interesting board game in which you see who can buy and keep 60 cows first. Our first game lasted 2 1/2 hours. The children were all busy playing with their toys and other games while we played ours. Benjamin and Loretta are finishing up their breakfast now. I have to keep a close watch on them. For some reason they started thinking its fun to throw food at each other. I guess a 2- and 3-year old can think up almost anything. They both had the flu so I am glad they are feeling better.

My husband Joe is at work. They are pretty busy right now. My oldest daughters, Elizabeth and Susan, are at school. They dreaded to end their Thanksgiving vacation. My 4-year-old, Verena, is sitting beside me on the rocker, rocking baby Joseph. Her birthday was Dec. 10, and she was counting the days until then. She thinks I should sew her bigger dresses since she turned 5 and she's really going to grow fast. Benjamin is tall for his age and Verena is scared that he'll be "bigger" than her. Children are so enjoyable.

We sure have had some cold mornings the last while. Joe put up wash lines in the attached garage where we keep our buggy, so I can hang clothes in there to dry when it is too cold to do it outside. Only so many clothes can fit on the racks by the stove in the house, so I have to dry the laundry gradually. During these cold days I hang the laundry on the lines in the garage until there is space on the racks by the stove in the house. During the summer you can wash, dry, and fold the laundry all in the same day.

DECEMBER 2002

Christmas Day is almost over. Everyone here at the Eichers has retired for the night. I hope everyone had a safe and Merry Christmas. Another week left of 2002. What will 2003 have in store for us? It is good we don't know our future. God will not give us a heavier burden than he'll help us carry. We do need more prayers in this world, though. As we thank God for his many blessings, let us also pray for peace on earth.

We had an enjoyable Christmas, although we missed our parents very much. My sisters Verena and Susan spent the day with us. We awoke to a nice surprise this morning: the ground was covered with snow. It snowed most of the day. Joe is hoping it will keep snowing so we can use my parents' bobsled to go help my sister Liz and Levi butcher hogs Friday. I remember how we would take the bobsled to church during snowy times. Dad would put bales of straw with blankets over it to sit on. It was so much fun. Those are just memories now.

We had a big Christmas dinner. Our menu was: fried chicken, mashed potatoes, gravy, corn, lettuce salad, celery sticks, green peppers, bread, etc. We enjoyed the cake our neighbor lady sent over for dessert. I will have to ask her for the recipe and share it with you readers. Joe fried the chicken for me tonight in the new stainless steel skillet he gave me for Christmas. I was very surprised and glad for the skillet.

We spent Saturday in Michigan at Joe's sister, Mary Ann and husband Jake. She had a delicious meal for all to enjoy, plus all the food that was brought in. The afternoon was spent visiting, singing and playing games. We arrived home at 7 p.m., safe and sound.

Sunday morning we all went to church. Brrrrr! The wind sure was cold. The umbrella really helped. The children must've had a good night's sleep, as they were all wide awake. Joe had his 34th birthday Sunday, Dec. 22. Joe barbecued chicken and mushrooms as some of my family came for supper. We love grilled mushrooms. I fixed the rest of the supper in the house.

We are enjoying our week with everyone home. It's nice to not have anyone leaving early in the morning. We started a 1,000-piece puzzle. It is a puzzle showing an Amish scene called "Autumn ride." We had gotten pretty far along with it today. While we were making supper, my older girls came and told us Benjamin and Loretta had just pushed the whole puzzle onto the floor. SIGH! And so we started over and have it almost back to where we had it. I can see them doing it all over again. At least they are healthy.

JANUARY 2003

This is the second day into 2003. My husband Joe has left for work and the children are still asleep. We have no snow here, but ice all over. I do hope there won't be any accidents. Today is the first day of school for the girls after their Christmas break. They are not very excited about ending their vacation. We had a nice time together while they were home from school and Joe off from work.

We have completed the 1000 piece puzzle we started on Christmas Day. We had one more breakdown with the puzzle when 2-year-old Loretta was sitting in the middle of it playing with her dolls. This was the day after her and Benjamin had pulled it off the table and we had to begin all over. With six children around it's hard to believe we still had all the pieces. I would like to glue the completed puzzle together sometime.

Last Friday we helped my sister Liz and husband Levi butcher five hogs. It was a lot of hard work. I am sure they were very tired that night, but also glad to have their jars filled again with fresh meat. We also made "Pon Hoss" with the juice of the liver pudding, adding flour, salt, pepper and some liver pudding to it. This is put into containers to cool and harden. Levi's sent some "pon hoss" and sausage home with us, so we enjoyed it sliced and fried for breakfast. Liz got all or most of her meat processed yet that day. She has a very big pressure cooker that processes 18-19 quarts at one time. She also had several smaller ones going. I'm sure it was a great relief for her to have it all done that day.

Since there was enough snow, Sister Emma and Jacob, sisters Verena and Susan, and our family took Dad and Mom's bobsled to Levi's. We had our horse and Jacob's horse hitched double. This was the first time any of these horses were hitched double, but they did a real good job of pulling together. It was a cold day but we kept warm sitting on straw bales covered with blankets.

This is now later and the girls made it off to school just fine even with the ice. The children have had breakfast and I must get the dishes washed. I hope to get the house cleaned and then start ironing clothes. Best wishes to all you readers in 2003! Following is a snickerdoodle cookie recipe that a reader requested:

SNICKERDOODLE COOKIES
1 cup soft shortening
1 1/2 cup sugar
2 eggs
2 3/4 cup flour
2 teaspoons cream of tartar
1 teaspoon soda
1/4 teaspoon salt

Stir shortening, sugar, and eggs. Sift together flour, cream of tartar, soda, sand salt and stir into shortening mixture. Stir well and roll into balls the size of small walnuts.

Roll into mixture of:
2 tablespoons sugar
2 teaspoons cinnamon

Place 2 inches apart on ungreased cookie sheet. Bake until lightly browned but still soft. Bake 8-10 minutes in 400 oven. Makes around 5 dozen cookies.

JANUARY 2003

This is Wednesday evening and I should be in bed where the rest of the family is. But I need to have this column ready for the mail tomorrow, so I think I'll sleep better knowing this is done. I'm searching my tired mind what I could write that would interest you readers. I do not want to bore you readers. I do appreciate the many words of encouragement I have received and expressions of sympathy in the loss of my dear mother. Oh, how greatly she is missed.

My daughters Elizabeth and Susan didn't have school today on account of high snow drifts covering the roads. By tonight, though, a lot of the snow had melted as it warmed up and the sun was out. The roads are now very slushy. My husband Joe said he seen quite a few cars stuck on the road. The roads were nice for sleighing up until today. The ice underneath the snow made the sleigh ride even smoother.

My 5-year-old daughter, Verena, has a very bad chest cold and baby Joseph has diarrhea so we had to miss going to church on Sunday. I appreciated that Joe offered to stay home from church and help me care for the sick ones. In the afternoon Joe hitched the horse to the sleigh and told me to take the children that weren't sick for a sleigh ride. I didn't go far but it was so refreshing after being inside with sick children. Everything looked so beautiful outside. Our evergreens looked so nice with snow clinging to the branches. Only our Master Artist could make such a lovely scene. It can get depressing caring for sick children, but do we appreciate our good health enough? Baby Joseph is 5 1/2 months and has pushed through his first tooth. I wonder if that is what was making him sick? It's always exciting to see that first tooth pop through.

We have no way of knowing how many hours the bus is delayed or if school is cancelled. (Editor's Note: Many Amish children go to public schools and ride a regular yellow bus. Although without a radio or TV, finding out about school cancellations is an impossibility). Every hour we had to watch for the bus. It interrupted my morning watching for the bus. After we knew the bus wouldn't come anymore, I had the girls help me around the house and they did a good job.

After chores were done the children all went outside and made snowmen. I let little Verena go outside with them as I thought a little fresh air might do her some good. But she came in coughing again so maybe I should've kept her inside. Sometimes a person doesn't know what's best. I think I will join the rest now and get some sleep.

This is now Thursday morning at 7:15 a.m. The girls have left for school at the regular time, little Verena is rocking baby Joseph, Benjamin is finishing his breakfast and Loretta is still sleeping. It's time I got my dishes washed and get started with my day. Meanwhile, here is a good pizza dough recipe which will please the whole family.

PIZZA DOUGH
2 teaspoons yeast
2 tablespoons sugar
1 cup water
2 tablespoons oil (vegetable or oil)
1/2 teaspoon salt
2 1/2 cups flour

Mix water, yeast, and sugar well. Then add oil, salt, and flour. Let set and then pat into pizza pan. Add your favorite toppings. Bake pizza at 425 for approximately 20 minutes.

JANUARY 2003

Our snow had almost all disappeared, but this morning it started to snow and the ground is pretty well-covered again Our temperature dipped down to the lower teens this week. That's the coldest we have had this winter.

Last week, the children made some snowmen. The next day it really warmed up and they melted down to a little ball. When the girls came home from school, my 3-year-old, Benjamin, went out to greet them. He couldn't believe the snowmen were gone. He walked around the house looking for them. Finally, he looked up at the fluffy white clouds and said, "There they are!". So this morning he was pretty excited to see his snowmen coming down again from the sky. He said he can fix them again as they probably broke falling from the sky. Oh, how sweet and innocent children can be.

A lot of people around here are busy butchering and processing pork and beef. A very big job! We haven't done ours yet. We don't plan to butcher beef anytime soon as I still have a lot of beef left in jars.
We had supper one evening this week at my sister Liz and Levi's. On the menu, among other things, was "rare beef." This was always a family favorite. For those of you who don't know what it is: you slice a chunk of beef thin-like. Then you season it with salt and pepper. Put lard in a small frying skillet. The skillet should be half-filled when the lard is melted. Make the lard real hot and then stir in a slice of seasoned beef twice with a fork on each side. Put it in a bowl and it's ready to eat. Mom always made the best rare beef. She liked a lot of black pepper on hers and that's probably why most of us like ours seasoned good with pepper. Our children like it too, now. For the young ones we do a few pieces without so much pepper. We also deep-fried mushrooms and onion rings at Liz and Levi's. My sister Emma and Jacob and family were also there.

Baby Joseph is feeling better after being sick almost a week. He now has his second tooth. I think that's what was making him sick. Now he is happy again and gets around all over in his walker.

Jan. 17 will be four long months since dear mother has passed away. There are so many times when it seems you have to ask her a question. In May it'll be three years since Dad passed away. Oh, how we miss them. God's ways are the best.

JANUARY 2003

4:30 a.m. We're ready to begin another day. My husband Joe begins the day by going outside to do the barn chores and he also adds some coal to the stove. It's a cold winter's morning. My sisters Verena and Susan are here so they help me pack Joe's lunch and prepare his breakfast.

5 a.m. Joe eats his breakfast of eggs, fried potatoes, bacon, cheese, toast and grapefruit juice.

5:30 a.m. Joe leaves for work and we prepare breakfast for the rest of us, fixing the same meal as he had.

6:15 a.m. The children are all awake except baby Joseph. We all eat breakfast. Then I help the girls get ready for school, while sisters Verena and Susan start washing the dishes.

7 a.m. My daughters, Elizabeth and Susan, leave for school. Sister Verena is sweeping the floors and sister Susan is finishing the last of the dishes. I put water on the stove to heat to do the laundry and gather the clothes that have to be washed. Joseph wakes up and I feed him.

8:30 a.m. Susan is sewing and Verena is cleaning all the windows. They are full of fingerprints. It's too cold for the children to go outside so they hang around the windows a lot, looking outside. I start with the laundry.

10 a.m. Susan helps me hang some clothes in the garage and then goes back to her sewing. It is 15 degrees outside, so we decide to hang all the clothes to dry inside and save us from getting cold fingers. I fill both clothes-racks with clothes, trying to fit on all I can. I look forward to nice spring days when everything can be hung outside.

11:30 a.m. Verena makes a quick lunch of grilled cheese sandwiches. We like homemade V-8 juice with those. She also makes a cheese-ball. The children love cheese-ball on crackers. It makes a good snack.

1 p.m. The noon dinner dishes are all washed. I rearrange the clothes on the racks, then I rock the children (Little Verena, Loretta, Benjamin, and Baby Joseph) to sleep for their afternoon nap. Susan returns to her sewing. Verena cleans the entrance area to our house, which doesn't stay clean long with snow being tracked in. She also fills all the kerosene lights and cleans the glass globes.

3:30 p.m. The girls are home from school and the children are awake from their naps. They all enjoy a snack of crackers and cheese-ball, plus some fresh apples and oranges. My daughter Susan is getting excited and counting the days until her 7th birthday which is Friday, January 24th.

4 p.m. Joe comes home from work. He has a quick snack and goes out to do the evening chores. Verena and I prepare a casserole for supper.

5 p.m. Joe leaves to go get our sleigh at the blacksmith shop as it was getting repair work done on it. Verena and Susan go home to get some more clothes so they can stay another day. I sure appreciate their help. With six small children in this house, the works seems endless at times. But children are such a joy to have around -- so sweet and innocent.

6:30 p.m. We all sit down together to eat a supper of casserole, sloppy Joe sandwiches, lettuce salad, cheese, pickles, fruit and homemade cookies.

7:30 p.m. Dishes are washed and everyone is ready to get to bed early after a long day.

8 p.m. Everyone has gone to bed. Goodnight.

HOMEMADE CHEESEBALL
 2 (8 ounce) packages cream cheese
1/2 teaspoon garlic salt
1/2 teaspoon parsley flakes
1/2 teaspoon minced onion
1 2 teaspoon seasoning salt
2 (3 ounce) packages chopped dried beef (or use your own homemade, dried beef)

Place all ingredients in the order given into a mixing bowl. Mix all together until you have a smooth, creamy consistency. Shape into a ball and put on serving plate. Serve with crackers.

FEBRUARY 2003

This is 5:45 a.m. and my husband Joe left for work awhile ago. It's another cold late January morning. Our thermometer shows 2 degrees. The children are all still in bed yet. They had fun playing in the snow outside last night. So I thought I'd let the school-age girls sleep a little later. They had a 2-hour delay yesterday on account of snow drifting the roads.

It warmed up into the 30s yesterday and now this morning it is so cold. Yesterday morning another blanket of snow had fallen and covered the ground. The world looked so pure and white. Snow was clinging to every tree branch. A very lovely scene!

Memories come of the January blizzard we had 25 years ago. I was six years old and not old enough to have to worry about it. I remember in the mornings the snow was blowing so bad that my brothers, Amos and Albert, helped my sister, Liz and I, out to the barn to help milk the cows so we wouldn't get lost on our way out. We were milking around 12 cows so with all of us, it didn't take long to get the cows milked and go back into the warm house. The milkman couldn't get through for quite a few days so we had all our milk-cans filled, stainless steel canners, plus anything else we could think of full of milk.

I know mother had written in her column before about there being 10 foot drifts in our yard. We could walk over fences, over the mailbox and walk up to the shed roof and write our names on it. Our neighbors came and plowed our lane out, which created a huge snow hill right in the middle of our yard. I wasn't going to school yet and I remember standing on top of that huge snow hill when the bus came to pick up my sisters after the blizzard. I didn't think back then how my parents must've worried about fire breaking out or someone getting sick and needing to get to the hospital. It would have been impossible to get through the roads then. I tried explaining to my children how much snow we had when we had the 1978 blizzard. They are just hoping we will have one. Elizabeth and Susan think that would be great to miss a week from school.

We received an invitation to our oldest niece's wedding for April 10th. This is exciting for us as it's the first of our nieces or nephews to get married. This would be Joe's oldest sister Maryann's daughter and she turned 21 this month. They live in Michigan so it's nice to have time to plan ahead. We have 40 nieces and nephews on Joe's side and 35 on mine. Looks like we'll have plenty of weddings to attend in the future.

FEBRUARY 2003

Monday, February 17 will be a sad day in this household. It would be Dad's 72nd birthday and five long, lonely months since Mother passed away. Dad passed away in May of 2000. The day before Dad had his stroke we had spent the day at my parents. Joe and Dad went to get our running gears home from the blacksmith shop as it was being repaired. Dad was helping Joe fasten the buggy box and the running gears. Little did we realize how our life would change and that we only had one more week with Dad. It was later until they had the buggy ready to use. I thought it was unusual that Dad didn't go to the barn to do his chores, he just stood there and talked while Joe was finishing up. He talked about happenings years ago and about worries he had for the future. That day seems so precious to us now. I'll never regret spending three days and two nights there the week between when Dad had his stroke and when he passed away. We stayed at the house to help out however we were needed.

Emma and I washed walls and ceilings and just helped keep the house clean while Mom stayed by Dad. The Saturday that Dad died we had come home the night before and Jacob and Emma had also gone home. My sister Liz and her husband Levi had come to Mom & Dad's to take a turn staying overnight. Jacob's and us thought we would go home and get some rest.

The next morning Joe went over to my folks to help with the outside chores. He wasn't gone long when he came back home and told me to get the children ready to go as Dad isn't too good. When we got there the EMS was there and they were taking him out. He had passed away already. Dad was a great father and a man of few words, but he had a great sense of humor.

 He had nine brothers and three sisters. My Uncle Emanuel also has a birthday on Feb. 17, being one year older than Dad. Every year we would take turns going back and forth to celebrate their birthdays. One year the weather was so bad and snow was blowing that Dad and Mom didn't think Uncle Emanuel's would come. So Mom didn't prepare anything special for supper. Uncle Emanuel and Aunt Leah lived around seven or eight miles away. Mom hadn't started our supper yet when Emanuel's and their children and also their married children and families arrived for supper. We were so surprised but Emanuel's were afraid if they didn't come we would have prepared food for them. But Mom had supper prepared in a hurry with everyone pitching in to help. Along with the food everyone bought we had a good supper.

This is 4:30 a.m. and Joe has left for work. He will start at 5 a.m. this morning. It makes a long day when they put in extra hours but I am thankful that he has work. I fixed breakfast for Joe and the guy that takes him to work. I made fried eggs and potatoes, cheese and toast so I hope that'll hold them over till lunch.

PEANUT BUTTER BROWNIES
2 1/4 cups flour
2 1/2 teaspoons baking powder
1/2 teaspoon salt
2/3 cup butter
2/3 cup peanut butter
1 1/4 cups sugar
1 1/4 cups brown sugar
1 teaspoon vanilla
3 eggs

In a small bowl, mix flour, baking powder, and salt. In a large bowl, mix butter, peanut butter, sugars, and vanilla. Beat until creamy. Add eggs, one at a time, beating well after each egg. Gradually beat in flour mixture. Spread evenly into a well-greased 13-inch pan. Bake at 350 for 30-35 minutes.

FEBRUARY 2003

It is Wednesday evening and everyone has retired for the night. It is later already and I should go join the rest in sleeping, but thought I'd write this column while all is peaceful.

We went to Jacob and Emma's for supper tonight. They were surprised to see us drive in. The children weren't ready to come home tonight, since we had such an enjoyable evening there. It warmed up into the upper 30s today, so Joe thought I should get out of the house. It's amazing what a ride in a buggy through the fresh air can do. The children are over the flu for now and I hope it'll stay that way.

We sure had a lot of snow this last week. We couldn't open our front door as a 4-5 foot drift was in front of it. Joe done his share of shoveling snow.

I will answer some reader mail now. Thank you all for your wonderful, encouraging letters. Someone wondered if we have "top buggies" (buggies with a roof). No, we have the open buggies, so we use umbrellas to head off the wind. Although when it gets really windy, it's hard to keep the umbrella up or from going inside out. Another reader wrote to me about the chicken pot pie recipe. She said the recipe doesn't say to take the bones out before adding the rest and that some new brides might not know this. So, yes, separate and remove the bones from the meat before adding the rest.

A reader asked what I use when I have a recipe that calls for shortening. I use lard that we get when we butcher our hogs. If I run out, I buy shortening. It really doesn't matter which kind you use unless a recipe calls for a certain kind. Another reader wrote in asking what kind of stove I cook Joe's breakfast on. We have a kerosene stove in which you turn up the wick and light it. After you're done with the burner you have to turn the wick down until the flame is out. She also asked what kind of sewing machine I use. I use a "Singer" treadle sewing machine and I also have a New Home treadle. Another question from the same reader was "how do we obtain water to wash clothes and how we wash clothes?" I have a cistern pump inside the house in which I pump water into 20 quart stainless steel canners to heat for laundry. I put one on the heating stove and the rest on the kerosene stove. I like to put water on over an hour before I start the wash to get it good and hot. I have a gas motor on my washing machine. A lot of people around here still have the washing machine that you have to pull the handle back and forth and also turn a handle that makes the wringer go. I grew up with one like that. I don't use or make the homemade laundry soap. Mom used to make it and when we'd get poison ivy she made us take a bath with it. I just buy my soap as there is hardly any time to make my own. And, yes, we have to iron our clothes, although a lot of people are buying materials now that you don't have to iron. We have hand-held irons that we heat on the stove and switch back and forth when one cools off.

Another question asked was if I buy store-bought bread. Yes, I do, sometimes. I also bake my own bread. Nothing beats a fresh slice of bread still warm out of the oven. A reader wrote in requesting my homemade noodle recipe. We use a hand-cranked noodle maker which speeds up the process. Try this recipe, it's delicious and easy.

MOM'S HOMEMADE NOODLES
1 egg
1 tablespoon water
pinch salt
1 cup flour

Put flour in a bowl and make a well. Drop egg, water, and salt into well. Mix in center moving to the outside of well until a stiff dough is formed. Divide dough in half and set one half aside. Roll dough as thin as possible, about 1/16" thick. Lightly dust top of dough with flour. Roll dough up as a log. Cut half inch wide strips. Unroll and lay dough strips on cookie sheet. Follow same for remaining dough that has been set aside. Let air dry one hour, turn over and let dry an additional hour. Keep noodles on a cookie sheet and let them dry for one week. Rearrange the noodles on the cookie sheet every day to ensure they dry out.

MARCH 2003

We are having our share of snow this winter! There was a very small attendance in church on Sunday because of the weather. My husband Joe went and picked up my brother-in-law, Jacob, to go to church. There was ice in with the snow, which made it hard pulling for the horses. Some churches cancelled because of the weather. I stayed home with the children as I didn't want to take them through the bad weather. Also, I didn't feel too good. I'm having a sore throat and stomach-ache and fever once in awhile. So besides sweeping the floors and washing dishes, nothing much is getting done this week Baby Joseph has pushed another tooth through, and his fourth one is almost through. This is making him feel sick.

On Friday evening, Joe's brother Benjamin, his wife Miriam and their three children, Joe's sister Esther and her friend, David, gave us a visit. We hadn't seen Benjamin's in over a year, so it was a nice visit.

Jacob and Emma's daughter, Emma, had her fifth birthday on Feb. 15th. Our daughter, Verena, who turned five in December, cannot figure out why she is older than Emma, but not taller. She asked me if I could make her dresses longer so that she would look taller. She stands on her tip toes to make herself look taller. She has such a big imagination. Children are so sweet!

Joe had a friend come plow open our driveway with his tractor as there is so much ice in with the snow, it makes it difficult to shovel. He did a very good job. My three-year-old, little Benjamin, said he wishes the snow would go back up in the sky as he can't walk very good on it. I guess I agree with him. I'm ready for good ole springtime.

A reader wrote to ask what "liver pudding" is. had mentioned it in an earlier column. Liver pudding is made while butchering pork. It comes from head meat and meat cooked off the bones. The meat goes through a grinder and gets mixed up. We usually put ours in jars right away to process. Some Amish in this area put it in an iron kettle to fry it down a little before putting it into jars to process. In that way it is more like sausage. I also received a lot of mail about "pon hoss." Pon hoss is the made with the juice that is left from the pork bones that have been cooked in the iron kettle. It is made with a thickening of flour or corn meal and some liver pudding. We season it with salt and pepper. After it is cooked and thickened we pour it into loaf pans to chill. When chilled we cut it into slices and fry in a skillet until golden brown. Some Pon Hoss you can fry without lard, but some is dry and you need to add lard to the skillet. Dad would always get his just exactly right where you wouldn't have to add any. We sure miss having him around to help butcher meat. Mother was also so good at cutting out all the good steaks when we butchered beef.

I hope I have answered your questions about Pon Hoss. There were too many letters in the batch my editor brought to answer each one individually. Thanks for your encouraging words! Here is a smaller size recipe for Pon Hoss that you can try at home.

PON HOSS
3-4 lbs. Pork shanks or hocks
cornmeal or flour
salt
pepper

Over a medium heat in a large pot, cook pork until tender. Remove bones and skim fat from broth. Return meat to broth and add corn meal or flour, just enough to thicken (editor's note: amount of flour to be added with vary widely depending on the meat used, add flour one cup at a time until broth is a thick paste) Season with salt and pepper. Pour into loaf pans. Chill overnight in a cellar or refrigerator. The next day, slice and fry over medium-high heat until golden brown on each side. Serve

MARCH 2003

We are now well into March and, again, we awake to a fresh layer of snow on the ground and it was still snowing. We sure have had a long winter.

I am having a busy week! With the help of my sisters, I am getting new clothes sewn. On Tuesday, Emma and I cut out eight shirts and eight dresses and aprons. Then we sewed a couple of shirts yet. The material we have had to be cut out, as it won't tear, so that makes extra work. This material doesn't have to be ironed though, so I will gain time after it's done.

Yesterday, sisters Liz and Emma and I sewed all day. My sisters Verena and Susan cooked the meals and washed dishes and took care of our children. That really helped so we could keep on sewing. I hope to finish up today on the sewing. Susan will sew snaps on all the new outfits. This is such a relief to have done. I still want to cut out a couple more shirts for the boys and some white aprons for the girls before our niece's wedding, which is April 10. I really appreciated my sisters' help with my sewing. I think I will head back to the sewing machine now. I enjoy sewing!

A reader in Viola, Minn., asked for a "snickerdoodle cookie" recipe. Try this one! If you keep the cookies sealed, they'll keep fresh for weeks
:
SNICKERDOODLES
1 tablespoon sugar
1 tablespoon ground cinnamon
1 cup shortening
1-1/2 cups sugar
2 eggs
1 teaspoon vanilla extract
2-3/4 cups flour
1 teaspoon baking soda
1/2 teaspoon salt
2 teaspoons cream of tartar

Preheat oven to 400°. Combine tablespoon sugar and cinnamon in a small mixing bowl and set aside. Cream shortening in a medium mixing bowl; gradually add 1-1/2 cups sugar, beating well. Add eggs; beat well. Stir in vanilla. Combine flour, baking soda, salt and cream of tartar in mixing bowl. Add to creamed mixture; mix well. Shape dough into 1-1/2-inch balls, and roll in reserved cinnamon-sugar mixture. Place 2 inches apart on a lightly greased cookie sheet. Bake at 400° for 8 minutes or until lightly browned. Remove to wire racks to cool.

MARCH 2003

The children are all asleep except Benjamin and Loretta. My husband Joe is rocking them while I get this written. I'll be ready to get to bed when I am done with this - it has been a long, busy day. I did a huge laundry today. I ran out of clothesline, so I had to wait until some of it was dry before I could hang out the rest, so it didn't all get dry. I have it drying on clothes racks beside the stove now.

It warmed up into the 50s today, so after being stuck inside much of this long, cold winter the children had fun playing outside. They even took 7 1/2-month old Joseph outside and gave him rides in the little wagon. He really enjoyed it! Everything is muddy, though, from the melting snow. I made a big pot of vegetable soup for dinner. I made a big enough kettle to have an easy supper, but I also made cheeseburgers to go along with it. I remember when Mom used to make a big kettle of chili soup. Dad would take his finger and measure down the outside of the kettle, saying: "Monday, Tuesday, Wednesday," etc, teasing Mom that he would only have to eat leftover chili soup for that many days, but it never really lasted that long. Dad would also tease us girls when we baked cookies that he has to wait to eat one until he puts his shoes on. So that if he'd drop it, it would break his toes (our cookies were nice and soft, Dad just liked to joke that they were hard). One time his joke backfired as our company brought the cookies. Dad was very embarrassed when he found out they had brought the cookies and he said he should put his shoes on before trying them. I have so many good memories of Dad and Mom.

I mopped the living room and both bedroom floors this afternoon. I didn't get the kitchen done, hopefully tomorrow. The floors get dirty when it is so muddy outside. Joe took our new horse for a ride tonight before supper. The roads are so muddy and our buggy now needs to be washed off. This is the time of year when I am constantly washing coats that get splattered up from the roads. We got a little 8-week old puppy from some friends for our children. They really enjoy her. I think I'll go to bed and join the rest. Joe has put Benjamin and Loretta to bed now. Goodnight.

Meanwhile, you readers try this recipe that I got from my Mom. We tried it and it's really good:

DEEP DISH TACO SQUARES
2 cups biscuit mix
1/2 cup cold water
1 pound hamburger
1 Tbsp. chopped onion
1 green pepper
8 ozs. of pizza sauce
1 pkg. of taco seasoning
8 ozs. of sour cream
1 cup cheddar cheese (shredded)
1/3 cup salad dressing

Mix biscuit mix and water and press into bottom of a lightly greased 13- by 9-inch pan Bake at 375 for 8 minutes. Brown hamburger, onion, and pepper. Add taco seasoning and pizza sauce. Spoon over warm crust. Combine sour cream, salad dressing, and cheese. Spread over meat mixture. Bake uncovered at 375 for 25 minutes until golden brown and bubbly.

MARCH 2003

I had a nice surprise today when my sisters Susan, Verena, Emma, and her children came this morning. They came for breakfast, so we had eggs, potatoes, bacon, toast, cheese, grape juice, milk, and doughnuts. After dishes were washed, Verena and Susan took Emma and Jacob's horse to be re-shod. Emma stayed here and sewed Elizabeth a dress and apron for me. Meanwhile, I made a one-kettle soup for lunch, which is always quick and delicious to make on a busy day.

It was raining when they left for home this afternoon., I hope they didn't get too wet. The children were all tired tonight from playing so hard. Benjamin fell asleep at the table when we were eating supper. Poor little boy just didn't want to take a nap today because his cousins were here to play with him.
We had a beautiful day on Monday. It warmed up into the 70s. I took advantage of the nice weather and did my laundry. I washed some quilts and blankets and coats since it was such perfect drying weather. Then I mopped my floors, but I didn't get my laundry all folded and put away. It was so nice to be outside on such a day. Makes me anxious to plant the garden, but I know we'll still have some cold weather ahead.

On Tuesday I had a nice surprise. My uncle Emmanuel and Aunt Leah, five of their married daughters and some of their children came for a visit. I knew they were going to visit Verena and Susan, but hadn't realized they were coming here also, so they found my house a mess. I guess it's like the saying goes: "If you come to see me, come anytime. But if you come to see my house, let me know." They visited with all six of us sisters on Tuesday. They helped me fold my laundry while we visited. Aunt Leah is my mother's older sister, so it brought back memories of Mom. Hard to believe it's been six long months since Mother passed away to that Great Beyond.

Here is the recipe for One Kettle Soup which I prepared for lunch:

ONE KETTLE SOUP
1 quart canned, cooked beef
1 quart Homemade Noodles
4 medium potatoes, diced and peeled
salt and pepper to taste
1 medium onion, chopped

Fill 6 quart kettle with 3 quarts of water and bring to a hard boil. Add potatoes, noodles, and onion together in the kettle on top of the stove and return to a hard boil (about 8 minutes).Then add cooked beef and hard boil for 12 more minutes. Do not overcook or too much liquid will be lost. Beef soup base can be used in place of the beef. If using soup base, no salt should be added until serving, as soup bases are already high in sodium. Add two more quarts of water. Change heat from high to low and cook for about 15 minutes.

APRIL 2003

6:30 a.m. This is a Saturday, so we slept in a little longer than during the week. I start breakfast, while Joe carries water to the stove to heat. I plan to do my laundry. Joe starts the stove as we are burning wood and it didn't last all night.

7:15 a.m. Children are all awake so we sit down to eat breakfast. Sausage gravy, biscuits, fried eggs, cheese, milk, and grape juice is on the menu. Saturday morning breakfasts are always enjoyable and relaxing since no one has to leave for work or school.

8 a.m. Breakfast is over and I wash dishes, while my daughters, Susan, 7, and Verena, 5, dry them and put them away. Elizabeth, 8, sweeps the floors. My husband Joe goes out to do his morning chores with Benjamin, 3, and Loretta, 2, tagging along.

9:30 a.m. I gather the clothes to wash. Joe starts to take off our old storm door and will replace it with a new one. Our other one was in bad shape already.

9:45 a.m. Joe carries water to the washing machine for me and I start with a huge laundry.

11:30 a.m. I just finished filling up all the clothes lines and have more clothes that didn't fit on. Joe has the storm door on and it sure looks better now. He helped me with the laundry in between working on the door. Benjamin's shoes got a good washing, too. He walked through the muddy garden and got stuck, so he stepped out of his shoes and walked the rest of the way to the house in his socks. His socks looked a fright.

Noon We eat a quick lunch of sandwiches and chips.

12:45 p.m. I get some laundry off the lines and hang up the rest. Joe rocked Benjamin, Loretta, and Joseph to sleep for their naps.

1:30 p.m. Joe starts fixing our pump. It wasn't throwing up water very good. I cut out two caps (head coverings) for Elizabeth and Loretta, then I sewed them. I cut out and sewed Susan and Verena each one last night.
3 p.m. I iron some clothes that we need for church tomorrow. Joe gave up on the pump, as he'll have to have another man here to help lift it. He is washing off our buggy as it is all splattered up from the dirty stone roads around here.

4:30 p.m. I get the clothes in off the lines and leave them in clothes baskets until Monday. Time in this day is running out so I won't take the time to fold them yet. Joe is doing his evening chores.

5:15 p.m. I wash all the children's hair and give them all a bath. After playing outside all day they sure needed it.
6 p.m. Joe is making supper tonight -- homemade soup and fried chicken.

6:45 p.m. Supper is ready and it looks delicious. It always does when I don't have to do it.

8 p.m. Dishes are all washed and we're all ready to call it a day. Goodnight. Let us pray for peace in the world.

APRIL 2003

We have had an enjoyable late March Sunday. This morning we started out to attend church in another church district, it was at my husband Joe's Uncle Jake and Aunt Mattie's house. This would be my sister Emma's husband Jacob's parents. Joe and Jacob's mothers are sisters. Joe's mom died almost eight years ago at the age of 54. Jake and Mattie live about 12 miles from here, so we started out before 7 a.m. We took our new horse and she did very well to go that far. It was a nice morning to drive with the buggy and horse, but rather chilly until the sun came out.

Joe's 89-year-old grandma lives on the same place as Jake's, so it was nice to visit with her. She does very well for her age. Jake's had a good lunch for all of us after church. The lunch consisted of ham, Swiss and Colby cheese, homemade bread, pickles, red beets, peanut butter, butter, jelly, coffee, etc. They wanted us to stay for supper as well, but we were a long ways from home with the horse and buggy.

My sisters Verena and Susan were also along with us. My sister Liz and husband Levi, were there, as this was their church district. We stopped in at Levi and Liz's on the way home and had popcorn. This gave our horse a break, as

Levi's would be almost halfway home. Levi's wanted us to stay for supper but we were anxious to get home before dark after a long day.

Next week my girls will have spring break, so we are all looking forward to that. The girls can really help me out with my work at home. I am hoping for a nice, warm week. We hope to clean the upstairs bedrooms while they're home. I also hope to sew Joe a couple of work shirts. The wood he carries at work is very hard on his shirts. Sometimes the work seems endless with a growing family, but I'm glad I'm healthy to be able to work.

Try this recipe to help you use those hard-boiled eggs this Easter season:

CREAMED EGGS
6 fresh eggs
Sauce:
6 tablespoons butter
6 tablespoons flour
1 1/2 teaspoons salt
dash of pepper
3 cups milk

Hard boil eggs (We put them in a kettle and after the boiling point is reached, boil for 5 minutes. Then take them out of the kettle and peel them). Peel and set aside. Melt butter in heavy saucepan. Add flour, salt and pepper. Stir until well-blended. Slowly add milk, stirring constantly. Cook until smooth. Pour sauce into 2 1/2 quart casserole dish. Chop eggs and stir into sauce. Serve on hot toast.

APRIL 2003

We are having lovely spring weather this week. Joe worked up the garden tonight and hopefully I'll be able to get something planted yet this week. I'd like to plant peas, lettuce, radishes, onions, and potatoes soon. Mom was never an early bird with her garden, but she always had the best garden.

We did some cleaning in the front yard. We had 10 tree stumps removed so it looks a mess right now. I will be glad once we get it all straightened out and grass planted. We also had a circle driveway put in, which makes it nicer to get in and out of our place.

We had a nice time in Michigan. We left on Wednesday afternoon and came home around 9 p.m. on Friday. Thursday was a very nice day for the wedding. The wedding services were held at the neighbors. The meals were served at Melvin's (my niece Verena's husband) parents. They could seat around 200 at one time so there were a lot of dishes to be washed in between settings. Their menu was mashed potatoes, gravy, meat loaf, ham, dressing, mixed vegetables, taco salad, homemade bread, pies, cakes, fruit, puddings, and ice cream. I was supposed to go help on Wednesday as that's when the women and girls get together to bake pies and peel potatoes. So there's not so much to do on the day of the wedding. Some communities do the food preparation on the Tuesday before the Thursday wedding. There is a lot of work in getting ready for a wedding.

On Friday we stopped at Joe's sister, Carol, husband Pete, and family to see their new house. Then we headed to the hospital around an hour from there yet to visit with Joe's brother. He had a bad accident recently and has a broken arm and leg, two shattered knees and internal injuries. He wasn't doing too well when we were there. He was in a lot of pain. He is lucky to be alive. God had his protecting hand over him. It took us around 3 1/2 hours to get home from the hospital so we were a tired bunch. My sisters Verena and Susan went with us, so they spent the night here.

I did a huge laundry on Monday. The clothes dried so nice. I just love wash days like that. We are enjoying dandelions these last couple of weeks. Also, winter onions. We make a sour cream and pour it over the dandelion greens. Then we put in diced up, hard-boiled eggs. We eat this with cooked potatoes and bacon. My 5-year-old daughter, Verena, asked me why I was picking and washing grass to eat.

The rest have all gone to bed, so I think I'll call it a day.

We saw Joe's Uncle Solomon from Dundee, Ohio, at the wedding and he requested a homemade horseradish recipe. This is my Dad's brother Andy's recipe:

HORSERADISH RELISH
1 cup grated horseradish
1/2 cup vinegar
1/4 teaspoon salt

Wash horseradish roots thoroughly and remove the brown outer skin (a vegetable peeler is useful in removal of the outer skin). The roots maybe grated or cut into small cubes and put through a hand food chopper or an electric blender. Combine ingredients. Pack into clean, sterilized jars. Seal tightly and store in refrigerator.

APRIL 2003

It is around 8 a.m. and I have water heating on the stove to do my laundry. It looks like it'll be a nice day. The temperature is already up to 53, so I'm hoping it'll warm up to stay. Warm temperatures will help bring along the garden, which has now begun for the year.

On Good Friday, we got quite a bit of garden planted. We planted 1/4 pound of early sweet corn. It is a 63-day corn, so hopefully it'll do good, and we'll have corn by late June. We also planted a lot of onions, radishes, several different kinds of lettuce, peas, green beans and 50 pounds of seed potatoes and some flowers. We had a full day. My husband Joe mowed the grass for the first time this spring and I did a huge laundry. We also cleaned out the shed and moved my washing machine back out there for the summer. My washing was done in an entrance area to the house during the winter as the shed doesn't have heat.
We helped our children color 66 eggs on Good Friday after everything else was done. I think Benjamin and Loretta's clothes were almost colored too, but they had so much fun doing it. The children wanted to color eggs during the day, but I wanted Joe to be there to help show the younger ones how to color their eggs. It was enjoyable to all do it together. The children grow up so fast. It makes a person wonder what the future holds in store for us all. Only God knows and He will help us through the hard times, if we put our full trust in Him.

We spent Easter Sunday at my sister Emma and Jacob's. Emma had a delicious meal of barbecued ribs, mashed potatoes, gravy, corn, dandelion salad, cheese, winter onions, etc. Then she served a homemade rhubarb crunch and ice cream for dessert. After dishes were washed, my sisters Verena and Susan hid eggs outside and the children hunted for them. They had an exciting time until they found them all. Emma had filled some plastic eggs with candy, so that was fun for the kids to find. Meanwhile Joe and Jacob were going to go hunting for mushrooms, but then it began to rain so they gave it up.

The girls have only 4 1/2 weeks of school left. I am eager to have them home for the summer. They have had really good teachers at school. Elizabeth brought home a bluebird house they made at school so Joe fastened it to a post outside for her. She is looking forward to seeing it get used. I think Elizabeth takes after my Dad as he loved to watch birds and always had purple martin houses up.

My water should be almost hot enough to start the laundry, so I'll go gather all the clothes. I done some ironing after Joe left until it was time to wake the girls up to get ready for school.

Now that rhubarbs have advanced and are ready to use, I'll share the rhubarb crunch recipe that my sister Emma made on Easter Sunday:

RHUBARB CRUNCH
3 cups fresh rhubarb
1 cup sugar
3 Tablespoons flour
Topping:
1 cup brown sugar
1 cup raw rolled oats
1 cups flour
½ cup butter or shortening

Preheat oven to 375 degrees. Mix rhubarb, sugar, and flour well and place in a greased baking dish. Combine the topping ingredients and sprinkle it over the rhubarb mixture. Bake at 375 degrees for 40 minutes. It's done when a toothpick inserted comes out clean. Serve warm with milk or cream.

MAY 2003

I can hear it thundering in the distance. It looks like a storm is brewing in the west. Our neighbors are still outside working up our fields and hope to plant oats and pasture mix yet tonight. They are trying to beat the rain. I'm sure those horses will be glad when they're done pulling the plows. We sure appreciated the neighbors help. They have helped us out a lot already.

I have radishes, lettuce, peas, onions, and green beans peeping through in my garden. This is the time of year when the gardens look so nice, before all those nasty weeds start to pop up.

I was helping my sister Emma sew on her new clothes today and yesterday. Her husband Jacob's brother is getting married in June. I want to help her get her wedding outfits sewed as she helped me out when I needed help to sew. Yesterday, it was eight years ago that Joe's Mom died. We only had Elizabeth at the time, and she was just 10 months old. Joe's Mom was in a hospital two hours away. We went with some of Joe's family that day to the hospital to spend time with his Mom. On the way up, the man driving us there had a flat tire on his van. So the men changed it and that delayed us a little to get to the hospital. The last we had heard was that Joe's Mom was improving and would be able to come home soon. So you can imagine the shock when we got to the hospital and Joe's Dad told us she died five minutes before we got there. A blood clot had entered her lungs and took her life.

My Uncle Toby passed away also on this same date, four years ago. He found out he had cancer and died four months later. My Aunt Lovina (Mom's sister) is getting married again on May 15th to Abe Raber. Abe lost his first wife around the same time Uncle Toby died. Abe has 10 children, all married except for one daughter. Aunt Lovina has nine married children. They will have big gatherings when both their families get together! I wish them God's richest blessings in the years ahead. My sisters Susan and Verena plan to attend their wedding. Aunt Lovina moved an hour north from here after Toby died so she could be with her daughter and son-in-law.

This is now Thursday morning, May 1st. Our neighbors got the oats all planted last night. The storm blew over yesterday and we only got a little shower, not enough to chase them out of the field. Although this morning we had a thunderstorm and a good soaking rain.

I have water heating to do laundry. Looks like it'll be a nice day. The school principal just brought my daughter Susan home from school sick. Hopefully it's nothing too bad.

A reader in Harmony, Minnesota requested a buttermilk cookie recipe. Try this one, and feel free to add your own frosting to it:

BUTTERMILK COOKIES
1 cup shortening
2 cups white sugar
4 eggs
4 cups all-purpose flour
4 teaspoons baking powder
2 teaspoons baking soda
1 teaspoon salt
1 cup buttermilk
4 teaspoons vanilla extract

Preheat oven to 425 degrees. Grease cookie sheets. In a large bowl, cream together the shortening, and sugar. Beat in the eggs, one at a time, then stir in the vanilla. Combine the flour, baking powder, baking soda and salt, stir into the creamed mixture alternately with the buttermilk. Drop by rounded spoonfuls onto the prepared cookie sheet. Bake for 6 to 8 minutes in the preheated oven. Allow cookies to cool on baking sheet for 5 minutes before removing to a wire rack to cool completely.

MAY 2003

It is May 7th already! I heard it rain and thunder during the night. It was quite loud. My 3-year-old Benjamin came to our bed as he's so scared of thunder and lightening. We've had our share of rain this past week. The farmers will probably be glad when it dries up, so they can get back in the fields. This rain should help the hay grow. I'd like to plant more garden when it dries up again. Joe is going to work up another garden for me as I hardly have enough room left for everything I wanted to plant. The corn I planted is up a couple inches now.

Spring is such a lovely time of year. Lilacs and tulips are in full bloom. The girls keep bringing me a fresh bouquet of lilacs to refill my vases. They smell so good! Spring is also a time of outdoor chores. Joe did some mowing last night. All this rain sure makes the grass grow in a hurry. I went out and did some raking here and there.

My sister Emma, husband Jacob, and their children stopped in on the way home from town last night, so I told them I'd make a quick supper and they could eat before heading home. I made tacos and soup.

We have some little chicks that just hatched yesterday. Not all of them are hatched yet. And of all things our cat had seven kittens in our dog Skippy's doghouse. So far Skippy hasn't bothered the little kittens. Joe thought about moving them but is afraid the cat wouldn't like that. When the mother cat leaves the doghouse another cat stays with the kittens.

A lot of people are having luck finding mushrooms. Joe wants to go, but hasn't been able to because of so many chores at night to do. I must get busy I have the irons heating on the stove and hopefully I'll get some clothes ironed. I would also like to do some mending. The pile just keeps getting bigger.

On Friday I plan to attend the Mom's picnic at school with daughter Susan, who is in kindergarten. She is so excited that I'm going to school to eat with her.
I made breakfast burritos for breakfast this morning. I put scrambled eggs, sausage, green peppers, mushrooms and cheese into the burrito shell and rolled it up. Makes an easy breakfast. Meanwhile, some readers have requested recipes to use those spring rhubarbs. Here is a good one:

RHUBARB CAKE
1/2 cup butter
1 egg
1 Tbsp vanilla
1 1/2 cups brown sugar
1/2 tsp. salt
2 cups flour
1 tsp. soda
1 cup buttermilk
1 1/2 cups finely chopped, fresh rhubarb
1/4 cup of sugar and cinnamon mixed together

In a large mixing bowl, cream together butter, vanilla, brown sugar, and salt Add flour, soda, and buttermilk. Fold in finely chopped rhubarb. Pour into cake pan and then sprinkle sugar and cinnamon mixture over the top. Bake at 350 for 30 to 35 minutes or until golden brown on top

MAY 2003

Rain, rain, rain! That's what we've been having almost every day. I think some of my lettuce has been drowned out. One corner of my garden was flooded, luckily though, it's the corner where I hadn't planted yet. I am hoping it'll dry up soon. It hasn't dried off for over a week now. The weeds are taking over the garden.

May 10 was my sister Susan's 27th birthday. My family -- sister Leah & Paul, brother Albert and Sarah Irene, sister Liz and Levi, sister Emma and Jacob, and Joe and I, plus all our children -- spent the day with my sisters Susan and Verena. We were sorting through our parents belongings. The men were gathering tools, etc, outside. The women emptied Mom's cupboard which she had packed with dishes. It was sad to think that Mom was the one to put the dishes in the cupboard. Mom has been gone eight months and Dad died three years ago on May 20th. Oh, how we miss them! I get such a longing to talk to them once more, but we must leave it all to our Heavenly Father, who doesn't make any mistakes. Someday we'll understand it all. We never know what the next day has in store for us.

My brother Amos and Nancy and family couldn't come help on Saturday as they were blessed with their 10th child. Baby Samuel was born on May 5th. This makes two boys and eight girls for them. I imagine Amos and his son, Ben, age 12, were excited to see another boy. This is the first grandchild born since Mother died. There are seven grandchildren born since Dad died.

This is our first nice day now for awhile. The sun is shining and it's 65 degrees at 9 a.m. Daughter Susan is going on a field trip with her grade so I'm glad it's nice for them. Daughter Elizabeth has a summer birthday on June 14th so she is treating her class today for her "happy unbirthday." She will bring two of her friends home with her to spend the night and then go back to school together tomorrow.

Yesterday I had a bad laundry day. Some of the clothes dried between showers. I have some clothes hanging on the rack that I'd like to hang out today now. I have laundry to fold, dishes to wash, floors to mop -- so I better get started. Although I don't think my work will run away. Sometimes I wish it would. Ha!

JUNE 2003

Another cool, windy day, but the sun is shining. Hopefully the wind will dry up the garden. It has been two weeks now that we could last hoe the garden. All these rains have kept it from drying off. We have enjoyed, though, our first taste of lettuce, radishes and green onions from the garden. These garden goodies taste so good and fresh again after the long winter.

Tomorrow, May 22, I will have my 32nd birthday. Three years ago I had a sad birthday. It was the day before Dad's funeral. I think this was the only birthday I had that nobody sang "Happy Birthday" to me. When I was a child, I remember how I would count the days until my birthday. Birthdays were so special to me back then, but the only birthdays I enjoy now are someone else's.

Tomorrow is my daughter Susan's last day of kindergarten. Daughter Elizabeth has three more days yet. They are very excited! I am also looking forward to having them home this summer. They are such a big help to me here at home. Our hen that had the little chicks now struts around outside with her eight little chicks in tow. They are really growing. So are the seven baby kittens I wrote about last week. The dog was getting rough with them, so Joe moved them to the barn and they are doing good in there.

Joe's sister, Ruth and her husband, Chris, and four of their children are finally on their way home from Mexico. They were there for more than three months for doctoring. I am sure they will be excited to join the rest of their family at home and be all together again. I just can't imagine how that would be. Chris's Dad died while they were in Mexico and they were unable to come home for the funeral as their daughter was very sick.

This is now Thursday, May 22 and I am another year older. My sister Emma and children and my children and I are spending the day with our sisters, Verena and Susan. We finally have a nice, warm day! The children are having fun outside. Jacob and Emma's baby Benjamin turned a year old on May 12. My baby Joseph will be 10 months old on Saturday. It seems we should see Mom rocking the babies.

Speaking of Mom a reader in Crab Orchard, Kentucky requested Mom's recipe for homemade biscuits and gravy. Mom would use a milk gravy often. Here is the recipe:

HOMEMADE BISCUITS
 2 cups sifted flour
 1 Tbsp. baking powder
 1 tsp. salt
 1/4 cup mayonnaise
 1 cup milk
 1 tsp. sugar

 Preheat oven to 375. In a large bowl, sift flour, baking powder, and salt. Add mayonnaise, milk, and sugar and mix till smooth. Mix two to three minutes with a spoon until you have a soft white dough. Dough will be slightly sticky. Drop by lightly-floured tablespoons onto a greased 11- by 7- inch cookie sheet or fill 12 muffin tins 2/3 full. When baking on a cookie sheet the batter will spread out during baking. Bake 18-20 minutes. When the biscuits are done, they will look a light, golden brown in color. Biscuits will be about 3-inches wide and 1 1/2 -inches tall. Texture will be light and fluffy. Makes one dozen 3-inch biscuits. Serves 4 to 6

HOMEMADE MILK GRAVY
2 quarts milk
 thickening of 3 Tbsps. flour and 3 Tbsps. milk
1 tsp. margarine

salt and pepper to taste

Heat two quarts milk in a 10-inch skillet. When milk is hot, but not boiling, add flour mixture. Then add margarine. Season with salt and pepper. Stir on medium heat till thickened. Gravy will be very light in color. Serve hot over biscuits. Makes 4 one-cup servings Serves 4 to 6

JUNE 2003

We spent Memorial Day at sister Emma and Jacob's. Joe is helping Jacob train their 2-year old colt. They hitched her to the buggy for the first time on Monday. There can be some anxious moments when training a colt, but she did very well. Joe enjoys training colts.

While we were at Jacobs, Joe went back home to retrieve some items. When he didn't come back right away, sister Verena and I started home to see what was going on. When we came closer we saw lights flashing in front of our house, but they started leaving as we came closer. There had been a car/tractor wreck almost in front of our house and Joe went to see if he could help. So he had been waiting to come as he couldn't get through the blocked road. The man in the car died yet that night. This must've been a shock to family and friends. Life is so uncertain. It's good we don't know what the future holds.

Also on Monday, Emma had done her laundry so we helped her get it in and folded. Sisters Verena and Susan helped get mine out early and most of it was dry before we left for Jacob's. Joe, Jacob, and Susan did some hoeing out in the garden. I think Jacob's family were glad for all that got done. Emma had deep-fried fish, creamed potatoes, salad (with fresh lettuce), onions, radishes, cheese, and ice cream for our dinner.

Sunday we went to church at Joe's sister Loretta and Henry's in Michigan. We started out at 4:30 a.m. and had breakfast halfway there. I always enjoy when I get a break from cooking! The children mostly slept on the way there. Jacob, Emma, and children and sisters Verena and Susan went also. In the afternoon we visited with Joe's Dad before starting for home. We stopped in at Joe's sister Ruth and her husband Chris to see how their daughter, Lydianne, is getting along. She's on the road to recovery but still very weak. They're glad to be together after three months in Mexico for doctoring.

Last Saturday, Jacob helped Joe form up new walkways in front of our house. Tuesday evening they cemented the walks. It looks so much better now with the new walks and our yard has been leveled out and grass sown. Our yard has been torn up since we had 11 tree stumps removed. Another of our hens has hatched 13 baby chicks so we have 21 chicks so far.

A reader in Devils Lake, N.D. requested a chicken-corn soup recipe. Try this delicious one!

LANCASTER COUNTRY CHICKEN CORN SOUP
1 (4- to 5-pound) chicken, cut into 8 pieces
2-1/2 to 3 quarts water, or as needed
1 large onion
8 to 10 black peppercorns
2 tsps. salt, or to taste
10 ears of corn, (or 4 cups frozen corn kernels)
3 celery stalks, diced with leaves
6 ounces wide egg noodles (or use your own homemade equivalent)
Freshly ground white pepper
2/3 cup finely chopped fresh parsley
2 hard-cooked eggs, chopped

Place chicken in soup pot with enough water to cover. Bring to a boil, reduce heat, and skim foam as it rises to the surface. When it has subsided, add onion, peppercorns and salt. Simmer gently but steadily, partly covered, for about 1-1/2 hours or until tender. Remove chicken. Trim and discard bones and skin, and onion. Let soup cool, then skim fat from surface. Tear meat into spoonable pieces and return to soup. Cut kernels from 4 ears of corn, then grate kernels from remaining 6 ears. Add whole kernels and grated or pureed corn to soup along with celery and noodles. Simmer gently until corn and noodles are cooked. Add salt and white pepper to taste. Stir in parsley and serve, garnishing each portion with chopped egg. (This soup freezes well, but do that before adding the noodles). Yield: 4 to 6 bowls of soup

JUNE 2003

The sun is shining brightly which is nice to see after a few cloudy days. This spring has sure been cool. I'll be glad when it warms up to stay. I am writing this at Mom's living room table, where she wrote most of her columns. Oh how I wish she would still be here to do this writing. I will never be able to write like her. She was very special to me and a very good example, so I shall try my best with this column, and hope you readers enjoy it.

We are staying here at Mom and Dad's place for a couple of days getting ready for the upcoming auction of my parents 104 acre farm and all their personal property. How sad to see all this take place. I never realized how much work there is in getting ready for an auction. I'm sure sisters Verena and Susan will be glad when it is all over. After the sale, we'll help Verena and Susan move their belongings to their new home and help them get settled in. The house will be a lot smaller than this one, so I think they'll like it better. Although it'll be a big change on them as they were born here and have lived here all of their life. Life brings changes and we must go on. God is a great help! There are three apple trees here in the front yard, which Dad and Mom planted in 1971, the year I was born. They are very nice now and looks like they're loaded with apples. There are so many memories around here, but a place doesn't bring happiness.

There is a new set of buildings going up around the corner from here. It looks like they are making good progress. They have the basement poured and the foundation done for the new barns. There must be a lot of work to building everything new like that.

We spent last Saturday at Joe's uncle Jake's (sister Emma's husband's parents). Joe helped them cement their new barn floor. We drove the 12 miles with horse and buggy. It started raining when we were almost four miles from there. This is when the umbrellas really come in hand. We have a two-seated buggy so we need two umbrellas. Daughter Elizabeth can hold the one in the back. It quit raining after we were there awhile. We stopped in town on the way home for groceries.

Sister Emma was here the last couple of days helping get ready for the auction. They washed off most of the walls and ceilings. The bedroom and porch still have to be done. We would also like to get the grass mowed today. The house is starting to look empty as some of the furniture has been carried out to the wash house for the sale. Sister Liz and children just drove in so we'll have more help today. Thanks to all you great readers for your encouraging letters and notes

JUNE 2003

It is 5:30 a.m. and my husband, Joe, just left for work. We are here at my sisters' new home. Verena and Susan are renting from the lady across the road, not far from the home place. My sister Liz, her husband, Levi, my sister Emma and husband, Jacob, and a couple of friends helped move most of my sisters' belongings here last night. We have a lot of boxes to unpack and some cleaning to do today. This is the first time Verena and Susan have had to move. It'll be a big change in their lives.

Jacob, Emma, and their children also spent the night here. The children are all still asleep. They are tired from a big day yesterday. We decided to stay for the night, as it was so late when we got done moving things. This way, we can get an early start, and the children can sleep in. My sister Liz and her children plan to come help today.

Dad and Mom's house is almost empty now. Such a sad change has taken place. The farm was sold to some neighbors (also Amish), so it won't be in the family anymore. Dad and Mom's belongings were all sold at the public auction on Saturday, June 14th. Most of the furniture was bought by family members. I bought their cherry bedroom suite, which we have set up in our bedroom now. It rained the day before the sale, but most of the good things were inside the barn, tool shed and wash house. We had a nice day for the sale. It wasn't too hot, and it didn't rain. My daughter Elizabeth had her 9th birthday on the day of the sale. She said she won't ever forget her 9th birthday, when Grandpa and Grandma's things all were sold. My, how fast these years fly by. It's so hard to believe it's been nine years ago that our first child was born.

Baby Joseph will be 11 months next week. He is awake now. He's pushing teeth again and doesn't seem happy.

The weeds in my garden have taken over with all this rain. I hope I'll be able to get in and work the garden tomorrow. We want to plant a small garden here for Verena and Susan today, if we get time. It won't take much for them, but it's nice to go out and get fresh vegetables whenever you want them.

I better get this (letter) to a close and go help my sisters. There are a lot of dishes to be washed. A reader in Erlanger, Ky., requested a rhubarb recipe. Try this one for coffeecake:

RHUBARB COFFEECAKE
2 cups all-purpose flour
1 teaspoon baking soda
1 teaspoon salt
1 1/4 cups brown sugar
2 eggs
1 cup solid vegetable shortening at room temperature
2 teaspoons vanilla extract
1/2 cup buttermilk or soured milk (made with lemon juice; don't use old milk because it would have a high bacteria count)
2 1/2 cups diced rhubarb (stems only)
For topping:
1/3 cup sugar and 2 teaspoons cinnamon.

In a large mixer bowl, beat together the shortening, brown sugar, eggs, and vanilla. Add the buttermilk or soured milk. In a smaller bowl, stir together the dry ingredients (flour, soda, salt). Have oven heating to 375 degrees.
Add dry ingredients to the shortening mixture and stir to make a thick batter; do not over-mix. Fold in the rhubarb and spread batter in a lightly greased 9-inch square baking pan. For topping, stir together in a small bowl the 1/3 cup sugar and 2 teaspoons cinnamon. Sprinkle over rhubarb batter.
Bake coffeecake at 375 degrees

JULY 2003

It is now 8 a.m. and I have water heating on the kerosene stove to do the laundry. Another hot day! But there is a nice west breeze coming in now. I want to get the wash on the lines and then get some clothes ironed that we'll need for the wedding tomorrow. Joe's cousin, Martin (Jacob's brother), is getting married. Hope it'll be a cooler day as we plan to go with horse and buggy. We want to start out earlier before the sun gets too hot. The wedding is 12 miles from here, so that's a long ride with horse and buggy. A hot day can also be very difficult on the wedding cooks, with all the hard work around the warm stoves.

Next week Joe will have his vacation, so the children and I are looking forward to that. We want to go help Jacob and Emma prepare for church services, which will be held there a week from Sunday. Emma was busy sewing for the wedding this week yet. Today she went to go help bake pies and all they do the day before a wedding. There is a lot of work to be done in getting ready for a wedding. We were surprised to get an invitation to Joe's cousin, Denny's, wedding in Milroy, Ind., in July. We would like to go if Joe can have a day off work again. Meanwhile, with all the preparation for the wedding, weeds have taken over in my garden. It needs to be hoed so badly, but when will I find time? Maybe next week. I didn't get much of anything done this week. I had a high fever for a couple of days and now I'm battling a real bad cold. I guess when a person gets sick they appreciate their good health a lot more.

On these hot days the children have been filling the little swimming pool out back with water. It sure helps keep them cool. Joe was mowing the grass last night until dark. He mowed over our newly planted grass for the first time. We had the right rains to make it grow fast. We haven't had rain for a week so the farmers are getting their hay in. That's another hot job in this heat. A good shower would cool off everything. We will probably have church services here at our house in about five weeks. So the house will get a thorough cleaning before then. It's always a good feeling to have everything cleaned again. Last week I was cleaning out drawers. The children outgrow some of their clothes so fast. Little Joseph is 11 months old now and has eight teeth. He seems a lot happier since his new teeth are through.

A reader in Zanesville, Ohio, asked about a salad recipe that can use some of the fresh garden goodies. Try this one for Seven Layer Salad:

SEVEN LAYER SALAD
1 head lettuce
2 cups fresh (frozen is OK also) peas or cauliflower

1 medium onion, sliced
Chopped hard-boiled eggs, to your taste
Celery, if desired
1 pound bacon, fried and chopped
2 cups mayonnaise
1/3 cup sugar
2 cups Cheddar cheese, grated

Chop or tear lettuce into one inch pieces. In the bottom of a 2-quart casserole dish, place a layer of lettuce along the bottom. Then layer the peas, onion, eggs, celery and bacon. For the seventh layer, mix the mayonnaise and sugar until thin. Spread mayonnaise-sugar mixture on top. Do not stir. Chill for 12 hours. Before serving, sprinkle with grated Cheddar cheese and bacon bits. Serves 6.

JULY 2003

It has been a hot, humid day. We left early this morning to go help my sister Emma and her husband Jacob prepare for church services which will be held at their place on Sunday. Joe and Jacob hauled manure and cleaned out the barn where they will have the church services. Emma and I washed down walls and ceilings, etc. We hope to go help Jacob's again tomorrow. Emma would like to wash her curtains and clean her windows. There is a lot of work to get everything clean, but it's a good feeling to have everything clean again.

On Friday, we went to the wedding of Jacob's brother, Martin. We started out early for the long, 12-mile ride with the horse and buggy. It was a nice, cool morning so it was better traveling for the horse. In the afternoon, after the wedding, we visited with Joe's sister Ruth and family. They insisted we stay for supper so we had a good barbecued chicken supper. Our children really enjoyed the evening. We all piled into the horse and buggy for the remaining nine miles home and arrived back to our place around. 10:30 p.m. The children all feel asleep in the buggy on the way home.

July is a month full of special dates in our family. Our daughter Loretta had her third birthday yesterday, July 1. We made a cake for her and had her blow out the candles. She enjoyed the day so much that she keeps telling us that today is still her birthday. Benjamin will be 4 years old on July 14, so we will have two 3-year olds until then. Meanwhile, our baby Joseph will be a year old on the July 24. Joe and my 10th anniversary is on July 15 and my brother Albert's 39th birthday is also on that date. My sister Emma will be 30 on the July 19. Mom's birthday is July 18. She would have been 67. She is missed so much! This is now Thursday morning. I was too tired to finish this last night. Everyone is still asleep so I thought I'd finish this while all is peaceful. There is a nice breeze coming in the window. Looks like it will be a beautiful day.

We want to eat a quick breakfast and go over to help Jacob again today. With Jacob's brother's wedding last week it put them a little behind in preparations for their upcoming church services.

A reader in Bradenton, Florida asked about a homemade ham salad recipe. Try this delicious one:

HOMEMADE HAM SALAD
2 cups ground, cooked ham
3 small stalks celery, diced fine
1 large dill pickle
1 1/4 tsps. dry mustard
1/4 tsp. onion powder
1/2 cup mayonnaise
1 Tbsp. lemon juice
1/2 tsp. salt

Chop ham and grind through a hand-grinder or electric food processor, for those of you with electric. Pack ham firmly into each cup and then put into a bowl. Then cut celery, and pickle with a sharp knife and add into ham. In a separate bowl, add dry mustard, onion powder, mayonnaise, salt, and lemon juice and stir. Additional mayonnaise may be added to suit your taste. Then stir this mixture into the ham. Mix and spread onto sandwich bread. Ham salad tastes even better the next day after being refrigerated overnight. Also tastes great spread on crackers. Makes one pound of salad.

JULY 2003

It was a busy work day today, with some projects unfinished. The girls and I cleaned the upstairs bedrooms at our house. It took longer than I expected as I went through the closets also. I did some weeding out in the garden tonight, but the mosquitoes were so bad that I gave up. Joe was mowing the yard but didn't get quite finished. Everything is still pretty wet from all our recent rains.

We had fried chicken, creamed potatoes, fresh green beans, cheese, etc for supper tonight. Some of my green bean plants are turning yellow, probably it's been too wet for them. I heard of others that are having the same problem. We did haveour first meal of sweet corn from the garden last night which we all enjoyed.

There has been a lot of clean-up going on since the flooding of the past weeks. Around 227 homes in this area were damaged and six have been lost completely. I feel so sorry for the people that lost their belongings, but these things can be replaced. The lives that were lost can't be and my deepest sympathy goes to these families. God has a purpose for everything. Someday we'll understand it all.

My brother Albert and some of his children visited today and gave us some exciting news. They had another boy, named Andrew. He was born yesterday, July 15, on Albert's birthday. Albert Jr., age 11, was also born on his Dad's birthday so they have three in their family with a July 15 birthday now. This was also our 15th wedding anniversary. Our baby Joseph gave us some excitement this week as he started taking his first steps. The children are so excited they make him try again and again. It seems seeing the sixth child take those first steps is just as exciting as seeing the first one.

My sister Liz and her husband, Levi, had church services at their house on Sunday. They had a good lunch and supper for all who attended. There were well over 100 for supper. Levi made chili soup outside in the kettle. Liz had three different salads, ham, cheese, pickles, red beets, hot peppers, fruit, puddings, cakes, pies, and other desserts. They had a very nice day. The services were held in their big barn and lunch was served in the house.

My sister Emma and her husband, Jacob, gave us a scare on Monday. Jacob passed out a few times Monday morning. They were able to take him to a local emergency room where he was there a couple hours while doctors took X-rays and tests. They think he inhaled too much of the fly spray he uses to spray his horses with. We are glad it wasn't anything worse. Jacob was off work for three days as he was very weak after that. He must've not had enough ventilation where he sprays his horse. A person just doesn't know what God has in store for us from day to day. We only need to take one day at a time and leave it all in "His" hands.

Meanwhile, here is a recipe for zucchini casserole since the zucchinis are plentiful in the garden right now:

ZUCCHINI CASSEROLE
4 cups grated zucchini
1 cup Bisquick
1 /3 cup vegetable oil
1 /2 cup grated cheese (any kind)
1 /2 teaspoon garlic powder
1 tablespoon parsley flakes
4 eggs, beaten

Mix all ingredients together. Make sure you mix everything together well. Put in casserole and bake at 350 for approximately 50 minutes. Casserole will be golden brown and bubbly when ready.

JULY 2003

Our baby, Joseph, is a year old today, July 24. I want to make a little cake for him. We'll all enjoy watching him dig in and eat it tonight.

It's 5:15 a.m. and my husband, Joe, is almost ready to leave for work. The children are all still asleep yet. I made Joe a cheese toastie and eggs for his breakfast, then I decided to get this written and ready to put in the mail. We are having real busy days right now, with church services having been set here for Aug. 3.

Joe has been working outside until dark every evening. He's building a loft in the tool shed so he'll have more storage space. We would also like to have church services in there. We ordered new windows for our house, which will be ready to be put in next Thursday and Friday. Ours are pretty old and we were in need of new ones. I will be so glad for the new windows as they will be so much easier to clean. They will tilt inward so everything can be cleaned from the inside. No more dragging the step ladder from window to window. Whew!

My sisters, Emma, Verena, and Susan, have been helping me this week in preparing for church services. We washed down walls and ceilings and were cleaning the basement. It takes time to clean all the jars of food on the shelves in the basement. We need to clean the floor yet. We had water in the basement from all that recent rain. What a mess! But we can be thankful it wasn't worse. Joe hopes to get that problem fixed sometime. There is so much work to do and so little time. I cleaned two of the upstairs bedrooms and have one yet to go. So I'm hoping to get to that today.

We are enjoying fresh potatoes out of the garden. We didn't get as many as we should've, as some are rotted from too much wet weather. We had our first tomato yesterday from the garden, but I wouldn't be surprised if some of my tomato plants don't survive. I put out around 45 plants, though, so hopefully we'll still have enough. Susan gave us a lift in helping weed our garden yesterday. We also dug out the onions. Those did pretty good this year. We have another meal of sweet corn yet, then the stalks will be ready to be pulled.

Tomorrow night we'll help Verena and Susan move the remainder of their belongings. Next week will be closing and the new owners will take over the old homeplace. Meanwhile, cousin Toby's wife has everyone in our church invited for dinner on Sunday to surprise Toby for his 40th birthday, which is July 31. So lots going on around here. I hope all you readers are well!

A reader from London, Ohio, remembered the pie my mom used to make by the name of "Bob Andy Pie." Yes, I can share that recipe. Here it is:

BOB ANDY PIE
2 cups white sugar
2 cups milk
1/2 teaspoon cloves
1 teaspoon cinnamon
3 heaping tablespoons flour
1 tablespoon butter
3 eggs (beat yolks and whites separately)

Mix together sugar, flour, cloves and cinnamon. Add butter, beaten egg yolks and milk. Also, whites of eggs. Pour into two unbaked pie crusts and bake at 350.

AUGUST 2003

4:30 a.m. It is Saturday morning and my husband, Joe, is leaving for work. He has to work until 9 a.m. today, which he dreaded to think of going into work with all the chores that needing to be done here at home. As he got ready for work, I folded laundry that I washed yesterday but didn't get put away.

5:15 a.m. I sweep the the floors and do some organizing. Then I get some mail ready to send. I know it'll be a busy day so I thought I would get that off my mind.

6:30 a.m. I make a big pot of homemade sausage gravy, which is a delicious way to begin a day! We'll have a full house today, as my sister Emma, husband Jacob and their children, plus my sisters Verena and Susan are coming to help us, so we told them to come for breakfast. We'll be having church services here Sunday so there's lots of cleaning and preparation involved. So nice to have family come over to help.

7 a.m. Jacob's, Verena and Susan arrive and we make homemade biscuits and fry eggs. My sleeping children are surprised and excited to be woken up by Jacob's children. I was glad they slept longer as they will have a big day.

7:45 a.m. We all eat a breakfast of sausage gravy, biscuits, fried eggs, cheese, fresh hot peppers from the garden and tomatoes.

8:30 a.m. Breakfast is over and the children are all outside playing except for Emma's 1-year-old, Benjamin, and my 1-year-old, Joseph. It's so cute to watch them play. It seems no matter how many toys they have, they always want the same toy. Verena washes the breakfast dishes while Susan goes out to weed the garden. Those weeds just come up so fast. I go out and dig up some more potatoes and pull enough sweet corn for lunch. Emma gets the worst job of cleaning: my three kerosene stoves. This is a big job to clean out the pipelines and get the burners all cleaned.

A fire could result if a pipeline would get clogged up. I usually clean the pipelines twice in a year. Jacob is pulling down the old cow stable, where Joe used to milk our cow.

9:25 a.m. Joe comes home from work and Jacob and he are working on the new loft in the tool shed where we plan to have church services Aug. 3.

11 a.m. Verena starts the grill to grill some pork steaks for lunch. Then I help her husk the sweet corn from the garden and get that on the stove. I also wash fresh potatoes and put those on the burner. The two-burner stove is all cleaned and looks and works a lot better.

12:30 p.m. Lunch is ready and everyone comes in to eat. We enjoy a meal of barbecued pork steak, sweet corn, potatoes, cheese, lettuce, tomatoes, hot peppers, watermelon and cookies. Hard to believe the children will all head back to school soon. It's nice to have them home.

1:15 p.m. Joe and Jacob head back out to the tool shed to finish the loft. Verena and I wash dishes while Emma finishes up on the stoves. My sister Susan heads back out to the garden. I make some fresh lemonade, which always goes so good on a hot day.

3:30 p.m. Emma and I wash the children's hair, which needed it after a day of playing in the barn and outdoors. Verena swept and mopped the kitchen floor. Susan helps Joe and Jacob unload a wagonload of hay.

5:30 p.m. The loft is finished and everyone is ready to call it a day.

5:45 p.m. Jacob's and Verena and Susan head for home. We sure appreciated their help.

Here is the recipe for biscuits that we fixed for our breakfast. I hope you readers enjoy them. Thanks for all of your encouraging cards and notes. They are much appreciated!

HOMEMADE BREAKFAST BISCUITS
2 cups sifted flour
1 tablespoons baking powder
1 teaspoon salt
1/4 cup mayonnaise
1 cup milk
1 teaspoon sugar

Sift flour, baking powder and salt. Add remaining ingredients. Mix 'till smooth and drop by tablespoons on greased cookie sheet or fill 12 muffin tins 2/3 full. Bake 18 to 20 minutes at 375.

AUGUST 2003

Church services were held in our tool shed on Sunday. (Editor's Note: Old Order Amish families hold church services every other week at the home of a church member. Often, especially during nice weather, they'll hold the service in an "out-building." Lovina has a spacious tool shed that is very comfortable for holding services.)

Quite a few families attended from other church districts, so we had a big attendance. My brother Albert and his wife brought their baby Andrew to church for the first time. We had rain on Sunday morning, so some of the people were caught in the rain on their way to church. Some had to detour because of water being over the roads again.
We've had lots of flooding this summer. We had rain Friday night and Saturday. I never took time to go to the rain gauge until Monday morning. By then, it showed almost 5 inches. The rains stopped for a while Sunday morning, just until we had the first table seated to eat after church, then we got another good shower. We could seat 40 people at one time to eat in our attached garage area. We served ham, hot dogs, cheese spread, peanut butter spread, lettuce, pickles, hot peppers, red beets, sandwich spread, strawberry jam, butter, and coffee.

I didn't invite anyone back to our house for the evening supper. This is the first time that I didn't, but I think we were all ready for a break. Next week my husband, Joe, will be starting to work at 5 a.m. every day and putting in 10-hour days. So we were glad to get to bed early.

A lot of work goes into preparing to hold a Sunday church service at home. My sisters Susan and Verena were here helping Saturday. Jacob (sister Emma's husband) also came awhile to help Joe haul some more manure out of the barn. We cleaned the windows in the garage and tool shed, then mopped both floors. The basement windows and floors were cleaned, also. The church benches were all set up in the tool shed, and the tables for eating were set up in our garage. We mopped all the floors again in our house.

Also on Saturday, we mixed the peanut butter spread that is traditionally served for an after-church meal. (Editor's note: This spread is served in other Amish communities as well.) The spread is a mixture of peanut butter, marshmallow creme and corn syrup. Later on Saturday afternoon, Verena and Susan took all six children home with them and washed their hair and gave them all a bath. That really helped me out, and I could get the dishes all ready for the next day and do the last-minute things.

Monday was cleanup day. Verena and Susan stayed Sunday evening so they could help me. We did laundry, swept and mopped the floors, cleaned the garage and washed a lot of dishes. It is a good feeling to have the house all cleaned again after church. Now, I hope to sew some school dresses for Elizabeth and Susan. School will start Aug. 19 -- already. This summer flew by so fast. Elizabeth will be in third grade and Susan in first grade.

Thursday and Friday we had 22 new windows put in our house. I am so excited for the new windows. They are so much easier to clean. But now if my windows get dirty, I have no excuse not to clean them.

A reader in North Newton, Kansas, requested a recipe for a zucchini cake to use up all the fresh garden zucchini this time of year. Try this delicious recipe:

ZUCCHINI CAKE
3 eggs
2 cups sugar
1 cup vegetable oil
1 tablespoon vanilla extract
1 teaspoon salt
1/4 teaspoon baking powder
1 tablespoon cinnamon,
2 teaspoons baking soda
1 cup finely chopped nuts
4 tablespoons unsweetened cocoa powder,
2 cups flour
2 cups grated zucchini, unpeeled.

Have oven heating to 350 degrees. Lightly grease a 9x13-inch baking pan or coat it with cooking spray. In a large bowl, combine the eggs, sugar, oil, vanilla and salt. Mix well. In a smaller bowl, stir together (or sift) the baking powder, cinnamon, baking soda, cocoa and flour. Blend into the egg mixture along with the nuts and zucchini. Turn batter into the baking pan and bake at 350 degrees for about 1 hour or until cake tests done.

AUGUST 2003

On Saturday our family enjoyed a day at the zoo in a nearby city. It was cloudy in the morning, but turned real nice with the sun shining. I think the children enjoyed the monkeys the most. This was the first time we took the children to a zoo. We went when we only had our daughter, Elizabeth, but she was too small to remember. She is now 9 years old. My sister Emma, her husband, Jacob, and family, and my sisters Verena and Susan also went. We had some tired children when we arrived back home!

I had told Jacob's family, Verena, and Susan to all come for a brunch on Sunday forenoon. We had fried eggs, potatoes, bacon, cheese, tomatoes, hot peppers, toast, butter and jam, milk, and juice for our meal together.
It was nice to sleep a little longer on Sunday morning, as my husband, Joe, has been leaving for work at 4:30 a.m. every morning.

On Sunday afternoon we all went to the viewing of our good neighbor, who passed away at age 46.
Our sympathy goes out to this family. We do not know what God has in store for us from day to day, but we do know He makes no mistakes.

On Monday I did an extra-huge laundry. Around 2 p.m., my cousin Daniel and his wife came with a load of hay that we had ordered. Joe wasn't home from work yet so Daniel and his wife and I put the 155 bales up in the haymow.
I could tell this morning that I'm not used to putting up hay anymore. Mom and we girls always helped Dad and the boys put up hay years ago. We only had two brothers, so we girls helped a lot. Joe was so surprised when he came home and saw that we had put the hay up in the haymow already.

In the evening, Joe was working on taking down the old tool shed door while I did some work in the yard after taking the clothes off the lines. It was thundering and lightning real bad, but we never got more than some sprinkles.

This is now Wednesday at 4:30 a.m. Joe has gone to work and, in a little while, I plan to go to town to get school supplies for the girls. They found out who their new teachers will be and are getting excited about school coming up. I will miss their help at home. My baby Joseph will be lost without Elizabeth here. She is his favorite, and he always wants her to hold him. He's giving us so many scares as he has started climbing now. He pushes a chair up to the table and crawls on top of the table. Such a sweet innocent age!

AUGUST 2003

It is 8:30 a.m. on a very nice, breezy Thursday. I just finished washing the breakfast dishes. The mornings are a little more "rushy" now with school having started. My girls, Elizabeth and Susan, have to be ready to go to school by 7:10 a.m. My younger children wake up earlier now, too, so that I can feed them all breakfast at the same time.
I ironed some clothes after my husband, Joe, left for work this morning, but I still have quite a bit to do yet. I want to get this written before the mailman comes. If the clothes get hung out later today, they should still dry nicely with the breeze we have.

This is Elizabeth's and Susan's third day of school. They were excited to meet their new teachers and very pleased after they did. Next year, my daughter Verena will be in kindergarten. She can really be a big help to me here at home, so I'll miss her. She does a very good job of sweeping the floors and wiping off dishes. On Monday, after doing the laundry, I sewed Elizabeth and Susan each a new dress for school. I didn't get the aprons sewed yet, so I hope I can do that later today. I ordered peaches for next week, so I'll be busy getting those into jars. I always think peaches are easy to process.

My sister Verena will turn 37 tomorrow, Aug. 22. She and my sister Susan are still getting settled into their new house (following the auction of their parents' farm, the late Ben and Elizabeth Coblentz).

This has been an enjoyable week so far. On Monday evening, our neighbors helped Joe put in our hay, so I think we now have enough hay for the coming winter. My garden has dried off well, so I want to dig out the rest of the potatoes before we get more rain. I have had only a few tomatoes this year, but my sister Emma gave me some from her garden. Hers are doing pretty well. My brother Amos gave us some pickles, and my sister Liz gave us some sweet corn. I sure appreciated it all. This was the first year my garden was this bad. It had too much water standing in it too often. Last year, I had more tomatoes than we could possibly use, and this year I only have a few. It's been such a wet summer, which has not been good for the gardens.

A reader in Gig Harbor, Washington, requested a hot ham salad recipe. Try this tasty recipe.

HOT HAM SALAD
3 cups diced ham
1/2 cup sweet pickle relish
2 teaspoons minced onion
2 teaspoons prepared mustard
3/4 cup mayonnaise
1 cup diced celery
2 hard-cooked eggs
1 tablespoon lemon juice
1/4 teaspoon each salt and pepper
1 cup crushed potato chips.
(Editor's note: The salt should not be necessary, due to the salt content of the ham, mayonnaise and potato chips.)

Combine all ingredients except potato chips. Place in a 2-quart casserole. Sprinkle potato chips on top. Bake, covered, for 20 minutes at 425 degrees, until top is bubbly and golden. Yield: 8 servings.

SEPTEMBER 2003

Supper is being prepared as I write this column. My nine-year-old daughter, Elizabeth, is frying ribs for our supper. She asked if she could do it, so I lit the kerosene burner for her and got the pan ready. I showed her how to roll the ribs in flour and then put salt and pepper on it. I sliced the ribs in thin pieces so they wouldn't take so long to get ready. After the first pan was done I told Elizabeth to give her brothers and sisters a taste to see if they like it and they did. She was excited to be able to fry the meat. I guess that's the only way they'll learn how to do it. It's just hard to believe I have a daughter old enough to do that.

Elizabeth and Susan washed and dried the dishes after they were home from school and had their homework done. I often leave the dishes from lunch for them to wash after they come home. It is another rainy and dreary evening. It has been rainy the last three days and water is across the road in some places. It's not too high yet. Our rain gauge shows we have had 4 1/2 inches since Sunday night. My garden was in need of rain but it's almost too much for it now. It sure has been a wet summer. I am hoping for a nice day tomorrow, as I haven't done any laundry this week yet, on account of rain. We cannot choose our weather - we have to take whatever the Good Lord sends us.

I want to go check if my potatoes are soft and finish supper. My husband Joe will be in soon and I want to have supper ready so we can eat. I will finish this later.

This is now Wednesday morning and the girls just left for school. I have water heating to do laundry but I'm not sure if it will be nice enough of a day yet.

My daughters Elizabeth and Susan and some of their cousins are going straight from school to my sisters Verena and Susan's house. They will spend the night there and go to school from there in the morning. The house here will seem so empty tonight. It's good for them to get used to being away from Dad and Mom, but I know I'll miss them so much. Probably more than they'll miss me. I know they will be taken good care of at Verena and Susan's. They were very excited!

Meanwhile, my other children, Verena, Benjamin, and Loretta are outside playing. Baby Joseph is inside with me. They came in awhile ago and asked for coats to wear. It's 65 degrees so it is probably chilly to them after those 90 degree days last week.

I'm anxious to try out my new sewing machine today. We bought it last week but I haven't had time to sew.

A reader in Bloomsburg, Pennsylvania requested an omelet recipe. Try this good one:

DELICIOUS OMELETE
¼ cup shredded Monterey Jack cheese (or other in you prefer)

Filling:
1 teaspoon butter or margarine
2 tablespoons chopped onions
1/4 cup chopped green or red pepper
1/4 cup chopped baked ham or fried bacon

Omelet:
2 eggs
1 teaspoon butter or margarine
2 tablespoons water
pinch of salt and pepper

To make filling: In a small non-stick skillet or omelet pan, heat butter over medium heat. Add onion and peppers, cook two minutes. Stir in meat. Cook two more minutes or more. Empty filling onto a plate; set aside. Wipe skillet clean.

To make omelet: In a small bowl, beat together eggs, water, salt and pepper just until blended. Add butter to skillet. Melt over medium heat. Pour egg mixture into skillet; with a fork pull cooked egg toward center. Repeat all around edge of omelet until it's barely moist on top. Sprinkle cheese over half of omelet. Top cheese with filling mixture. Using a spatula, carefully flip unfilled half of omelet over filled half. Run spatula around edge of omelet and slide onto plate. Makes one omelet.

SEPTEMBER 2003

Everything has quieted down here at the Eichers. It's been a long, hard day and everyone has gone to bed for a good night's rest. I will join them as soon as I get this written.

The girls had a nice surprise this morning! They went out to the bus and the bus driver said there would be no school for the elementary school students (Editor's note: most Old Order Amish children in Lovina's community attend public schools) They had a water main break at the school. I had some very excited girls! They were so tired yet and weren't ready to get up and get ready for school. After they heard they didn't have to go they were far from being tired.

Last night we were at my sister Emma and Jacob's for supper. Joe helped Jacob load hay. Now tonight, Jacob's came here and he helped Joe get ready to put in new doors on the tool shed and garage.

My sisters Verena and Susan also came tonight, so Emma, Verena and Susan helped me process peaches. We have over half of them done and I want to finish the rest tomorrow morning. It sure goes faster with that many people helping. Processing peaches is simple: you peel them, cut them in half (some people slice them), and put them in jars. Then you make a syrup of sugar and water and pour it over the peaches and cold pack them for 10 minutes. If you cook them too long they will be too soft. During the winter, we open the jars of peaches just to serve on the table with meals. The kids like cake and peaches, they mix it together on their plate. Sometimes I put peaches in Joe's lunch-pail for work. Another way I like to fix peaches is in a peach upside down cake.

I also ordered two bushels of grapes as I want to process some grape juice. I am always glad when that job is done. I don't put in as much sugar as the recipe calls for and the children don't seem to mind. I put in just enough sugar where it tastes good. I like to stay away from using too much. After we have our own home-canned grape juice the store bought doesn't taste good, it's too sweet.

SEPTEMBER 2003

This is Sept. 17th at 9 p.m. and the children have all gone to bed and are sound asleep. The children and I spent the day at my sisters, Susan and Verena's house, helping them get ready for an upcoming yard sale. My sister Emma and children were also there helping.

Our minds go back to a year ago tonight when we received the shocking news that dear Mother had passed away in Missouri (Editor's Note: Elizabeth was in Missouri, traveling with her editor and two daughters, Verena and Susan). . We had gone to bed and were awakened to hear Levi (sister Liz's husband) knocking and calling our name at our bedroom window. I didn't realize what dreadful news they had come to tell us. Oh, it couldn't be true! We kept Levi's children here while they left to go tell my brothers and sisters the sad news. I had been so tired when I went to bed, as Emma and I had been washing walls and ceilings for the upcoming church services that would be held here at our house.

After the sad news, sleep would not come anymore. Around 1 a.m. my brother Albert arrived and asked if I'd like to go to the phone with him and talk with Verena and Susan in Missouri. I was glad to go and Joe stayed here with the children. The phone is around 3 miles from here and when Albert and I got there, Jacob and Emma were also there talking on the phone with Verena and Susan. It was so hard to grasp that Mom had passed away and to try to think how different life would be.

Jacob's took me home and they stayed here until daylight. Emma helped me clean up my house and we ironed some clothes - anything we could do to occupy our minds. In the morning we went to the homeplace to start getting ready for the funeral. As the news traveled around, friends and relatives came to see if they could help. The furniture in the house was all taken out to clear room for benches that would set up for the funeral service. Some of it was carried upstairs and the rest was put out in the wash-house. The tool shed was cleared out to make room for church benches in there also. Mom died on a Tuesday night but her body did not come home until Saturday, and the funeral was held on Monday.

Funeral services were held in the house. Every room was filled with family members. The tool shed was filled with friends as services were also held in there.

Life would be different from now on, I told myself. It is so nice to be able to ask your parents for advice, and now in less than 2 1/2 years they had both passed away. Appreciate your parents if you are lucky enough to still have them.

Without God's help we wouldn't have made it through it all. "He" makes no mistakes, so we do not want to question "His" ways.

When we got back from the graveyard, the young boys and girls had mopped the floors in the house and put the furniture back in place. We stayed with Verena and Susan in the homeplace that night and they came to our place the next day. The rest of the week we were busy cleaning here as church services would be held here on Sunday. Life goes on. We have so many precious memories of Mother.

Here is a recipe for "Oatmeal Pie", the very first recipe to run in Mom's column back in 1991

SEPTEMBER 2003

Fall has arrived! We're having very chilly mornings these last few days. We don't have a wood and coal-burning stove yet for this winter. Our other one wasn't in good shape anymore so we moved it out last spring. A little heat feels good on these first cool mornings of autumn. With the kerosene lamps lit and a burner lit on the stove the house can warm up in a hurry.

Yesterday, I got a big job accomplished. I had such a huge stack of clothes that had to be ironed, so I started right after the girls left for school and continued with it for most of the day. What a relief to have that done! Before I had children, I could have the clothes ironed in a hurry. Now I have to stop ironing to check up on them, change a diaper, or keep them from getting into things. While I am doing that, the iron - which gets its heat from sitting on the burner of the stove - will get too hot, so I then have to let them cool a bit, etc. Now don't get me wrong, I wouldn't give up any of my children. Children take a lot of time and patience, but they are so sweet and innocent and so precious!

Today I want to do my laundry if the weather permits. My week has been so busy and it has also been rainy so I haven't done any laundry yet this week. I'll have a very big pile of wash to do today.

My sister, Emma, will drop off her three-year-old, Jacob, and one-year-old, Benjamin, for me to watch today. She has to take her daughter Emma to the dentist and her Elizabeth to the eye doctor. Her Benjamin and my Joesph, who is also age one, are both walking, so it'll be fun to see what all they'll try to get into today. My four-year-old daughter, Verena said last night that she'll help me baby-sit the babies. She is excited that they are coming.

This past weekend we made a trip to Michigan to visit Joe's Dad. We took along pork steak and some other food. Joe grilled the pork steak at his Dad's house. We got to visit with three of Joe's sisters and their families who also came with food. This was good for Joe's Dad to have us all there for the day. Living alone you know he has lonely days. He sent us home with some cabbage out of his garden, which looks like it really did good this year. So we've been enjoying home-grown cabbage this week.

Tomorrow, my daughter Elizabeth, along with all the third-graders, will spend the day on a field trip to a farm in Ohio. She is excited about going! They won't be back home until 5 p.m. It'll be a trip she'll never forget. I hope they will have a nice day.

I now need to go wake up the girls and get them ready for school. I also want to get the water heating on the stove so I can start the laundry. Emma will be bringing her boys over at 8:30 so I should get started. I hope you readers are all having a good week!

OCTOBER 2003

We are enjoying a week of warmer summer-like weather. It sure is appreciated after the early cold snap we had last week. The children were tired of wearing shoes after a mainly barefoot summer. I'm sure this weather won't last too long, but hopefully it will hold out until our new stove arrives.

Farmers are busy taking off their beans and doing plowing. Some of the leaves are starting to fall. All of this makes a person think of the upcoming winter. Will we have a lot of snow? On Sunday we had dinner with my sisters Verena and Susan. My other sisters Emma and Liz and their families were also there. Liz's children were at Verena and Susan's house from Saturday evening until Sunday evening. The children all enjoyed their day together.

For dinner we all had fried chicken, mashed potatoes, gravy, corn , lettuce salad, cheese, celery and carrot sticks, green and hot peppers, tomatoes, bread, butter, cake, apple-crisp and ice cream. It was an enjoyable time together.

In the afternoon, we enjoyed playing a board game called Aggravation. It can be aggravating if you're not on the winning team.

Some of the children and I have been battling the flu this week. I always hate when I get sick the same time the children do. My 7-year old daughter Susan was home from school on Monday and Tuesday, missing her first days. I had such a big laundry to do on Monday, but I didn't feel well enough to do it. Susan had vomited three times during the night on Sunday. So that adds up the laundry in a hurry. What a relief when Verena and Susan came to get my laundry and brought it back later all clean and folded. What would I do without their help at times like this? This morning everyone seems to feel okay again. I still feel weak. I haven't been getting much done besides meals and dishes. Hopefully by tomorrow I'll feel okay to do the laundry. These nice days make the clothes dry real nice, but we're bothered with ladybugs getting on the clothes. In the morning you don't see them around, but by noon they come from all directions. I'll deal with the ladybugs, though, if the weather just stays nice.

Today, Oct. 9, is Joe's Dad's 65th birthday. We won't be able to make it for his birthday. Too many miles in-between us and Joe is putting in long days at work.

I'm expecting the grapes I ordered to come soon so that'll be another big job to do all that canning and processing. Sure am glad they didn't come while I was sick! Here is the apple crisp recipe we had for dinner the other night:

HOMEMADE APPLE CRISP
6 cups fresh apples, sliced
1 tsp. cinnamon
1 cup quick oats
1 /2 tsp. salt
3/4 cup brown sugar
1/2 cup soft butter

Preheat oven to 350. Slice the apples in an 8- by- 8-inch pan and sprinkle with cinnamon. Combine the rest of the ingredients and mix until crumbly. Sprinkle over apples. Bake at 35-40 minutes. Is good served with milk or ice cream!

OCTOBER 2003

The morning rush is over on this Thursday morning, October 16. The girls just left for school and my husband Joe left at 5:30 a.m. for work. They have been working 9- and 10-hour days at my husband's workplace.

Last night, after work, Joe helped put up a new fence at my sister Emma and Jacob's. My sisters Verena and Susan were also there, so Verena came with the buggy to get me and the rest of the children to go over to Jacob's. Some other of my children had gone with Joe earlier in the day. I still had laundry on the line so I wasn't quite ready to go when Joe was.

Tonight Joe will go straight from work to my sister Liz and Levi's house. Levi is changing their house roof, so Joe wanted to go help him. The days are getting shorter now as we head deeper into autumn.

We decided that the men could get more accomplished if they got an earlier start. I will go with the children this afternoon to Liz and Levi's to join Joe, and my daughters, Elizabeth and Susan, will go straight from school to Levi's.

Yesterday I had a nice day to do my huge pile of laundry. The temperature had warmed into the 70s. On Monday I took my daughters, Elizabeth and Verena, to the dentist while my sister Verena watched my three youngest children.

It was such a nice day that I hated that I couldn't do my laundry. Then on Tuesday it rained all day. Soon the nice fall days will give way to winter and I'll have to hang clothes inside, at least sometimes.

Earlier this week I got my mending pile down to a few pieces.

I had a lot of Joe and the little boys pants that had buttons missing I can sew on buttons with my new sewing machine. Wow, this beats sewing them on by hand!

(Editor's Note: Amish customs vary greatly from community to community. In Lovina's area church members are permitted to have buttons on shirts and pants, but not zippers. Other Amish churches only allow "hooks and eyes," straight pins or snaps.)

I have some shirts cut out that I would like to get sewed. I don't think I'll get started this week yet, though.

Joe's sister, Ruth and brother-in-law Chris, baby-sat all six of our children for us on Sunday. Their youngest is 10, so it was different for them to again have smaller children around and there all day. They had their hands full! Ruth fed them breakfast, lunch, and supper. This was very much appreciated. The children enjoyed their day.

I know they were probably tired after caring for six active little ones all day. It's so nice to have family to help out.

OCTOBER 2003

Sunday was a nice, warm and very beautiful autumn day! My sister Emma, her husband Jacob, their children and my sisters Verena and Susan joined us for a "brunch" on Sunday forenoon. We opened our dining room table to its full length of 12 feet. My nine-year-old daughter, Elizabeth, enjoyed setting the table for 16 people. She did a good job! Our breakfast consisted of bacon, eggs, fried potatoes, cheese, toast, tomatoes, hot peppers, jelly, butter, chocolate chip cookies, coffee, tea, juice, and milk. This was so enjoyable to all sit down together and enjoy the meal.

Earlier in the morning, when Joe went out to do the chores he saw that our horse, Jenny, was bleeding real badly. She had a three-inch gash close to her mouth. We tried to get the veterinarian in town to come out but his son said he was on another call, so we decided we had better try something ourselves. My husband Joe tied rags around her mouth to put pressure on the wound to stop the bleeding. When that didn't work, I decided to try what Mom always did to stop bleeding: I took a piece of cloth and made it damp, then poured red pepper on it. We held this to the wound. In a matter of minutes the bleeding stopped. We have been tending to the wound since and it is healing nicely. We aren't sure how she was cut, but Joe thought she might have run into a nail or something. He checked the barn but didn't find any nails. Alls well that ends well, I guess.

After the breakfast dishes were washed, we decided to once again play "Life on the Farm," a board game that is really fun. (for more information about this game, go to www.theamishcook.com) We hadn't played that since last winter. Our one-year-old, Joseph, was taking a nap and my sister Verena took the eight other children (Emma and Jacob's kids and ours) for a walk to her house. They walked through the fields part-ways making the 1 1/2 miles a little shorter. The children all held out walking all the way, except our three year old, Loretta, gave up 1/4 mile from Verena's house. Verena carried her the rest of the way and she was asleep by the time they got there.

Meanwhile, Jacob, Emma, Susan, Joe and I had a nice uninterrupted game. Jacob's decided to go to his parents for supper. Verena and Susan told us to come there for a pizza supper. We came home around 8 p.m. and we all ready for a good night's sleep. Joe was to leave for work at 4:15 a.m. on Monday morning for another 10 hour day of work. My sisters Verena and Susan have started working at a nearby restaurant.

NOVEMBER 2003

This morning's weather is a change from yesterday when we had 70-degree weather. Now it's 34 degrees outside. The children enjoyed having another day of barefooted weather. The trees have shed all their leaves now and the rest of the English walnuts have fallen off the trees. They need to be picked up yet. Farmers are busy plowing the fields and gardens in the area. Ours is done but we have some flower beds to clean up still. Signs of autumn are everywhere. We haven't had any snow yet, but I'm sure we will one of these days soon. Brrrr! I dread those cold, snowy days!

We had a lot of wind during the night and have a lot of small branches off the trees scattered around. It is still very windy outside. I gave up doing my laundry today and trying to hang it outside to dry. I would like to have my husband Joe move my washing machine onto our enclosed back porch. I still have it in the garage and it gets chilly to do laundry when there is no heat in there.

We spent the day on Sunday in Michigan. We attended church out there and then visited with Joe's family in the afternoon. We had a very enjoyable day. The children were all tired after the hours of traveling and so were we. It made for a long day.

Thanksgiving Day is two weeks from now. Joe will be off work over this time (for two weeks). He will have surgery on Wednesday to have his gall bladder taken out. Hopefully this will make him feel better. I will be glad when it's over with and I hope everything goes OK. This is the first surgery he will have. It'll be hard for him to have to take it easy for awhile.

I must get busy as I want to get started cleaning the house. We will have some visitors from Michigan tomorrow. With six children around sometimes it doesn't pay to clean too early before company. I want to have the house looking halfway decent, though. I guess it's like the saying goes: "If you come to see me, come anytime, but if you come to see my house, let me know ahead of time."

I hope you readers will try this recipe, it is one that I use when Joe grills meat and everything gets done at once:

POTATO AND MEAT CASSEROLE
6 medium potatoes
4 medium onions, peeled and sliced
salt and pepper to taste
8 ounces cheddar cheese, cut into cubes
6 bacon strips, fried crisp and crumbled
YIELD: 4 to 6 servings

Place potato and onion slices on heavy duty aluminum foil. Season with salt and pepper. Sprinkle with cheese cubes and crumbled bacon. Wrap foil tightly. Cook about 1 hour on grill or in covered casserole dish at 375 degrees.

NOVEMBER 2003

It is 6 p.m. here at the Eichers on Thursday, Nov. 20. It has been dark for quite awhile already as we head into the shortest daylight hours of the year. Joe put in a long day of 11 hours at the factory where he works. Makes for a very short night.

My children -- Susan, Verena, Benjamin, and Loretta -- are outside helping or trying to help Joe do the chores. Benjamin brought in the eggs. He loves shining his little flashlight out in the dark. Nine-year-old Elizabeth is reading: She is a bookworm and enjoys every spare moment with her books.

We are going to have a different supper tonight. I'm going to make eggs, toast and bacon, along with cheese. I'll wait to fry the eggs until they come in, so the eggs will still be warm.

My 15-month old, Joseph, has pulled a chair up beside me and is trying to grab my pen. He seems to know when I want a little peace.

This is Thursday already, and I still haven't finished this letter to all you readers. Today, my sister Verena came and helped me do my laundry and cleaning. Sister Susan came after work and also helped. The laundry sure dried nice. I was glad for their help. It was such a beautiful day again. The children sure enjoy these warm days, which I know won't last much longer.

On Monday, Joe will have his gall-bladder surgery. It was moved to Monday instead of this week. I'll be glad when it's over with, and everything goes OK. He'll be off work for a couple of weeks, if everything goes well.

* Saturday morning, Nov. 22: Joe is working at the factory. They are very busy with Christmas orders. It's hard to believe that Christmas is that close, and that Thanksgiving will be this week.

My girls helped me get the breakfast dishes washed and dried. They are sweeping the floors and picking up toys. I have laundry that has to be folded still, and I also need to do some ironing of clothes for church tomorrow.

* Saturday afternoon: I finished washing the children's hair and have water heating to give them a bath.

Joe worked at the factory until 1 p.m. He did some repair work on the house this afternoon. I wanted to fill the kerosene lamps and discovered that our kerosene tank is empty, so we will have to shift around with lights and try to use the stove as little as possible until Monday, when we can order some kerosene.

This Saturday is just a quiet family day. Last Saturday, we had friends from Michigan visiting us. So, for their visit, we made cinnamon rolls in the morning, which sisters Verena and Susan helped me make. For dinner, Joe grilled chicken to go along with a menu of mashed potatoes and gravy, carrot and celery sticks, cheese, and tomatoes. For dessert, we had a pumpkin (cake) roll. Our friends also brought some food.

* Saturday night: Joe left with the children to go get ice for our ice chest. He took all the children with him except Joseph, 15 months old. Joseph is sleeping, so I want to try to have supper ready when they come home.

Happy Thanksgiving to everyone! I'll share the recipe for homemade cinnamon rolls that I made for our weekend guests. They might make for a nice start to a Thanksgiving weekend menu.

HOMEMADE CINNAMON ROLLS
1 1/2 cups milk
2 teaspoons salt
1/2 cup sugar
1/2 cup butter
2 packages active dry yeast
1/2 cup warm water
3 eggs
6 cups all-purpose or bread flour.
filling ingredients are additional butter, melted, brown sugar and cinnamon.

To prepare the yeast dough, first scald the milk by heating it in a medium saucepan to just below the boiling point. Stir in all the salt, the sugar and the stick of butter (or margarine), cut into pats so it softens faster. It doesn't have to melt completely. Set off heat and cool to about 115 degrees.

In a large mixing bowl, add both packets of dry yeast to the 1/2 cup warm water (not over 110 degrees F.). Let stand so yeast granules will soften, about 5 minutes. Stir well, then add to the mixing bowl the cooled milk-butter mixture. Add all 3 eggs, beaten to blend well first, and then 3 cups of the flour. Mix well. Add up to 3 more cups of the flour to make a soft dough. Scrape sides of bowl to make a ball of dough in the bowl. Cover loosely with plastic wrap and let rise in a warm place until the dough doubles in bulk, about an hour.

Punch down the dough, then roll out into a large rectangle on a floured work surface. Spread the entire surface of the dough generously with melted butter or margarine. Sprinkle evenly with brown sugar, then cinnamon. Roll up dough from the long side. Slice about 3/4- to 1-inch widths and turn on their sides on a large baking sheet with a rim. Cover rolls loosely with plastic wrap and let rise until nearly doubled in size. Meanwhile, have the oven heating to about 350 degrees.

As soon as the rolls have risen, bake at 350 for 5 to 7 minutes until rolls are light golden brown.

When they're removed from the baking sheet and completely cool, drizzle with a simple white frosting, if desired. (Editor's note: Simply mix a teaspoon or two of hot water or orange juice into powdered sugar and stir smooth.)

DECEMBER 2003

Tuesday evening, Nov. 25: We are home now, after being away for Joe's gall bladder surgery. The surgery went OK, but he still has a lot of pain. It will take time to heal. It's just so nice to be home again after being away from the children for one night and two days. It seemed longer. I knew, though, that they were in good care. My sisters Susan and Emma and her husband, Jacob, had them while we were gone. Jacob took care of our chores and kept the stove going, so we came back to a warm place. My sister Verena went on the journey with Joe and me, and she stayed with me while Joe was having his surgery. How nice to have family to help.

It is now Wednesday morning. Joe had a rough night, but is feeling a lot better now. The children are so glad to have him home that they don't want to let him rest. But the doctor told Joe that he needs to take it easy and not do a lot of heavy lifting. Joe will be off work for the next week or so while he recovers. I was teasing Joe that it'll be nice having him around to wipe dishes, sweep floors, and change diapers!

Our 16-month-old, Joseph, seems so unhappy. He can't figure out why he can't jump around on Joe when my husband is holding him. He thinks Joe should pick him up and carry him around. He's just too young to understand.

Our oldest daughters, Elizabeth and Susan, are at school now. This is the last day of school for them before the Thanksgiving break. Tomorrow is Thanksgiving Day, but we won't go anywhere. Joe will need to take it easy.

Last night, Jacob and Emma and family came over. Jacob did the chores for me. I was glad he did. Verena and Susan had sent over some homemade potato soup, and Emma brought some meat, so I heated supper so they could eat with us before they left for home.

I have the laundry all sorted and packed. Sisters Verena and Susan will come get it and wash it for me. I was so glad that they offered to do it. I washed on Thursday of last week, so I have a lot of dirty clothes piled up.

I want to thank the readers who sent Joe "get well" cards. Thank you for your thoughtfulness.

We had snow flurries on Monday -- enough to get the children excited. But they were disappointed the snow didn't stick. I told them we'll have more than we want soon enough. They are anxious for horse-and-sleigh rides again.

Christmas will be in four weeks. Time goes so fast. Joe will be 35 on Dec. 22. My daughter Verena will be 6 years old on Dec. 10. She said this morning that it's 14 days until her birthday. She's so excited that she's counting the days.

Meanwhile, it's time to start on holiday baking. Fruitcake is a favorite for many during the holidays. A reader from Gig Harbor in Washington State requested my fruitcake recipe made with dried, not candied, fruits:

FRUITCAKE
1 teaspoon baking soda
1 teaspoon baking powder
1/4 cup soured milk or buttermilk
3 cups all-purpose flour
1 teaspoon cinnamon
1/4 teaspoon ground ginger
1 cup diced dates
1 cup brown sugar
3/4 cup sour cream
1 cup molasses
1 cup chopped nuts
1 cup prunes, cooked tender, then finely chopped
2 cups raisins (simmered to plump them)
 2 eggs
1/4 teaspoon ground cloves
 pinch of salt.

Stir the 1 teaspoon soda and 1 teaspoon baking powder into the soured milk. (Editor's note: Not spoiled milk, but acidulated milk with a scant teaspoon of lemon juice.) Add enough flour to make a medium-stiff batter, about 3 cups, then add cinnamon and ginger. Stir in dates, brown sugar, sour cream, molasses, nuts, prunes, raisins, eggs, cloves and salt. Stir well and turn into a greased baking pan or mini-loaf pans (size not given). Bake very slowly (300-degree oven) for about an hour (less in small pans) or until it tests done when a slender pick is inserted. Other fruits may be added, such as dried apples.

DECEMBER 2003

We woke up to a ground covered with snow yesterday morning. It snowed most of the day and by evening we had a couple of inches. The children enjoyed making snowmen and giving sled rides. They had so much fun.

We went to Michigan on Thursday to visit Joe's family. Joe's dad wasn't home as he was working. We were sorry we missed him. We visited with Joe's sister, though, as they were cleaning at their dad's house. Also some women from their community were there helping. I'm so glad they do this for him since he is widowed.

Joe is still off work from his recent gall bladder surgery. The children enjoy having him home. I think he is getting anxious to get back to work, though.

It is early in the morning as I write this. Joe and the children are still in bed. I decided to get up earlier and write this before there's too much action around here.

Everyone is busy preparing for Christmas. It is such a busy season, but let's remember the reason for the season. Family gatherings are busy being planned. We will go to Michigan to have our Christmas Day with Joe's family at his sister Carol's house.

Dad and Mom used to have us all home on New Year's Day for our holiday gathering. We would all go there for breakfast and Mom would fix a big breakfast and have the tables all set. We would all sit down and enjoy the meal together.

It was beginning to take a lot of tables with the family growing. Without my sisters Verena and Susan at home to help her, she probably couldn't have done this. Mom would stand by the stove and fry eggs, eggs, and eggs. After breakfast we would wash dishes and sing Christmas carols. Then gifts were passed out which was the highlight of the day for the children. With over 30 grandchildren it took a lot of time to wrap all those gifts.

Oh how we miss them at this time of the year. The family has grown more since they were both laid to rest. Mom and Dad have 37 grandchildren now, 38 with Paul and Leah's daughter Mary, who died at age 5 in 1997.

Today is Joe's youngest sister Susan's 24th birthday. Yesterday was my sister Liz's husband Levi's 34th birthday. On Dec. 9, Joe's grandmother will be 90 years old. She does very good for her age. She just sewed a coat for my sister Emma's little boy. I think that's great that she still does that.

Thanks to all the readers who have sent get well cards to Joe. It was very thoughtful for you to take the time.

DECEMBER 2003

What a busy week! I am trying to get my fall cleaning done before the holidays. My sisters Susan and Verena helped me one day this week, and we got a lot done. I sure was glad for their help. Three people can do so much more than one.

On Monday, my husband, Joe, helped me do a big batch of laundry. I hung everything outside, as the temperature was around 40 degrees, chilly, but warm enough to still dry the laundry. The air was nippy, and my fingers were very cold by the time I got done. The sun was shining off and on throughout the day. The thicker clothes didn't dry all the way, but bed sheets, pillowcases, dresses and shirts were all dry by evening. Before dark, we brought two clothes-drying racks into the house and hung the clothes that still needed to dry. I use a bicycle wheel with clothespins hanging from the holes to dry certain items. I really like the bicycle wheel for hanging socks and other small things. Another nice thing about the bicycle wheel: During the wintertime, you can fill up the wheel inside the house and then take it outside to hang in the breeze. Then, you can also bring the whole wheel in and hang it in the house overnight to finish drying. Doing laundry in the winter is a lot more work than doing it during the summer months.

It's important to get all the clothes clean with all the flu going around in this area. Fortunately, my children all seem to be over the flu. It is always a relief when everyone is healthy again. I hope they stay healthy for the holidays.

This is now Wednesday morning. Another day is beginning, after a rainy night. The snow is all melted, and everything looks wet and dreary outside. We bought new boots for the children, which they really need now that it's so muddy.

My children Verena, Benjamin and Loretta are outside with Joe. He is doing the morning chores. Elizabeth and Susan have already left for school. Earlier, Joe fixed a breakfast of eggs, toast, sausage, juice, milk and rolls. This was a nice break for me. I'll miss him when he goes back to work. He is still recovering from gall bladder surgery.

My daughter Verena is 6 years old today, so she is excited that her birthday is finally here. She was very excited earlier this morning when we gave her a doll with a bottle and a little diaper bag filled with little things for her "baby." She was such a busy little mama this morning -- feeding her doll and changing its diapers. Loretta said she wants her birthday now so she can have a doll, too.

Joe has a doctor's appointment today to see how everything is since his surgery. I hope the doctor will give him a clean bill of health. Verena and Susan will stay with the children while we're gone. I asked them if they would bake a cake for 6-year-old Verena, so she can blow out the candles tonight.

I must get back to work. The children are back inside now. Benjamin said he only came in to warm up, then he's going back outside with Dad. He enjoys having Joe home, and so do I.

DECEMBER 2003

It is early Thursday morning and my husband, Joe, just left for work. My little Joseph is up already this morning. Usually he sleeps longer, so I'm sure he'll take a nap this forenoon. I gave him a cup of milk and sat him beside me on the rocker. He still looks tired.

I hope to get the rest of my Christmas cards sent out today. I think we are done with our Christmas shopping. Christmas is coming up fast. Where has the time gone? Somehow it seems like this month just flew by so fast. As we celebrate the birth of Jesus let us give thanks to the Lord for a life filled with many blessings.

It is Friday evening and we're invited to a wedding supper, but I doubt that we'll be able to go. The factory where Joe works is also hosting a Christmas party for the employees and their families, but we probably won't make it to that either. We plan to just stay home and prepare for Saturday. Joe's family will have their family Christmas gathering at his sister Carol and Pete's in Michigan. We will start out at 5:30 a.m. on Saturday morning, so we want to get the children to bed early on Friday evening. It will be a long day for the children and also for us. On Sunday we will have to get up early also to attend church services. It will be a full weekend but the girls can sleep in Monday as they have off school for two weeks over the holidays.

The children are all awake now and sleep is the last thing on little Joseph's mind. He is running around here now with his little ball. It seems to be his favorite toy. He'll toss the ball and then run after it. It's so funny to watch him try to jump up and down. He tries so hard but can't seem to get both feet off the floor at the same time.

I have the ingredients now to make peanut butter cups (a peanut butter mixture dipped in chocolate). I was going to dip some pretzels in chocolate, too, but forgot to buy pretzels when I was in town. Hopefully I'll get the peanut butter cups done today. I also have some clothes to iron before Saturday. Tomorrow I will make potato salad and "strawberry delight" to take along to the gathering in Michigan.

The children are ready for breakfast, so I better set this aside. It's getting hard to concentrate anyway. They all seem to be extra lively this morning, which takes a lot of patience. They're probably getting the holiday spirit! I'd rather see them like that than sick.

LATER: This is now late morning. I just rocked Joseph to sleep. The girls left for school a couple of hours ago. Merry Christmas to everyone!!

Try these Christmas cookies:

SOFT CHRISTMAS CUT-OUT COOKIES
3 cups flour
1 /2 teaspoon baking
powder
1 cup margarine
2 eggs, beaten
1 /2 teaspoon baking soda
1 1 /2 cup sugar

Mix all ingredients together. Chill dough overnight. Roll out and cut into shapes. Bake at 375 for 5 minutes and decorate with icing.

2004

This was a busy year for the Eicher family. The Eichers decided to move to an Amish settlement in Michigan, uprooting themselves from their life-long Indiana community. The family moved in the late winter/early spring, and quickly settled comfortable into their new surroundings. Joe and Lovina welcomed her little namesake into the world with the birth of Lovina, born on May 18.

Meanwhile, in the USA, voters returned President George W. Bush to office for a second term in November. Hillary Swank took home honors for best motion picture of the year for the film "Million Dollar Baby. " The average price of a gallon of gasoline was $1.75, with prices peaking just above $2 in March.

JANUARY 2004

It is almost 5:30 a.m. My husband, Joe, has left for work. He is over the flu and feeling better. So far, none of the rest of us has caught it. Baby Joseph was fussy for a few days, but he now has four new teeth peeping through. I figured that was his problem. He now has all his teeth except his 2-year molars.

The children are all asleep except Loretta. She's sitting beside me playing with the balloons that the girls got at the dentist's yesterday. Benjamin wants to go to the dentist now, so he can get a balloon. He said: "Mom, see how big I can open my mouth, and I'm only 4!" He doesn't realize there's more to going to the dentist than just opening your mouth.

We got to bed later than usual last night, so I'll let the school-age girls sleep until 6:30 a.m. The bus comes at 7:05, but I have their clothes and everything ready to go for them so they can get some extra sleep.

Yesterday we got a lot accomplished in preparation for church services. Services will be held at our home the next two church Sundays. My sisters Verena and Susan came, and we washed the walls and ceilings in both bedrooms. We also cleaned the furniture and took beds apart and polished everything really good.

After lunch, Verena took my daughters into town for their dentist appointments. She had to pick Susan up at school. This really helped me to not have to leave all the work here at home. My sister Susan rocked Joseph and Loretta to sleep for their afternoon naps, but she couldn't get Benjamin to take a nap. He says he's 4 years old and he doesn't need a nap every day. I gave him a book with horses in it to look at, and that kept him from getting into too much trouble.

Meanwhile, I did a lot of organizing. Those storage totes are so nice for storing extra blankets and clothes. With the children growing, I'm running out of drawer space in our dressers.

Today, my sister Emma and her children, Verena and Susan will come again. We plan to wash off more walls and ceilings. We'd also like to wash all the windows before church services. Susan will take my curtains, quilts and blankets to wash and dry them. With this cold weather, it's hard to get the curtains to dry without staining them. And the blankets and quilts take so long to dry. This will be a big job done and a great relief to me.

A reader in Federal Way (a mid-size town in Washington state) asked for a good casserole recipe. Most kids will like this one:

PIZZA CASSEROLE
1 pound ground turkey or beef
1 medium onion
salt and pepper as desired
1 can condensed cream of mushroom soup
¼ teaspoon dried thyme
¼ teaspoon dried oregano
¼ teaspoon garlic powder
1 cup instant rice
1 can condensed tomato soup
 grated cheese, any kind.

Have oven heating to 350 degrees. Brown the ground meat and onion in a large skillet, stirring to break up lumps. Drain as necessary. Add salt and pepper. In a separate saucepan over medium heat, mix mushroom soup (undiluted), the thyme, oregano and garlic powder, instant rice (Minute Rice) and the undiluted tomato soup. Rinse soup cans with a little water and stir into rice mixture. Let simmer for five minutes. Combine with the drained, cooked meat mixture. Turn into a casserole dish and top with grated cheese. Bake at 350 for 30 minutes

JANUARY 2004

4:30 a.m. It's time to start another long day. There's plenty to do in preparation for church services that will be held at our home this Sunday. My husband Joe goes outside to do the outdoor chores (feed the animals, etc).

5 a.m. Joe comes in from doing the chores. I have made for him a cheese toastie and eggs for breakfast. I also have his lunch packed and ready to go. Loretta and baby Joseph woke up so Joe tries to eat his breakfast and hold Joseph at the same time. Joesph is starting to hold one finger up when we ask him how old he is. His sister Verena also got him to wink his eye. He's at such a cute age when they try everything new.

5:15 a.m. Joe leaves for work. Yesterday morning he left at 4:15 a.m. so I was glad for the extra hour with him this morning.

5:45 a.m. The rest of the children are awake now. With the help of the girls we make beds and sweep the floors, get toys picked up, etc. I fold some laundry and put it away.

7 a.m. The girls are ready and waiting for the bus to come. Joseph has fallen asleep again. I was hoping he would as he got up way too early.

8 a.m. My help for the day has arrived! Sisters Verena, Susan, and Emma and her children are here. I told them to wait to eat and just have breakfast here with the children and I. We make a big skillet of "Egg Dutch", bacon, cheese hot peppers, tomatoes, and sliced-up a loaf of homemade bread that Verena and Susan made, along with grape juice and milk.

9 a.m. Dishes are being washed, and the kitchen walls and ceilings are being washed off also. I have kerosene heaters heating the garage and entrance area to the house. The windows are being washed and clean curtains are being hung.

12:30 p.m. We are ready to eat lunch. Verena has made homemade potato soup. After the children eat, we get four of the children to take a nap, which quiets the house down a bit. The other three are outside playing, the wind is a bit nippy so the children have been playing in the kerosene-heated garage this forenoon.

3 p.m. We have accomplished a lot and are starting to wind down. The stoves have been cleaned and the cabinets washed out. Joe and Jacob are home from work. The man that drives Joe to and from work takes Jacob to go get the church bench wagon. The bench wagon is a covered wagon that holds all the benches and song-books. It is pulled to the place where church is being held.

5 p.m. We have an early supper before they all head for home. I'm sure they are all tired from the hard day of work. Verena grilled pork steak, which must've been a cold job. All the children love pork steak and were glad Verena grilled some.

8 p.m. Bedtime! We helped the girls with their homework. We will all call it a day. It is so nice to know everything is getting cleaned

FEBRUARY 2004

It is Friday around 3 p.m., and my husband, Joe, just came home from work. He started work at 5 a.m., so it was a long day for him. The girls didn't have school today because of the icy roads. We got more freezing rain last night, making the roads very icy.

This is the third day the girls have missed this week, after snow canceled three school days last week, also. I suppose the teachers will be glad once the weather clears up, as I imagine these unexpected vacations mess up their schedules.

Benjamin and Loretta are taking a nap now. Joseph is awake, as he had a nap earlier today. Daughters Susan and Verena are playing with their dolls, and Elizabeth is writing a thank-you note to one of my readers who was so kind to send Elizabeth a book after reading in my column that she loves to read.

Church services were held here on Sunday. Everything is back in order now after the rush of preparing for the services. My brother Albert will hold church services at his house next. I didn't have anyone back to the house for supper after church, but I put out sandwiches, potato salad and cookies for my brother Albert, his wife, Sarah Irene, and family; sister Liz, her husband, Levi, and family; sister Emma, her husband, Jacob, and family; and sisters Verena and Susan.

Lunch is always provided for church members, and supper is sometimes offered to those who can stay.

Around 7 p.m. that same Sunday, Joe saw my brother Amos and his wife, Nancy, parked in front of our door with their big bobsled. They had been to sister Leah and Paul's for dinner and wanted to stop in and say "hi." We couldn't persuade them to come in, as they were ready to start for their 12- or 13-mile trip home.

Seeing them in their bobsled brought back memories of when I was a child and our family went to church in the bobsled. Sometimes, we would pick up a few families on the way to church.

The weather today was perfect for bobsleds. Joe will go into town today, though, with a buggy, not the bobsled. I need to make a list for Joe. He's harnessing up the horse to go to town to get groceries. After he gets back, we plan to go to sisters Verena and Susan for supper.

I miss the days when I could go home and spend a day at Dad and Mom's house. That's a thing of the past now, but memories linger on. God has a plan for everyone, and we know that. He makes no mistakes. We want to keep our trust in Him at all times.

This is now Saturday morning. We had a good supper at Verena and Susan's house last evening. The air was cold, so it was a refreshing ride in the buggy. It takes a lot more time to leave our house when it's cold because the children need a lot more coats, boots, scarves, etc. It takes a while until everyone is bundled up and ready to go. Everything is icy outside, so we loaded up right at the front door. We didn't want the children to fall on the ice.

A reader in Bloomsburg, Pa. , asked how we fix our pork chops. Try this recipe.

DELICIOUS BRAISED PORK CHOPS
5 pork chops
1 cup dried bread crumbs
 a grinding of pepper
salt as desired
1 egg, beaten to blend
1/4 cup milk
1/4 cup boiling water
3 tablespoons fat.

Add salt and pepper to the bread crumbs. Blend the beaten egg with the milk. Dip chops in the egg mixture, then coat with the bread crumbs. Have fat (shortening, part bacon drippings or oil) heating in a large skillet over medium-high heat. Brown the breaded chops in the hot skillet and turn once to brown both sides. Place chops in a shallow baking dish and add the 1/4 cup boiling water or enough to cover the bottom of the baking pan. Cover pan snugly with foil and bake in a preheated 400-degree oven for a little less than an hour, depending on thickness of the chops. Do not overbake or chops could dry out.

FEBRUARY 2004

What a morning! Our battery-powered alarm clock went off at 3:45 a.m. this morning, as my husband Joe had to leave around 4:30 a.m. for work. Before going outside to do the chores, Joe happened to look at the clock in the living room and it showed 6:15 a.m. So it was hustle and bustle for awhile until Joe found someone to take him to work and the girls were ready for school. Nineteen-month old Joseph just loves to play with our little alarm clock. I usually set it up higher but must've forgotten to yesterday. Coming home later last evening, I didn't check to see if the time was right on the clock before setting it. (Editor's note: While Old Order Amish don't have electricity, they are permitted in some areas to have small accessories like battery-powered alarm clocks or small flash-lights) Joseph didn't seem to mind that we all slept a couple hours later. He had the girls laughing before they left for school. He was winking at them and being a little show-off.

This week sure is going fast. Monday I did laundry and hung most of it outside as the temperature was in the 40s most of the day. Everything sure dried nice. By the next morning the rest was all dry on the clothesline racks. Sure gave me "spring fever" already, although Mr. Groundhog says six more weeks of winter.

I guess the main reason I'm hoping for an early spring is that we will be moving to Michigan in April. In our new place, we'll be quite close to Joe's family. It's going to take a lot of packing up with six children. Sisters Verena and Susan bought a house just around the corner from ours in Michigan, so they'll be going with us. We are excited that they found something that close to us.

We will regret pulling the children out of this school that they attend now, but after visiting their new school we were very pleased and the girls are less nervous now about moving. Everyone was very nice and helpful. There will be many memories to leave behind here in Indiana, but it's a new beginning for us.

Yesterday, sisters Verena and Susan came to help us do some packing. We would like to take a load with things we won't need until we're moved. We'd like to go clean the house and get everything ready for the move. It's a 2 1/2 hour drive each way so it's not easy to go clean unless we can go a few days at a time.

After supper we took Verena and Susan home. It was a nice evening to go for a buggy ride, although a little chilly. In Michigan they have covered buggies so that will be different, but a lot warmer than open buggies.

MARCH 2004

We are well into the first week of March now. Temperatures have warmed up and we're having rain off and on this week.

I'm planning to have a garage sale on Saturday to get rid of some of my extras before our move to Michigan later this month. They always say "one person's junk is the other person's treasure." My sisters Emma, Verena and Susan assisted me yesterday in setting things up and pricing things for the sale.

I was so glad for their help as I've been battling a bad head cold all week. I've lost a lot of sleep at night due to coughing, etc. I finally went to a doctor and now have medicine to take. It sure is helping.

We spent last weekend at our home in Michigan as we took another load of our belongings. While in Michigan, we slept at our new home for the first time. We all enjoyed it! A few more neighbors came to introduce themselves. It gives a person a very welcome feeling to be visited. I'll be glad when we have the rest of our things moved. It seems sometimes I want to go after something and then discover that it's in Michigan already.

There is a lot of hard work involved in moving that far with six children. I'm sure we'll like it, though, after we're all settled in. The children are asking to go back to Michigan so it helps that they like it there.

We hope to take a load of hay up to Michigan next week. The veterinarian came out last night to do tests or whatever they do to horses before you can take them across the state line. There are so many different things to do when you move.

I have to wake the school-age girls up to get them ready for school. They are having a hard time getting up the last few days. I could use extra sleep myself. I hope that things will slow down after awhile.

It's now 10 a.m. and I must finish this. After getting the girls off to school, I made breakfast for the four youngest children. I let them sleep a bit later. Then my sister Liz and her daughters, Rosa and Suzanne, stopped in for awhile. So now I have dishes waiting to be washed and floors that need to be cleaned. Floors don't take long to get tracked up when the children are going in and out. With the arrival of warmer weather, the ground is getting softer and with the recent rains there's plenty of mud. I also see windows that should be cleaned. There's too much work and not enough time. I will just do what I can and know that the rest won't run away.

I read some more letters that you readers sent and I want to thank you for the many encouraging words. Although I can't thank each of you individually, I want you to know how much I appreciate your kind words. May God richly bless all of you wonderful readers.

I will get back to packing and cleaning now, but, meanwhile, you all try this delicious dinner recipe:

HAMBURGER CASSEROLE
2 pounds of hamburger
1/4 cup of chopped onion
1/2 teaspoons of black pepper
3/4 cup of chopped green pepper
1/2 teaspoon of salt
1 tablespoon of chili powder
16 ounce can of tomato sauce
2 cups of shredded cheese
1 cup of cooked rice

Cook hamburger and drain excess grease. Mix cooked hamburger and the rest of the ingredients together in a large casserole dish, save one cup of cheese to spread on top. Bake at 350 for 20 minutes.

MARCH 2004

My sister Liz and her husband, Levi, had us over for supper on Sunday evening. She wanted us to come before we pack up the rest of our things for Michigan. The children had a lot of fun at Liz and Levi's. Levi Jr., age 9, gave my children pony rides with a young pony that he had trained. He did a good job training the pony. Benjamin just can't wait until we get a pony for him. Liz had a very good meal of fried chicken, mashed potatoes, gravy, dressing, corn, carrots, celery sticks, cheese, peaches, chocolate cake and ice cream.

After the dishes were washed up, we spent the evening singing and yodeling together. When we were all living at home with Mom and Dad still, we'd sing and yodel almost every night while doing the dishes. It made the work go faster. The evening with Liz and Levi ended too soon, and we all worked our way home. Jacob and Emma and their family and my sisters Verena and Susan were also there.

On Monday, I did the laundry and hung it outside. It snowed off and on, but some of the clothes still dried. What didn't dry, I hung on clothes racks by the stove and on bicycle wheels that have clothes pins hanging from them. I like to sort all the socks when I hang them on the wheels. After they're dry, I can put them away immediately and save time sorting them later. I'm looking forward to spring and warm, nicer wash days. It's so much better when everything dries in one day, and the clothes can be folded and put away that same day. "Rhubarbs" are peeping through the soil, so I hope that means that spring is near.

On Thursday, we took a load of around 100 bales of hay to our new place in Michigan. It looked like rain, and we didn't know if we should stop and buy tarps to cover it. We only got a few sprinkles before it slowed down and quit. This was a relief to get the hay there without it getting soaked. Jacob, Emma, and family went along; Jacob helped Joe unload the hay and put it up in the hay mow.

On Friday, we visited Elizabeth's third-grade class and Susan's first-grade class at school. We ate lunch with them. We decided to take time to do this before we all move. The girls have only four more days at this school. We will miss this school and all the nice teachers and the principal. We hope they will adjust to the new school and like it just as well. Next week will be a very busy week packing up the last of our belongings and moving.

Meanwhile, a reader in Tacoma, Wash., requested my homemade pie dough recipe. Here's how we do it:

PIE PASTRY (makes 4 crusts)
3 cups all-purpose flour
1 teaspoon salt
1 cup lard

Stir together the flour and salt in a large bowl and then cut in the lard to make a mealy consistency, using a wire pastry blender. In a smaller bowl, beat 1 egg to blend and stir in 1 tablespoon vinegar and 1/3 cup cold water. Stir with a fork into the flour mixture and form a ball of dough. Divide into four parts, wrap and chill to let the dough rest before rolling it out.

APRIL 2004

(Editor's Note: Friday, March 19, was Lovina and her family's first full day living in Michigan. They are settling in and seem to be enjoying the adventure of starting from scratch in a new place. To those who have inquired, Lovina will continue writing her column from Michigan. Also, to the many have asked, Lovina and her family hired non-Amish movers to take the bulk of their belongings in a truck. This is common practice among Amish moving long distances. Next week's column will be Lovina's first from Michigan.)

We headed to Michigan early this morning with another load of hay. My sister Emma, her husband Jacob, and their son Jacob Jr.. went up to Michigan with Joe, little Benjamin, and I. Sisters Verena and Susan kept the other eight children at their house. We started out around 6 a.m. and we were home by around 6:30 p.m.

Little Joseph was a lot more contented to stay with Verena and Susan. He just hates sitting in a car seat all the way there and back. I was glad they could stay at Verena and Susan's house. The children enjoyed the day at their house so much that they wanted to spend the night there. We brought them home, though, as I figured Verena and Susan were ready for a break.

In Michigan, Joe and Jacob unloaded the hay, which was a long, hard job. Then a load of lumber we had ordered arrived so they helped unload that. Meanwhile, while the menfolk were hard at work, Emma and I made chili soup for our lunch and we all ate our first meal at our new place. The realtor stopped by so we made him sit down and eat with us. He sure has been a good help to us already.

Benjamin and Jacob Jr. were quite tired by the time we were ready to go. Four-year-old boys can really get around looking for adventure. They enjoyed being in the hay-mow with their dads.

Before we started for home we stopped in to see where Mom's cousin and his family live, which is not far from our new place. The boys fell asleep on the way home. They were tired after a full day.

Joe quit his factory job after being there 7-1/2 years. With him not working during the day, we hope to have the rest of our belongings loaded up by Thursday afternoon.

We want to attend Susan's first grade musical at school on Thursday afternoon. That will be their last day of school in this school district.

We will start out early on Friday morning with the horses and chickens. Verena and Susan will go along. The driver will then come back and pick up Levi, Liz and children and Jacob, Emma and children and pull the 16-foot enclosed trailer out to Michigan with the rest of our belongings. It will be a busy week!

Reader questions: A reader in Sayre, PA asked for a simple icing recipe: take 5 cups powdered sugar, 1 1/2 cups shortening, 6 tablespoons milk and 1 teaspoon vanilla. Mix sugar and shortening first and then add milk. Beat hard and then add vanilla. Beat until soft enough to spread. Delicious!

APRIL 2004

We have been living at our new place in Michigan for almost two weeks now. So far we have enjoyed it here.

My husband Joe started his construction job yesterday. He really enjoyed his first day on the job. They changed a barn roof so the work was a lot different than factory work. Seems different to have him leave for work later, but he also comes home later. We have to get adjusted to a different place and different schedule.

Our daughters Elizabeth, 9; Susan, 7; and Verena, 6, started school here in Michigan this week. They really seem to like it. Verena only goes a half day but she likes it so well she would like to go all day.Benjamin, 4, and Loretta, 3, miss Verena not being home during the day. Benjamin and Loretta seem lost the last few days since the girls are in school and Joe leaves for work. They had been used to their Dad being home from work the past week or so. Joe was home working on the box-stalls for the horses. He got the box-stalls done just in time. Our horse, Itty Bit, had a colt on March 25th. She has a nice looking filly. The colt is active, always running around the field. Itty Bit had the colt only six days after we brought her here from Indiana so we are lucky she waited.

The chickens are getting settled into their new place in the barn. Joe had to find a way to keep Benjamin out of the chicken coop. He would keep checking on eggs, bringing one in as soon as it was laid. This was disturbing the hens. Our "little chicks" are now big and starting to lay eggs.

Last Monday afternoon, a few men from this area stopped in to say "hi" and welcome us to the area. Joe and my brother-in-law, Jacob, were talking with them outside. Jacob's were here for a few days helping us get unpacked. Joe was burning trash behind the barn before the men arrived. My sister, Verena, happened to look outside and see that the fire was spreading. We all ran outside to help put it out. The men carried buckets of water while we helped fill them. The fire came very close to our barn and luckily the wind was in our favor. We are so thankful there wasn't any damage. A good part of the field behind the barn was burnt and it had started in the corn field on the dry corn stalks. If we would've been by ourselves we would probably have lost the barn. So it was a rocky start to our move to Michigan!

We helped sisters Verena and Susan move here to Michigan last Tuesday and Wednesday. They walked over here yesterday and helped me do a big laundry. It's nice having them this close. And now we are even more excited as sister Emma and Jacob bought a 7 acre farm up here on Monday evening. It will be so nice having them in the area. The children miss each other as they were always together.

APRIL 2004

It looks like another beautiful day is beginning here in Michigan. The sun is shining so brightly. We are now an hour ahead. Being from Indiana, I have never lived in an area where there is daylight savings time. So far, though, it is not as bad as I expected it might be.

The girls are on spring break from school. It's nice having them home as we adjust to our new location. Everyone seems to really be enjoying the experience.

I hope to do some laundry today. I have to do laundry more often now, as I don't have much wash-line space. Joe hopes to get more clothesline put up after we get settled in a bit more. He works longer at night than he did in Indiana, but he likes the work better. Construction and carpentry work is a lot less stressful than his Indiana factory job was. When Joe gets home, he stays busy in the evenings raking and taking care of the yard. We have quite a bit of cleaning up around here still.

Sometime today, my sister Susan plans to walk over here to help the children color eggs. They always enjoy doing that. Little Benjamin is still going out to check on the eggs in our henhouse each morning, so we'll surprise him on Easter by putting colored eggs in the nests. It should be a cute reaction when he checks the nests and finds brightly colored eggs there.

I hope to get the upstairs cleaned now that the carpet is torn out and the new floor is done. I hope this week we can get the older girls moved up to their bedroom. We have three bedrooms on the main floor, which makes it nice for the younger children. The bedroom upstairs will be for Elizabeth, 9, and Susan, 7.

We cleared out the entrance area to the house last night. My sisters Verena and Susan came over to help me. We still had totes and boxes stored in there. They are now in the living room, and I hope to get them unpacked soon.

We tore the carpet out of the entrance area and discovered that there is cement underneath. That will be nice to do my laundry in there now. Joe moved my washing machine and laundry tubs in this morning. Now I'm all set to do laundry. Everything takes time.

Our horse's colt is still doing OK. Little Joseph just loves to look out of the window and watch it run around the field.

Jacob, sister Emma and family plan to come here to visit this weekend. The children are excited to have them come. They were all used to seeing each other more often than they do now. We will be glad once they are moved to this area by May. With Jacob coming, Joe will have help carrying the furniture upstairs.

We are seeing plenty of deer. They come pretty close to the house. I hope they won't bother the garden. Joe wants to get a part of the garden worked up so I can plant some early things. Garden goodies sound good again.

Daughter Elizabeth picked dandelion greens last night, so I want to fix them today. Dandelions can be fixed in so many ways. We like the young greens in salads, the bright yellow flowers in soups and jellies.

Try this recipe for homemade dandelion soup:

DANDELION SOUP
2 tablespoons butter
2 tablespoons flour
2 cups milk
2 cups dandelion flowers, all the green parts pinched off
a dash of celery seed, lightly crushed
a pinch of dried thyme leaves crushed between the fingers (or use more of fresh thyme, if possible)
1 bay leaf (optional).

To begin the soup, melt the butter in a medium saucepan over medium-low heat. Add flour and stir until it is well-combined and beginning to brown. Remove pan from heat. Whisk in the milk, a little at a time, until smooth, as you would make a gravy or white sauce. Return saucepan to heat. Mix in the dandelion flowers, celery seed, thyme and bay leaf. Simmer until the flowers are tender, 15-20 minutes. Remove bay leaf before serving.

APRIL 2004

These weeks are flying by fast. The girls are back to school after a week of spring break. It was nice having them home! Six more weeks of school is left for this term and then they'll have the summer off.

My husband Joe has worked up the garden for me now. The soil is really good here in Michigan. I hope to get some onions and potatoes planted today.

We missed seeing our sisters, Verena and Susan, this week. They are spending the week back in Indiana with Jacob and Emma. Jacob and Emma are starting to pack some of their things in preparation for their move here to Michigan. We plan to go Friday night to help them this weekend. Our little Benjamin can't wait to go as he's anxious to see Jacob's dog, Trixie, who had 5 puppies on Saturday.

Saturday we went to see the house that Jacob and Emma bought close by here in Michigan. It'll be nice having them so close. They plan to move the first week in May.

Our place in Indiana will be sold at a public auction in May. So we'll have to go back and clean some time and take care of the lawn, which is starting to grow. It'll be a busy summer getting settled in.

Yesterday I emptied some more boxes and rearranged my kitchen cabinets. Today I hope to get my cupboards filled with dishes. I think it's a lot easier packing up than unpacking and finding a place for everything.

The upstairs floor is done so we cleaned everything: floor, walls, ceilings and moved the girls up on Saturday. We have three bedrooms on the main floor. Benjamin and Joseph share the bedroom beside us. So far Joseph is doing well adjusting to sleeping in a regular bed instead of a crib.

Joe was doing some repairs on our roof one night recently, while Jacob's were here visiting from Indiana. That's when our Benjamin decided to show Jacob Jr. how to get on the roof through the upstairs window. There were some anxious moments until both boys were back inside the window. You never know what 4-year-old boys will think up to do next. One day I went out to the barn to check on Benjamin and Loretta and here they were mixing rabbit feed with chicken feed.

This past Sunday afternoon, Joe and I took all of the kids out for a buggy ride just to enjoy a beautiful day and explore our surrounding countryside in our new area. The kids really seemed to enjoy the ride and they seem to be adjusting so well, which is a relief. It was a perfect afternoon for a ride, but a little windy. The buggies in this area have roofs on them, which they didn't in our area of Indiana, so it takes some getting used to. Makes them a little top heavy on a windy day, but having a covered buggy is nice for those rainy days.

Well, I must get back to unpacking. Thanks again to all you readers for your nice notes and cards. Much appreciated.

A reader in Bloomsburg, Pa., requested a recipe for an easy cake. Try this one!

LAZY CAKE
1 1/2 cups pastry flour
1/4 tsp. salt
2 tsp. soda
1 tsp. vanilla
3 Tbsp. cocoa
1 cup white sugar
7 Tbsp. cooking oil
1 Tbsp. vinegar
1 cup cold water

Sift the dry ingredients into a 9-by-9 ungreased cake pan. Mix with fork. Make three holes in dry ingredients. Into one pour the vanilla, the next the oil, and into the third the vinegar. Pour over all this 1 cup cold water. Mix with a fork. Do not beat. Bake at 350 for 25 to 30 minutes or until done.

APRIL 2004

It is a windy Sunday evening, April 25, here in Michigan. It looks almost like we could get a thunderstorm. My husband Joe is anxious to go mushroom hunting whenever they start popping out.

Right now Joe is outside playing basketball, or rather trying to teach the children how to make a ball go through a net. I should be outside joining them but I felt tired. I'm enjoying the peace and quiet while it lasts. After awhile, though, it gets too peaceful and I long to hear the children's chatter.

I sat down and read a stack of letters from you wonderful readers. I received a batch of them in the mail yesterday from my editor. I feel so much encouragement from the nice written letters and cards. I appreciate all the good wishes on our move. May God's blessings be with you all! I wish time would allow me to answer each one, but with young children time is very limited. My mother always told me to take time for my children while they are young. I still am tempted to think my house has to always be organized. I've found out with six children that is not possible all the time. It's surprising, though, how the older children can really help out with the cleaning.

My sister, Emma, and her husband, Jacob, and family came out early this morning to attend church with us here in Michigan. It was nice seeing them again. We had a good but too short visit with them after church services. Sisters Susan and Verena went back home to Indiana with Jacob's this afternoon. Jacob's will load their belongings on Friday and Saturday (May 1) for their move to Michigan. We are all getting excited to think of having them close by again.

I hope they will like it here as well as we do. The people in this community have given us a very warm welcome and everyone is friendly, which helps a lot in making adjustments.

We had a good rain during the night. I am so glad for it as our garden needed it so much. I have onions, radishes, and lettuce peeping through. Mmm, garden goodies sound good again! The rain should give it a boost.

We plan to leave on Thursday morning, April 29, at 5:30 a.m. for Indiana. We want to go to our house in Indiana and do some cleaning before the upcoming auction. Then we'll spend Friday and Saturday helping Jacob's load up. We plan to return home on Saturday evening. Jacob's load of hay and their horses will come Monday in a week. Looks like we'll have a busy week of helping them get settled in.

MAY 2004

(EDITOR'S NOTE: Lovina and Joe Eicher welcomed a newborn baby early in the morning on May 18. The 5.15 pound baby is named Lovina. It's custom among the Amish to name their children after family. The baby was delivered three weeks early in an emergency c-section when Lovina developed severe gall bladder problems. Little Lovina was delivered early, but healthy - with lots of black hair. Lovina, however, battled severe complications because of the gall bladder problems and had to spend several days in the ICU. Lovina is expected to fully recover and both the baby and Lovina are now home and recovering comfortably. Lovina will take this week and next week off from her column while she recovers and tends to baby Lovina. Incidentally, while Lovina enjoys a close bond with her readers, she chose not to write about her pregnancy. It's common among the Amish not to announce and publicize a pregnancy, so she wanted to respect this church and cultural custom. This week and next will be spent answering some reader recipe requests.)

Dear Lovina:

I lost a treasured recipe that your mother ran in The Amish Cook column several years ago. It was called "Aunt Hilty's Cinnamon Rolls" and they were wonderful. I've wished for it many times, and I wondered if you could help me find it.

LaVonna

Fairfield, Ill.

Editor's answer: These are a favorite in Lovina's community. These deliciously sweet, sticky, yet solid cinnamon rolls are a staple on Amish breakfast tables in the Midwest. Enjoy!

AUNT HILTY'S CINNAMON ROLLS
1 1/2 cups milk
2 teaspoons salt
1/2 cup sugar
1/2 cup butter
2 packages of dry, active yeast
1/2 cup warm water
6 cups flour
3 eggs

Scald 1 1/2 cups milk. Add two teaspoons of salt, 1/2 cup sugar, and 1/2 cup butter or margarine. Add two packages of yeast to 1/2 cup of warm water and let stand five minutes. Add to above mixture. Add three beaten eggs and then three cups of flour. Mix. Add three cups more flour. Let raise to double bulk. Roll out and spread with melted margarine. Sprinkle brown sugar on top and then cinnamon. Roll-up. Cut about 3/4 to one inch width. Let rise. Bake in hot oven (about 350), five to seven minutes. Frosting can be added.

A reader in Gig Harbor, Wash., wrote to Lovina asking if she had heard of a recipe for "milk pie." This also is a family favorite, and a rather old, simple recipe. Here it is:

AMISH MILK PIE
3 eggs
1 cup molasses
1 cup granulated sugar
1/2 cup flour
1 teaspoon baking soda
3 cups thick sour milk
2 (9-inch) unbaked pie shells

Preheat oven to 400 degrees F.

Beat eggs. Add molasses. Combine sugar, flour and baking soda and add to egg mixture. Add thick milk. Pour into unbaked pie shells. Bake for 10 minutes; then reduce oven temperature to 325 degrees F and bake for 40 to 45 minutes. Sprinkle top of pie with cinnamon, if desired.

MAY 2004

It is a nice, beautiful morning, Wednesday, May 12, after some cloudy, rainy days. We've had a few thunderstorms this past weekend. Also a town near us had damage done from a tornado that touched down. We can be so thankful if all is well after a storm passes by.

It is a great relief to us that our property in Indiana was sold on Saturday at public auction. We had a nice day for the sale. The day before it was stormy and rained so we were so glad to see the sun on Saturday.

The children all seemed anxious to head back to Michigan. They were all tired from a long day and slept most of the way home.

The children were still tired early on Sunday morning when we woke them up to get ready to go to church. We took our horse, "Itty Bit", that had a colt six weeks ago to church. This was the first time she was separated from her colt, so she was eager to get back home. Needless to say we had a fast ride home. After we were home, my husband Joe put Itty Bit back with her colt and harnessed our other horse up. We then went to my sister Emma's as her husband, Jacob, and Joe went to look for mushrooms. You have to really know how to identify mushrooms as some are poisonous. They didn't have much luck on their hunt. On the way back from Emma and Jacob's, it rained steadily. It's so nice not to have to mess with umbrellas anymore when it rains. We are getting to like the covered buggies here in Michigan. Our buggies back in Indiana were not covered. It is also nice not to have coats all splattered up with mud when driving on the stone roads after a rain. We are still borrowing someone's buggy from our church. We sure appreciate it. Our new buggy should be ready in June.

Joe was working out in the yard until dark last night. We have a lot to mow and it's growing so fast with all the rains. I hope to get some tomato and pepper plants out this week yet.

Tonight there is a parent meeting at the school, which we plan to attend with Emma and Jacob. Our children will stay with my sisters Verena and Susan at Jacob's house until we get back from the school.

The children are outside now riding their bikes. Joe took Verena and Benjamin's training wheels off and they really can ride good without them. Loretta still has hers on. It seems that's one thing the children don't get tired of is riding bikes. Little Verena is ready for school. She only goes a half day and she really enjoys it. Yesterday she didn't have to go as it was only a half day. I was glad to have Elizabeth and Susan home to help me in the afternoon. We are having lots of asparagus right now, so I will share a recipe.

ASPARAGUS WITH HOMEMADE CHEESE SAUCE
2 cups fresh asparagus
one and one half cup of milk
seasoning to taste
3/4 cup soft cheese (cut-up)

Cook fresh asparagus just until tender. Add milk, then add seasoning to taste. When hot, add soft cheese. When cheese is melted, add this thickening:

2 tablespoons cornstarch
4 tablespoons water
Mix together. A person can vary thickness by using more or less cheese.

JUNE 2004

As you readers have already been told, Joe and I were blessed with a baby daughter named Lovina on May 18, 2004. She joins siblings Elizabeth, 9; Susan, 8; Verena, 6; Benjamin, 4; Loretta, 3, and Joseph, 22 months. She weighed 5 pounds, 15 ounces at birth and was 18.5 inches. She arrived three weeks early, but is doing great so far, for which we are thankful.

I will try to write about how everything went. At 3 a.m. on May 18, I awoke to very hard pain. I had been having gall bladder attacks throughout this pregnancy, and I thought it was another attack that would leave in an hour or so, as it usually did.

After a couple of hours, my pains got worse and to the point where I could hardly take it any more. My husband, Joe, went for my sisters Susan and Verena, who live just around the corner here in Michigan.

After they came over, Joe went to our non-Amish neighbor lady and asked if she would take us to the emergency room at the hospital in the nearby town. I had to have help getting out to her car. Susan and Joe went along to the hospital while Verena stayed here with the children.

At the hospital, they took tests and prepared me for an emergency C-section. They discovered I had pancreatitis, which caused me to be put into intensive care for five days.

Baby Lovina and I were in the hospital for seven days in all. I was battling fever, and my one lung almost collapsed, so I had to take breathing treatments. The doctor said it could have been too late for both of us had we waited much longer. Joe had wanted me to go to the hospital sooner. It was a relief once I could come home and not be all hooked up to everything.

Joe wanted to name the baby after me, as she was born four days before my birthday. I spent my 33rd birthday in the ICU, but my gift was that I could get moved out of ICU to a regular room that day. I couldn't see the baby for two days because of my fever. Joe would go down to the nursery and feed her, and she acted like she knew him already.

Jacob and Emma had their public auction for their property in Indiana on my birthday. My sisters Verena and Susan took our six children along out to Indiana. I think it was good for them to get away for a day.

I am so glad to be home again. I don't know what we would've done without Verena and Susan's help. The people in the community have been so caring and helpful. I will have to have surgery in several weeks to have my gall bladder removed. It will be a relief when that's over, too. God was above us, and we thank Him for saving us both. Thank you to all the readers for your cards and well-wishes.

Meanwhile, a reader in Berwick, Pa., asked if I had a recipe for homemade pretzels. This is one that is fun to fix. The children enjoy it because they can make the dough into fun shapes.

HOMEMADE PRETZELS (makes about 14 soft pretzels)
1/2 package (1/4 teaspoon) dry yeast
1 1/2 teaspoons sugar
2 cups all-purpose flour
3/4 cup lukewarm water
1/2 teaspoon regular table salt
1 egg beaten with 1 teaspoon water.
Use coarse salt to decorate the pretzels after shaping them.

For the dough: In a large mixing bowl, soften the yeast by sprinkling it over lukewarm water (105 degrees F.) with the sugar stirred in. After a few minutes, stir again to dissolve the yeast. Add regular table salt. Blend in the 2 cups flour with a fork to form a soft dough.

Clean the bowl and scrape dough out onto a lightly floured board or work surface. Knead dough until smooth. Pull off pieces of dough about the size of walnuts. Roll into 14-inch ropes and twist into pretzel shapes (animals or alphabet shapes are fun for young children.) Place on greased baking sheets. Brush pretzels with the beaten egg and water mixture; sprinkle with coarse salt, if using. Bake on greased cookie sheets at 350 degrees for 15-18 minutes.

JUNE 2004

It's Thursday forenoon, and I had better get this written and out in the mailbox before the mailman comes. Time just flies by in the mornings.

My husband, Joe, left at 7 a.m. for work. They are doing a lot of roofing jobs, but they also have some pole barns lined up to do. With all the rain lately they have lost a few days of work. Joe has been cleaning out the barn. A lot of trash stayed here at the new place we bought, so we're gradually trying to get it hauled away.

We took our brand new baby Lovina along on Tuesday to Indiana. We went out to do the closing on our property there. She did pretty good about traveling. She is sleeping a little longer during the night. I think she had her days and nights mixed up for awhile. She would sleep a lot during the day and, at night, be bright awake.

The closing had been scheduled for May 21, but then I ended up in the hospital, so we had to cancel it until I was able to travel that far. I will probably have my gall bladder surgery in three weeks. I will be so glad to get that over with. Then, I hope I won't have to be so careful what I eat.

My daughter Elizabeth had her 10th birthday on June 14. It is so hard to believe that our oldest child is already 10!

Gardens are starting to look better since we've had a few sun-shiny days. My garden needs to be hoed so badly. Joe didn't come home until 6:30 last night, and we had visitors, so it just hasn't seemed like the nights have been long enough to get everything done lately. I will be glad when I can help with the harder work again.

We have our new covered buggy now. Sunday, we went for a ride in it. Sister Emma and Jacob told us to come to their house for dinner. It was nice to get out of the house for awhile on such a pleasant day, although I was upset that we missed some visitors from our church who came to see the baby.

Sisters Verena and Susan did my laundry on Monday and swept and mopped the floors. I don't know what I would've done without their help.

Benjamin, Loretta, and Joseph will all have birthdays next month. Joe and I will also have our 11th wedding anniversary, so July will be a busy month around here.

Little Joseph seems to accept baby Lovina more than he did at first, although it still bothers him at times not to be the baby. We got one of Jacob's puppies, and Joseph just loves that little puppy.

I want to thank all of you readers who have sent baby, birthday, and get-well cards. I appreciate all the good wishes, and may God bless each and every one of you for your kindness.

A reader in Quincy, Ill., asked for a strawberry muffin recipe. Here is a good one to try:

STRAWBERRY MUFFINS
3/4 cup regular margarine, softened
3/4 cup sugar
1 1/2 teaspoons vanilla
3 eggs
3 cups all-purpose flour
3/4 teaspoon salt
3/8 teaspoon baking soda
1 1/2 cups fresh, homemade strawberry preserves
3/4 cup buttermilk
1/2 cup chopped nuts (optional)

Preheat oven to 325 degrees. In a large bowl, cream margarine. Add sugar and vanilla. Stir vigorously until fluffy. Add eggs, one at a time, beating well after each addition.

In a medium bowl, sift together flour, salt and baking soda. Combine preserves and buttermilk in another small bowl. Stir well and add alternately with the flour mixture to the margarine mixture.

Beat only until just blended or the texture of the muffins will be changed, then stir in nuts (optional).

Spoon batter into greased muffin pan or paper-lined muffin cups. Bake until toothpick comes out clean when inserted into middle of muffins. Turn muffins out onto a wire rack to cool completely. Makes approximately 4 1/2 dozen small (1 3/4-inch) muffins

JUNE 2004

It is Tuesday evening, June 29, and we are over here at my sister Verena and Susan's. Jacob and Emma and family left for home a while ago. It sure is cozy riding in a covered buggy when it cools off at night.

In our new covered buggy we can open the back seat up so that it lays flat for the children to lie down if they get tired. But tonight we walked to Verena and Susan's since the weather was nice and they live so close.

Jacob and Joe were taking steel and doors and everything that's still good off of an out-building here at Verena and Susan's tonight. They have three older sheds outside and have decided to tear all three down and have a new one put up. It will be a lot nicer for them when it's all done. Joe will try to finish it tomorrow.

We decided to just stay here for the night. Some of the children fell asleep early in the evening. Instead of waking them up and walking home with all the tired children it was easier just to stay.

I did laundry today, Wednesday. It was a very nice afternoon to do it. My daughter Elizabeth, 10, is sure a big help doing the laundry. The girls are getting older and can really help with housework.

Everyone wants the job of taking care of little Lovina. She is a sweet addition to the family and doesn't lack attention. We have to keep our eyes open with Joseph, though. He wants to be nice to her sometimes, and sometimes not. He wants to try and sit in her seat or crawl into her crib. We try give him more attention so he doesn't get so jealous.

Meanwhile, daughter Loretta keeps asking me how many times she has to sleep before her birthday, which is Thursday, July 1st. She will be 4 years old. She and Benjamin will both be 4 for two weeks and then Benjamin will turn 5 on the 14th. Benjamin doesn't care to have Loretta being the same age as him for very long.

I have to go to the hospital tomorrow to have some tests done for my upcoming gall bladder surgery. It seems like I'm finally getting back my strength to work and hate to think about having the surgery. I will be glad to be able to eat and not be afraid of having a gall bladder attack. Hopefully after I heal from surgery I'll feel a lot better.

Everyone is now sound asleep so I think I will join the rest. It's been a long day and tomorrow will be, too.

Friday we will head to Indiana and spend the night at sister Liz and Levi's. Then on Saturday we plan to attend the Coblentz reunion. It will seem sad to not see Dad and Mom there. The children are excited and can't wait to get to Levi's.

Here is a good casserole recipe to use those garden zucchinis which are becoming plentiful:

ZUCCHINI CASSEROLE
2 medium-sized zucchini, peeled and cut into cubes
2 eggs, slightly beaten
1/4 c. milk
1 teaspoon baking powder
2 tbsp. flour
2 c. cheddar cheese, grated
1/2 c. onion, chopped
1/4 c. green pepper, chopped
2 cloves garlic, minced

Preheat oven to 350 degrees. Steam or boil zucchini until almost tender. Drain and cool. In a medium-sized bowl, combine eggs, milk, baking powder, cheese, onion, green pepper and garlic. Stir in zucchini. Bake in a greased casserole dish for about 30 minutes. Let it sit for a few minutes before serving.

JULY 2004

Everyone is getting settled down for the night. It is thundering and lightning, and we have received some rain. We hope to get a little more because the garden is looking dry.

We were at Jacob and Emma's today. Joe was helping Jacob, as they are in the process of building a new barn. They have only a small shed to keep their horse and hay in, so this will be a lot better.

Emma and Jacob will have a "frolic" (barn-raising) on Saturday for the community. There were quite a few men there today helping to dig holes and setting poles.

I went along to help Emma cook for the men and wash dishes. I'm sure they will be glad when it's all over and done.

Friday afternoon we left to go to Indiana. We went to Levi and Liz's and spent the night at their house. We also visited cousin Heidi's for a pizza supper where a lot of Dad's family had gathered.

We had breakfast at Levi's on Saturday morning, and then we headed to the park for the Coblentz reunion.

Levi hitched the team of horses to the wagon and we all rode together. Jacob's family, Verena and Susan also went to the reunion. Jacob and family went to his parents for the night, and Verena and Susan were at Levi's with us.

All of Dad's 12 brothers and sisters were at the reunion. I saw a lot of cousins I haven't seen for a while. These years fly by and there have been a lot of changes. This was the first time we went to the reunion since Dad died. It seemed like something was missing.

Liz prepared a big breakfast of biscuits, sausage gravy, eggs, potatoes, cheese, coffee, tea and juice. We had an enjoyable time with them.

The children enjoyed the pony rides at Levi's. Our little Benjamin followed Levi Jr., age 10, around all over. Levi doesn't have any brothers, so I think he enjoyed having another boy around.

We got to see brothers Amos and Albert and their families at the reunion, also.

We started for home later and had to get up early on Sunday morning to go to church. It was the first time we took baby Lovina to church. She was pretty good and slept through church services.

Thank you to everyone for the kind words and cards while I've been recovering from gall bladder surgery.

A reader in Sullivan, Ind., asked for a corn casserole recipe. This one calls for ground beef, so it's a main dish.

CORN BAKE
1 pound lean ground beef
1/3 cup chopped onion
1/3 cup ketchup
1/2 teaspoon salt
1/2 teaspoon chili powder
1/4 teaspoon dried oregano
1 1/2 cups fresh corn, cooked
1 package (8.5 ounces) cornbread mix (or make your own from scratch)
3 tablespoons butter or margarine, melted (divided)
1 (16-oz.) can tomatoes with liquid, chopped (or use your own equivalent from the garden)
1 tablespoon cornstarch

In a skillet, brown beef with onion, stirring to break up lumps of beef. Drain off dripping. Add ketchup, salt, chili powder and oregano. Cook for 5 minutes. Cool slightly.

With a spoon, press meat mixture into the bottom and up the sides of a greased 10-inch pie plate. Spoon corn kernels into crust. Prepare cornbread batter according to package directions. Stir in 2 tablespoons melted butter. Spread batter over corn. Bake at 425 degrees for 20 minutes. Meanwhile, combine chopped tomatoes with juice, the cornstarch and remaining butter in a saucepan. Cook and stir for 5 to 10 minutes or until thickened. Cut pie into wedges and serve with tomatoes.

JULY 2004

It's another beautiful day but it feels like it could get pretty hot. My laundry is drying on the lines now, which is one thing this warm weather does well. My sisters Verena and Susan helped me with the laundry which allowed it to get done much quicker.

I had my surgery last week and I feel like I'm on the road to recovery finally. I ended up back in the hospital 3 days after my surgery as I had a fever of 102. The doctor said I don't have an infection but thinks I caught the flu. So after resting I feel good again.

Between the surgery and being on the go a lot this summer, I haven't been able to get into the garden as much as I would like, so weeds are taking over. Even with the weeds, though, we are getting lots of fresh vegetables. We are enjoying all the garden goodies. It seems so easy to make a meal at this time of year. My sweet corn is behind but hopefully it'll still produce something. We need to water our garden more often here in Michigan as the soil dries off so fast. It sure is different than last year in Indiana when my garden was flooded a lot. A year ago is when we had that awful flood in Indiana, many people were left homeless and lost most of their belongings.

Saturday, July 17, Jacob's had their barn-raising. Around 26 men came to help and the barn is now up and enclosed. It still needs some doors and finishing touches done. I was, unfortunately, back in the hospital on that day so Joe couldn't go help. Our children went to Jacob's while we were in the hospital.

My sister Liz, her husband Levi, and family came here from Indiana on Friday and spent the night here. Then they went to Jacob's on Saturday to help with the barn. It was nice to see them again. We had a hard time getting the children settled down for bed as they were excited to see each other.

Baby Lovina is still doing well. She weighs almost 9 pounds and will be 2 months old on Sunday. She really smiles and is very alert. Little Lovina can somehow manage to sleep through all the racket in this house. With six other kids around here it can be noisy. Meanwhile, 2-year-old Joseph is adjusting a little better to her. I let him hold her and he'll smile at her and kiss her. As times, though, he'll try to slap her, so I try to be careful.

Sunday, July 18th is Mother's 68th birthday. I get such a longing to show her my new baby. And also our new home. I told Joe I wish we would've all moved out here when Dad and Mom were still living. I think Dad and Mom would've liked living in this area. Joe enjoys the lakes close by. He has done some fishing but doesn't get enough time to go often. Dad also liked to fish. There is a lake down the road just a bit.

Our new barnyard fence is up now, so that is one major project completed around here. Hopefully things will slow down as we gradually get settled. I feel like I'm gaining strength to do more. I want to thank all the readers that have taken time to send a card. It's nice to know you care.

With the garden now in full swing, here is a good recipe to use those tomatoes:

GREEN TOMATO BREAD
3 cups all-purpose flour
1/4 teaspoon baking powder
1 teaspoon baking soda
1 teaspoon salt
2 cups granulated sugar
1 tablespoon cinnamon
2 large eggs, lightly beaten
1 cup vegetable oil
1 teaspoon vanilla extract
2 cups finely chopped or ground
Green tomatoes - about 2 medium
1 1/2 cups chopped pecans

Preheat oven to 350 degrees F. Grease and flour two 8 x 4-inch loaf pans.

Combine first 6 ingredients in a large bowl; make a well in center of mixture. Combine eggs, oil and vanilla extract; stir well. Add to dry ingredients, stirring just until moistened. Fold in tomato and pecans. Spoon batter into prepared loaf pans. Bake for 1 hour or until a wooden pick inserted in center of bread comes out clean. Cool in pans on a wire rack for 10 minutes. Remove from pans, and let cool completely on wire rack.

JULY 2004

I will try writing this column tonight, even though I'm holding baby Lovina. She's being fussy again. I'm hoping she isn't a "colic" baby. She has a hard time burping after her feeding at night. Our little Verena was a colic baby, and I remember how often she kept us awake during the night. My husband Joe could usually hold her just right, and she would settle down. It seems Lovina, too, settles down easier when he holds her. I remember at the hospital I couldn't see her for two days because I had a fever, so Joe spent more time with baby Lovina than I did.

They took me down in a wheelchair to see her after I was feeling better. As soon as I held her and she started crying, Joe would take her, and she was quiet right away. She must've known who Joe was already. I was used to having my babies beside me all the time after they were born. But the nurses told me there will be plenty of time for bonding, and they were right. Things have been going pretty smooth since we've been home from the hospital.

I continue to thank you readers for all your cards and well-wishes.

After my gall bladder surgery, I was so tired. Joe would get up and heat Lovina's bottle and feed her. I hated to have him do that and lose sleep, as he had to get to work the next day. But Joe told me that he knows he wouldn't have felt like feeding a baby right after his gall bladder surgery.

Right now, Joe is out working in our yard. He hopes to get our hay mowed tomorrow. We hope we can get it baled and in the barn before it rains. If it rains, I guess we won't complain because our other fields need rain, also our garden.

Daughter Elizabeth, age 10, is washing supper dishes and Susan, 8, is picking up toys and sweeping floors. I had to hold baby Lovina, so I figured I might as well write this and get it ready for tomorrow's mail pickup.

Yesterday, July 19, was sister Emma's 31st birthday. We surprised her by all getting together for supper. Sisters Verena and Susan were there, also. We had an enjoyable evening and a good meal. Baby Lovina didn't enjoy her evening, as she was fussy. Maybe we'll have to switch to a different formula. She seems real contented until evening, though.

We had an easy supper tonight -- no cooking. Our neighbor lady brought supper in for us. How thoughtful! She was on her way to town and dropped it off. It really gave me a lift, as I was doing some unpacking. I emptied quite a few totes and was just starting to think about what I should fix for supper when she dropped by. I hope I can repay her sometime.

Joe's sister Loretta and her husband Henry were blessed with a baby girl on Saturday. They named her Rebecca. We would like to go see her sometime. They live in this Michigan community. This makes three boys and three girls for them now.

I plan to go spend the day tomorrow at sister Emma's. The children can't wait to visit with their cousins. They always have a fun time playing together. Emma and Jacob are enjoying their new barn, which looks really nice.

Meanwhile, try this moist, sweet bread that uses some garden zucchini and three spices:

ZUCCHINI BREAD
3 eggs
2 cups sugar
2 cups shredded zucchini (do not peel)
1 cup vegetable oil
2 teaspoons vanilla extract
3 cups all-purpose flour
1 teaspoon salt
1 teaspoon baking soda
1 teaspoon baking powder
2 teaspoons cinnamon
1/2 teaspoon grated nutmeg
1/4 teaspoon ground cloves
1/2 cup finely chopped walnuts or pecans
1/2 cup raisins
Yield: 2 loaves

Beat eggs until foamy in a large mixing bowl. Stir in sugar, shredded zucchini, oil and vanilla extract.

In a smaller mixing bowl, stir together the dry ingredients: the flour, salt, baking soda, baking powder, cinnamon, nutmeg and cloves. Gradually stir dry ingredients into the zucchini mixture. Stir in the nuts and raisins. Divide batter between 2 loaf pans greased on the bottoms only. (size not specified).

Bake at 325 degrees (preheated oven) for 60 to 80 minutes. Cool 10 minutes. Loosen around edges, invert and remove loaves from pans. Cool completely. Wait one day for easier slicing.

AUGUST 2004

It's so hard to believe that we're this far into August! Daughters, Elizabeth, Susan, and Verena will start school on August 23rd. The summer sure flew by. I'll miss their help while they're away during the day.

It's a rainy morning right now. Must be my husband Joe has inside work somewhere today as he hasn't come back home yet. He works as a member of a carpenter crew so outdoor work can be rained out. Yesterday was very hot and muggy and Joe was up on a roof putting on shingles all day. He was so warm when he came home from work.

I helped him mow the yard last night as I knew he was tired from the long day. We worked together until dark and got everything mowed. I'm glad we did since it rained overnight. The rain will do the garden good and cool everything down. It was hard to get up this morning since we worked so late last night. Hopefully we'll get a good night's sleep tonight. Joe will take off from work the next two days to help the carpenter crew that's putting up Verena and Susan's barn. Hopefully the weather will be nice for that.

There's a large empty field behind our house that we want to plant wheat in. But first we have to prepare the soil, which is so full of rocks and stones. We have been kept busy since we moved here picking stones out of the field so we can plant. The stones, while difficult to remove, are nice and colorful. We are saving some of them as Joe is going to make some flower beds for me, for which they will make nice borders. My sister Emma and her husband Jacob and my sisters Verena and Susan came over one night and helped us pick up stones.

Joe used our horse, Diamond, to pull the stones up behind the barn. It's a job to get all those stones picked up. All the children except baby Lovina were out in the field helping pick up stones. We had baby Lovina with us in a stroller and she really seemed to enjoy the evening. We were all so glad when it got too dark to see so we could quit. Many hands do make lighter work!

The move to Michigan, however, has been worth all the work! We enjoy it here so much and don't wish to move back. The children say they like our new home better so that helps a lot. We're always glad to hear from family and friends, though. We had a letter in the mail from my brother Albert, which we appreciated. I would like to send one back.

We are enjoying sweet corn and all those other garden goodies. My corn isn't ready yet, but someone gave us some. People sure have generously shared with us since I didn't get as much planted as I usually do between moving, a new baby, and surgery this past spring and summer. It sure has been quite a year already.

Baby Lovina is once more a contented little girl. I starting using a different kind of baby bottle called a "Vent Aire". She could drink too fast out of her other bottles and these bottles seem to swallow less air. So I am glad the problem was that simple. She was 11 weeks old yesterday and now weighs 10 pounds. It's so sweet how she coos and tries to "talk."

We were surprised to see friends that used to live close to us in Indiana come in to visit with all of us sisters on Monday. They wanted to come before the school year started.

Now to some reader mail:

To the Mansfield, Ohio reader about "The Amish Cook Treasury." (Editor's note: This is a new book with over 300 of The Amish Cook's never published recipes from Amish, Mennonite and German Baptist kitchens. The 200-plus page book, available for $28, is sprinkled with articles about quilting, canning and parenting. For more information, or to order, call 1-800-245-7515. All books ordered before August 31st will come signed and personalized by Lovina and arrive in time for Christmas. The Best of The Amish Cook, Vol 1 & Vol. 2, and The Treasury are available now for a package price of $50.)

I should get back to doing the many chores that need to be completed around this house, but have had lots of letters about zucchini recipes. Zucchini is so plentiful this time of year, try this delicious recipe:

CHOCOLATE ZUCCHINI CAKE
1/2 cup butter, softened
1/2 cup oil
2 eggs

2 1/2 cups flour
4 tablespoons cocoa
1 tablespoon baking soda
1/2 teaspoon baking powder
1/2 cup sour milk or buttermilk
1 3/4 cup sugar
1 teaspoon vanilla
2 cups zucchini (shredded)
1/2 teaspoon cinnamon
1 cup chocolate chips

Grease and flour a 9 X 13" pan. Mix all ingredients, except chocolate chips, together until smooth batter. Sprinkle one cup of chocolate chips on top. Bake for 30 minutes in 325 oven. Remove when knife inserted comes clean. Can frost, but cake is moist enough that it's not necessary.

AUGUST 2004

Elizabeth is giving Lovina her bottle. Usually, if she has a bottle before we go to bed, she will sleep all night. That sure helps me get more rest. She is an early bird, though, it seems that as soon as Joe and I are ready to get up, she starts waking up. Baby Lovina is a very happy little one. It's so cute to get her laughing. She really makes sounds already. Such a precious angel!

Joe started a new job today. He is back working in a factory. He liked working with the construction crew, but he likes the hours better in a factory. He will have a lot more time at home in the evenings. I'm excited to think of Joe coming home earlier and so are the children.

Tonight Joe and the children went to pick up more stones in the field again. Last week I wrote about how we want to clear that field out so we can plant wheat. After such hard work, a hearty dinner was needed, so I made a big casserole. I told sisters Verena and Susan to come get some for their supper also. Susan helped pick up stones for awhile. The weather made such hard outdoor work tolerable because it was a cold day for August. The whole summer sure hasn't been too hot, except maybe a few days.

I am still getting used to a different stove, but I like it better. In this Amish community they have gas stoves, which is what I have now. It sure is different and lots easier than the kerosene stove I had back in Indiana. We also have a gas refrigerator. This is the first time we've had one, before we always had to buy ice and use an ice chest to keep our food cold. We would keep the ice chest in the basement so the ice would keep longer. This refrigerator sure has saved me a lot of steps.

My tomatoes are really doing well. It looks like I'll have to process some juice in a few weeks if they keep doing good. I pulled the rest of the onions tonight and did some weeding in the garden. Those weeds sure are taking over. Verena and Susan's barn is up now, except for the floor. It will be cemented tomorrow. It sure looks good. They'll keep their buggy in the barn.

Saturday we headed into town and took the children to the park. We had a picnic there. Joe grilled chicken and we also had potato salad and cheese. The children enjoyed it and weren't ready to go home. Joe and I even enjoyed the swings and slides with the children. It seems sometimes with life so busy, we don't do things like that often enough. The years fly by, and before we know it, the children will be grown. It takes so much patience and a lot of prayers to raise a family. God is a great help! Do we thank him enough for all his blessings?

Try this recipe for a hearty casserole:

HEARTY HAMBURGER CASSEROLE
3 pounds ground beef
2 cans cream of mushroom soup
9 slices bacon
3 cups cooked spaghetti
3 onions, sliced
1 quart tomato juice
3 cups sliced potatoes
1 pound cheddar cheese
3 cups sliced celery

Brown beef and onions; drain and pour into a casserole dish. Layer the potatoes, celery and spaghetti. Pour the cans of mushroom soup over the mixture.

Fry the bacon and cut into small pieces and put on top. Pour tomato juice over the bacon and then sprinkle the cheese over the top. Cover and bake at 350 degrees for 1 1/2 hours.

AUGUST 2004

We spent Sunday, Aug. 22, with my brother Albert and Sarah Irene and family in Indiana. My sister Emma, husband Jacob, and their children (plus my sisters Susan and Verena) also went. We hired 2 vans to take us as we're a total of 17 (editor's note: While most Old Order Amish don't own cars, preferring instead to use horse-drawn buggy, they are permitted to ride in motorized vehicles to visit relatives, attend faraway weddings, etc.). We started out around 6 a.m. after we finally got all the car seats hooked up and the children belted in. That takes a while just doing that. My sister Verena's birthday was on Sunday, so she took us all out for breakfast on the way to Indiana. It was a treat to eat out and not do any dishes.

We stopped in at my sister Liz and Levi's on the way to Albert's. She has been busy this summer repainting her bedrooms upstairs and re-varnishing the wood floors. Liz and Levi's decided to join us at Albert's for the day. We were all glad to get to see Albert and Sarah Irene's 2 1/2 week old daughter, Susan. She's a sweetie! I didn't realize how my baby Lovina had grown until I saw her beside Susan. They are 2 1/2 months apart.

Albert had a big dinner, with the main dish being delicious barbecued chicken. We all had an enjoyable day together. Albert's oldest daughter, Elizabeth, had her 17th birthday on Sunday, as did sister Leah's son Paul Jr. who turned 9. Uncle Joe and Betty Coblentz and a couple of their grandchildren also had dinner with us at Albert's.

Before we started for home we stopped in for a short visit with my sister Leah and Paul's family. This was the first time they had seen baby Lovina. Leah set some snacks out and we stayed longer than we had planned to. Leah is preparing for the move to their new 50-acre farm that they bought 9-10 miles north of them. After leaving Paul's we stopped in to say "hi" to brother Amos, Nancy, and family. They weren't home so we headed back to Michigan. We arrived back around 9 p.m., so we made the children go to bed right away. They had slept on the way home after such a long day. As always, it was good to be back home in Michigan again!

We are trying to get back into a "routine" again as the school year begins. Joe and I now have four children going to school, which is hard to believe. Benjamin only goes half days. I'm sitting out here on the front steps with Benjamin, Loretta, and Joseph waiting on the bus to pick up Benjamin. He leaves around 10:25 a.m. (Editor's note: Amish children in Michigan, like many Amish, attend public schools until the eighth grade). So far he seems rarin' to go so that makes it easier to see him go. Loretta has a paper and pencil and says she's writing a column, too.

I processed 19 quarts of pickles already and have another bucket yet to go. I made dill, banana and also some freezer pickles. A lady from the community had extra corn and gave me quite a few bags. It was all bagged and ready. I hadn't met her until Tuesday evening at Joe's sister MaryAnn's. I thought that was so thoughtful for her to do that. It sure means a lot to me. A friend also gave us a big sack of sweet corn, so I hope to work that up today. I also have green beans to do that I got from Verena and Susan. My hot peppers are also ready to be picked and put into jars, but I'll leave that for next week. Meanwhile try this delicious way to prepare your garden green beans.

HOMEMADE GREEN BEAN CASSEROLE
3 slices bacon
1 small onion, sliced
2 teaspoons cornstarch
1/4 teaspoon salt
1/4 teaspoon dry mustard
16 ounces of home-canned or store bought green beans
1 tablespoon brown sugar
1 tablespoon vinegar
1 hard boiled egg, chopped

Cook bacon in large skillet until crisp. Crumble bacon. Pour off all but 1 tablespoon drippings; add onion, and saut until tender. Blend in cornstarch, salt and mustard. Drain beans, reserving 12 cup liquid. Stir reserved liquid into skillet. Cook, stirring constantly, until thickened and bubbly. Stir in sugar and vinegar. Add beans; heat until bubbly-hot. Sprinkle with crumbled bacon and egg.

SEPTEMBER 2004

It's a busy day here but I want to sit down and write this column. I need to get it in the mail on Wednesdays so my editor has it to send to all the newspapers in time. Before I sat down to write this I was in the middle of processing red beets, green beans and hot peppers. Last night I did some sweet and also some dill pickles. I now have over 40 quarts of pickles, plus I still have some left from last year. I think I have enough pickles now until next summer. I am running out of sugar and vinegar so I might not be able to finish today. I'll probably have to make a trip to town after Joe gets home from work. I don't like to run out of something in the middle of a task. But it feels so good to see the canning jars all filled up and ready for the winter ahead. I want to get more of my vegetables from the garden all worked up this week.

My sister Emma and Jacob will have church services at their house in a couple of weeks. We want to help them prepare all we can. They wanted to take their turn to have the services in their new barn before they start filling it up too full. It'll be different to take church in a new community. We'll probably host church sometime this fall if we can get our tool shed insulated and heat in it. Joe is thinking about using our coal stove that we moved up from Indiana.

Friday night Joe's sister, Christine, husband, Jake, and five children plan to come for supper and stay here overnight. So I want to get some extra beds made up. They live around 2-3 hours from here so our children don't see each other very often. We told the rest of Joe's family that are close by to also come. Jacob, Emma and family and Verena and Susan will also come over. Joe is planning to make barbecued chicken and I'll make mashed potatoes, gravy and all the trimmings. It'll be easy to make a big meal with all the fresh vegetables out of the garden.

The school children have off on Friday and Monday for the Labor Day holiday so that'll be nice to have them home. Joe will also have off on Monday. We are thinking about giving the basement a thorough cleaning so it would be done for church, unless we decide instead to go fishing and have a picnic and forget about work for a day. Wouldn't that be nice?

SEPTEMBER 2004

I feel like I hardly have time to sit down and write this column. It has been such a busy, busy week! But how could I let all you readers down with all the encouraging letters I receive? I am sorry that I do not have the time to answer back to each letter. I do want you to all know I appreciate all the kind and encouraging words and may God bless you all richly.

I have been processing grape juice. I have processed 114 quarts already. It will sure be nice to have our own this winter. I add less sugar than it calls for, so when we drink store-bought grape juice it seems way too sweet. Nothing is better than home-canned grape juice.

Loretta is having quite the time with her broken arm. (Editor's note: Loretta broke it during a fall from trampoline the previous week) She feels so handicapped. She was trying to sweep the floor with one hand. She has a hard cast on for four weeks. I feel so sorry for her. I just hope her arm is healing OK. As far as pain, she never complains of it hurting! She has lost her balance going upstairs and fell on it, so hopefully we'll get through without hurting it again.

Baby Lovina is 4 months old now and weighs almost 13 pounds. She is really getting lively and wants all the attention she can get. She started sucking on her thumb while she sleeps. Hopefully I can break her of that habit. I tried giving her the pacifier but she spits it back out. I never had any of my others do this.

Jacob and Emma had a nice day on Sunday to have church services at their house. They had it in the new barn and served lunch in there afterward. They served coffee, tea, homemade wheat and white bread, ham, pickles, red beets, zucchini relish, a peanut butter mixture (marshmallow cream, corn syrup and peanut butter), butter, jelly, cookies, etc. After dishes were washed we all enjoyed some popcorn.

Jacob's are coming tonight. Jacob will help Joe get started insulating our pole building so that we can have church services this fall. On Saturday, Jacob's and Verena and Susan and us plan to go to Indiana to Mom's side family reunion. It'll be a big reunion. There are 83 of us grandchildren and all married except a few. Some great-grandchildren are married and have children. Uncle Elmer and Aunt Emma will have it in their new building before they add it to the store they have. Mom and Dad will be greatly missed that day.

PUMPKIN PANCAKES
1 c. flour
Pinch baking soda
2 tbs. sugar
1/4 tsp. cinnamon
1/8 tsp. ginger
1/8 tsp. nutmeg
1 egg well-beaten
1-1/4 c. milk
2 tbs.. melted shortening
1/2 c. canned pumpkin or mashed sweet potato, cooked

Combine flour, soda, sugar and spices. Combine egg, shortening, pumpkin and milk; add to flour mixture, beating until smooth. Bake on hot, lightly greased griddle, turning only once. Serve hot with butter and syrup or powdered sugar.

OCTOBER 2004

This is already Thursday forenoon and I better hurry before the mailman comes. Where has this week gone?

Oct. 1 has passed and that marks two years that I wrote my first column. Taking over for my Dear Mother was the hardest thing I ever had to write. God has been a tremendous help and so have you readers with your encouragement.

My husband, Joe, is home today working on the pole barn. We're putting in new overhead doors for it. Our other ones were pretty old and these new ones are insulated to heat for church services. Joe and Jacob have a good start in insulating them but they ran out of insulation. Material is so expensive anymore.

So maybe we can do a little at a time and have it done by the time we have church.

I have a big laundry out on the lines. Sister Verena came over and had breakfast with us and then helped me with the laundry. We were at their house for supper last night and so were Jacob and Emma's. They had a delicious supper. It's always nice to eat someone else's cooking.

We have hay cut down and it'll probably be ready to be put in today. It got rained on but were so glad for the rain. It had been pretty dry. What a change from the flooding we had out in Indiana last year.

I brought home some of Verena and Susan's hot peppers and zucchini. They sure had a good garden this year. I want to process the hot peppers and make zucchini relish with the zucchini. I need to get the recipe off sister Emma. She made some and gave us a taste, it is very good!

Joe's nephew Emanul is getting married on Oct. 14. He is from this area. They would like all of us that will be cooks that day to wear dark blue dresses. So hopefully I can cut and sew me a new dress as I don't have one that color.

I sure got plenty of good used clothes at the Amish garage sales this spring. It helped out a lot with my sewing. I couldn't buy the material for the price I gave for it. Clothing customs are different in this community so we had to have all new clothes. A lady in our church also gave me a lot of clothes that her children had outgrown. I thought that was so nice of her. It was greatly appreciated and saved me a lot of sewing.

Tomorrow I take Loretta to the doctor for a checkup on her arm. Hopefully it is healing good. If it is, her cast can be taken off in two weeks. She says it is really itchy.

I made something different for breakfast this morning. We really liked it! I'll share my recipe. A hint: I put cheese slices on top after they are almost done. Very good!

BACON & POTATO PANCAKES
5 to 6 medium potatoes, chopped
1/2 cup chopped onion
2 tablespoons flour
oil for frying
5 bacon strips, cooked and crumbled
2 eggs, beaten
saltpepper to taste

Shred potatoes. In a bowl combine potatoes, bacon, onion, eggs, flour, salt and pepper. In a skillet, heat oil until sizzling. Drop by 2 heaping tablespoons into hot oil. Flatten to form patties. Fry until golden brown. Turn and cook other side. Drain on paper towels. Yield: 2 dozen.

NOVEMBER 2004

It turned out to be a warm and beautiful day for a wedding, the wedding of Joe's nephew Emanul. It was very foggy on our way there. It always makes me nervous to drive the buggy through fog. We had our blinking lights on but I'm always afraid someone won't see us in time. I appreciate the covered buggy even more now with cold weather coming on.

The wedding services were held at the bride's neighbors in a big buggy shed. The meals for those in attendance were served at the bride's home in a big building where they could seat over a couple hundred people at one time. In this community, when they have a wedding they rent a cook wagon and cooler. The wagon has 5 gas stoves, a sink with hot cold running water, cabinets, etc. It also has kettles, plates, silverware, bowls, towels, glasses, coffee cups and just about everything you need to prepare and serve a wedding meal. This makes it so much easier after the wedding not to have all the dishes to put away or return to people.

They assigned us cooks all to specific duties. My job and also five other women was to peel potatoes and put them into kettles to cook. Then get them all mashed after they were ready. It takes a lot of potatoes on a day like that. It wasn't too bad with all of us to take turns mashing. Some of us had babies to go tend to. They had women assigned to make homemade gravy, vegetables, chicken, salad dressing, etc.

The cooks and the table-waiters (which they choose friends and cousins and assign a boy and girl to every table to wait on) eat before we go over to see the couple get married, which is around noon. Usually only the cooks that are related to the bride and groom go and the rest keep watch on the food on the burners.

After the couple is united in marriage everyone comes over to the bride's home to eat. When Joe and I got married we had everything (services and meals) all at my Mom's, which made it nice.

After everyone was served, dinner dishes were washed, tables set again for supper and the bride and groom opened their many nice wedding gifts. Some singing takes place also and then it's time for us cooks to start all over again for supper. For dinner they served potatoes, gravy, dressing, corn, baked chicken, salad, bread buns, pudding, fruit, cake, and different kinds of pies. For supper, mashed potatoes, gravy, dressing, mixed vegetables, meatloaf salad bread, pies, cake, ice cream, and strawberries. Then after every meal they passed a bowl of candy bars around which I doubt not many people were hungry for until much later.

It was a long day but enjoyable. Was nice to finally climb into bed after a day like that. The children were also tired from a full day of playing with friends and cousins.

NOVEMBER 2004

This week is flying by way too fast. Church services will be held here on Sunday and we are still trying to get prepared. We are going to get our heat hooked up this week. We have gas heaters that we will only use when we have church or family gatherings in the out-building. The good side about all the preparing for church is that a lot of household jobs are getting done that will be nice to have done before winter anyway.

Joe's sister, Esther, and her friend David, came on Friday to help us prepare for services. Then Saturday Jacob's, and my sisters Verena, and Susan were here helping, so all of the family help has been appreciated! Uncle Joe and Betty Coblentz from Indiana dropped in and brought fresh chicken for dinner which Verena barbecued.

On Sunday, Joe and Betty and Joe and I and our children had a brunch over at Verena and Susan's house. They had a delicious meal waiting for us. After dishes were washed Verena and Susan gave Joe and Betty a ride in our covered buggy.

Jacob's family from Indiana were at their house on Sunday.

I have some questions that readers have asked. Sorry about not answering sooner. Thanks for taking time to send your encouraging letters, they really help keep me motivated to write this.

A reader asked what kind of lights we use. Before we moved here to Michigan we used kerosene lamps and lanterns. Out here we use gas lanterns. The gas lanterns make a very bright light. No, we never used candles, neither did my Mom or Dad when they were growing up. Before I was married we had only kerosene lamps, no bright lanterns.

A reader also asked how I wash off my walls and ceilings and what I use. I use Stanley products called Degreaser and Try It which I put into warm water. I always think the house smells so refreshed after the walls and ceilings are washed. Yes, I wring the rag out tight enough where it doesn't drip too much. I do the ceiling first as sometimes you'll splatter the walls while doing the ceilings. Those wall mops also come in handy. Hopefully this will answer some of your questions.

We have a gas freezer here in Michigan. I've never had one before, so I would appreciate any ideas, recipes on how to best freeze vegetables, meat, etc. Thanks in advance so much! It would surely save time to freeze some instead of processing everything. I did some freezer pickles and I'm surprised at how good they taste.

DECEMBER 2004

Sunday we had a very nice family day together. In the morning, my husband, Joe, fixed breakfast outside on the open fire. We have an outdoor fire-place which is great for cooking meals. Joe made bacon, fried potatoes, and eggs. We had a late breakfast, but we do that a lot when we're home on a Sunday. We have a late breakfast and an early supper. It was nice to get a break from cooking. Joe and I had coffee and the children had hot chocolate with our meal. We huddled closer to the fire while breakfast was cooking in the cold November morning air. It turned out to be a nice day, though, and really warmed up. We all pitched in to do the dishes together after we ate our breakfast.

Mom always told me: "This is your nicest time while your children are all young and under your care." I think I'm beginning to see what she means. When the children get older there are even greater responsibilities. Prayers are greatly needed while raising a family.

After dishes were done the younger children played with dolls and some of them read. Joe and I gave our oldest child, Elizabeth, some more German lessons. We usually wait to teach them to read German until between third or fourth grade. This way they won't get the German and the English mixed up.

Joe grilled hamburgers later on while I prepared some food in the house for our supper. Sisters Verena and Susan walked over and joined us. While we were taking the hamburgers off the grill, Jacob, Emma, and family drove in with their pony and pony wagon. What a surprise! We were happy to have them join us for our early supper.

After supper, the children enjoyed pony rides while adults played basketball. We took advantage of the sunny warm, day. Those days will surely be limited from here on out.

We planned to spend Thanksgiving Day with Joe's family at his Dad's house. We plan to drive the 12 miles with horse and buggy. At least if it's cold or rainy we have a covered buggy to travel in. I do not miss those cold, open buggies in Indiana.

We recently spent a day down in Indiana visiting family. We visited with sister Leah and daughter Elizabeth. They are busy packing for their upcoming move to a farm around 9-10 miles north of there. Next we stopped in to say "hi" to

Sarah Irene and children. Brother Albert was working so we missed seeing him. We had a dinner of fried chicken and all the trimmings at sister Liz's. On our way home we stopped in at brother Amos and Nancy. Amos came home from work while we were there. They wanted us to stay for supper but we wanted to get home earlier as the children had to go to school the next day

DECEMBER 2004

It is hard to believe that we are now well into December! This morning, we awoke to a very lovely winter wonderland. Our Master Artist has once again painted a world of such beautiful scenery. The trees are a sight to behold. With the rain we had yesterday turning into snow, the branches look very breath-taking with the glittering ice.

We had our first snow of the season on the night before Thanksgiving. The children had so much fun making snowmen and enjoying sled rides. They made a very big snowman and had their father, Joe, help. The next morning it was laying on its side. Our five-year-old, Benjamin, thinks "Frosty" probably got tired and laid down to take a nap.

We spent Thanksgiving Day at Joe's Dad's house. There was an attendance of 35 people. Joe's Dad had prepared the turkey and dressing, while the rest of us brought in all the other goodies. There was more than enough food for all! While there, the children had fun playing outside in the snow. We drove the 12 miles to Joe's Dad with horse and buggy. We saw a lot of nice scenery on our way. This is a very beautiful area with lots of trees and rolling land. We were used to very flat land in Indiana. Our horses seem to be toughening up to traveling on these roads with more hills.

Yesterday, Joe, Loretta, and I attended the funeral of a 79-year-old lady from this community. She is a mother and grandmother to a lot of the men Joe works with. We left Joseph and Lovina with my sister, Verena. The other children were in school. We drove the 11 miles with horse and buggy. It was raining off and on throughout the ride. We sure have appreciated these covered buggies so many times already!

After we came home from the funeral we had a nice surprise! Brother Albert, Sarah Irene and baby Susan, plus Uncle Joe and Betty stopped in for a short visit from Indiana. They also visited my sisters Verena and Susan and Jacob and Emma and family. They had spent the day with Sarah Irene's mother who lives around a half hour from here. They decided to give us a visit before heading home.

A reader in Independence, Mo., requested a recipe with ginger. Try this delicious cupcake recipe, which goes good around the holidays!

GINGER CUPCAKES
2/3 cup molasses
1/2 cup sugar
1/2 cup shortening
2 teaspoon ground ginger
1 teaspoon cinnamon
1 teaspoon baking soda
2 cups flour
1 cup sour milk
2 eggs, beaten

Heat molasses, sugar, shortening, ginger, and cinnamon to boiling, stirring constantly. Cool to lukewarm. Sift soda and flour together. Add to cooked mixture alternately with sour milk and eggs. Bake in paper cupcake liners in cupcake tins at 350 for 15 to 20 minutes. Makes about 16 cupcakes.

DECEMBER 2004

Today, December 22, is my husband Joe's 36th birthday. I want to bake a cake for him to mark the occasion. I asked our children yesterday if we want to make him blow out 36 candles and they all thought that it would be fun! It is 5 a.m. now as I write this and the children are all still asleep. Baby Lovina woke up Joe and I, wanting a bottle. So I decided to write this column while all is quiet. I don't think we need an alarm clock. For some reason she always knows when 4:30 a.m. comes around She sleeps all night, though, which I'm glad for.

Baby Lovina gets around everywhere in her walker. We sit her on the floor, but she flops onto her stomach and really gets around. She is now 7 months old and such a joy! It's always interesting to see babies learn new things. She likes to tease her 2-year-old brother, Joseph, when she's in her walker. She waits until he has all his little horses standing and then she pushes her walker right through them, knocking them all down. Joseph gets so aggravated at her and thinks he has to teach her how to behave.

We had a cold weekend with the temperature going down to 2 degrees and it was very windy. It's harder to keep the house cozy when that wind blows. Most of the snow is gone now. I keep hoping we might get just enough snow to cover the ground before Christmas. I always like to see a white Christmas. I guess we are never satisfied, are we? We should accept the weather however God sends it.

Saturday is Christmas Day already. We will be home and take time to spend the day with the children. Let us take time to thank God for his many, many blessings on this day our dear Savior, Jesus Christ, was born. We wish you all God's blessings throughout the holiday season and in the year 2005.

On Monday morning at 5 a.m. we plan to head out to Indiana to sister Leah and Paul's. We will have our family Christmas gathering at their new home. We haven't all been together for a family gathering since Mom died. It will be nice to all get together again, but our dear parents will be greatly missed. Five of us daughters have moved to different places this year. Six of the oldest grandchildren have a "special" friend now. So along with the two new babies in the family this year, the family is growing in another way. Life goes on and changes are made. What would we do without our Heavenly Father to guide us through these years? It takes so many prayers. God has been so good to us. We have so many blessings to thank "Him" for. Do we take enough time for "Him" in this busy, rushy world?

Have a safe holiday! Sauerkraut is a popular dish on the New Year. Try this delicious recipe!

SAUERKRAUT BALLS
1/2 pound ground pork
1/2 pound ground beef
1 medium minced onion
1 (16 ounce) can sauerkraut (undrained)
1 tablespoon chopped parsley
1 teaspoon lemon juice
1 tablespoon Worcestershire sauce
1 teaspoon soy sauce
1/2 tablespoon horseradish
1/2 teaspoon dry mustard
1 teaspoon Tabasco sauce
1 egg, beaten
1 tablespoon Parmesan cheese
1/2 teaspoon garlic salt
1 teaspoon poultry seasoning
1 cup saltine cracker crumbs

Combine all ingredients for meat mixture in large bowl and mix well. Roll into 1-inch balls.

Breading:
3 eggs
1/3 cup milk
1 cup (or more) dry bread crumbs
1 teaspoon poultry seasoning
Oil for deep frying

Combine bread crumbs and poultry seasoning. Dip sauerkraut balls into egg mixture, then roll lightly in bread crumbs. Deep-fry in hot oil (370 degrees F) for 4 to 5 minutes or until cooked completely through. Makes 60 to 70 sauerkraut balls.

DECEMBER 2004

This will be the last column I'll write for 2004. We have only two days left of this year by the time most of you readers see this it already be the new year. Another year will soon be past only what's done for Christ will last. We wish you readers all a blessed 2005!

We had a nice Christmas weekend. On Sunday we had the potluck dinner with the church. It was a nice time for fellowship and there was a good variety of food. It's always enjoyable to eat someone else's cooking for change.

Monday morning, Dec. 27, we headed out at 5 a.m. for Indiana to go to my oldest sister Leah's house for our family gathering. So did Jacob, Emma and family, and sisters Verena and Susan. The whole family was there making a total of 59 people present. Dad and Mom were missed so much, but I know they would be happy that we all got together. They now have 39 grandchildren.

After a good dinner we enjoyed the afternoon singing and visiting. Everyone brought snacks to share for the afternoon. Drivers took us there and back, and we arrived home around 7:30 p.m. Was nice to leave, but was good to be back home again safe and sound. A person can be so thankful to reach home safely with so many accidents that happen. The children slept most of the way back and also on our way out there. Baby Lovina doesn't mind her car seat so she also slept, which made it nice.

It warmed up into the 40s today. We haven't had it that high for awhile. The grass is peeping through the snow and it almost seems like a taste of spring in the air.

Jacob's and us had supper at sister Verena's and Susan's last night. They made homemade pizza and ice cream. It was all delicious!

I want to give the house a good cleaning over the next day or so because on New Year's Day we'll have Joe's family here for a Christmas gathering. Would be nice if it would stay warmer for that day. Joe has eight sisters and three brothers, so we'll have a good-sized crowd here if everyone's able to come. There are 42 grandchildren on Joe's side. Two of the grandchildren are married.

2005

For the Eichers, 2005 was a year of settling in to the rhythm of a new life in Michigan. It also brought the arrival of a new family addition: Baby Kevin joined the family in September.

In the rest of the world, "Crash" took home the best movie award for the year. And the wars in Iraq and Afghanistan continued to grind on……

JANUARY 2005

We are now into the first week of 2005. This morning we awoke to a white world once again. The last snow had melted with the rains we were having off and on. It is still snowing now and it makes a person's spirits lift to see it snow after all those dreary days of muddy rain. God is in control of the weather, though, so I should not complain, but be thankful for His many blessings. Our minds go out to the victims of that bad earthquake in Asia. I cannot imagine what those people are going through. Let us remember them in our prayers.

Sunday we were taking Verena and Susan home after having "brunch" at Jacob and Emma's. While traveling uphill the bit on our horse, Diamond's, bridle broke and somehow made him lose his footing and fall down. With Verena and Susan along to help we quickly had all the children out of the buggy. We immediately unhitched Diamond from the buggy, but had to work to get the shaft away. He finally got up, much to our relief. We were afraid he might've broken a leg. Joe walked home to get a new bit for the bridle. We were fortunate to not be far from home. Diamond was OK, just a little stiff and sore. He is our "Old Faithful," we raised him from a colt and Joe trained him. He is a trustworthy horse, now almost 11 years old. I told Joe I am glad that bit didn't break on us when we were traveling a busy highway in town. God had his protecting hand over us.

We had Joe's family gathering on New Year's Day. Not everyone made it but we still had a full house. We decided to empty out our living room and set up three eight-foot tables in there. It was nice to have everything in here and not have so much walking back and forth to our out-building where we were going to gather. If I'd have a stove and sink out there it wouldn't be so bad. Joe grilled 40 pounds of chicken for the occasion and I made mashed potatoes, gravy, ham, dressing, corn, punch, and coffee. The others brought in the salads, pies, cake, puddings, cookies, etc. We had more than enough food and everyone brought snacks to enjoy while we played games in the afternoon. Before they left Joe's family carried out the tables and benches and put my furniture back in place.

JANUARY 2005

It is a very busy week! We are cutting up a lot of beef this week. Jacob, Emma and I started yesterday during the forenoon while my husband, Joe, was at work. We did Jacob's half and then ours. It was a long, tiresome day. We missed having Mom with us to help, she knew how and where to get all the best steaks from a steer. My sisters Verena and Susan came here after work and gave us a hand. We have the beef chunks ready for canning jars and the steaks are sliced and ready to be put into bags for the freezer. Joe and Jacob grinded the hamburger last night. It was very late when we got done, so when 3:30 a.m. arrived (which is when Joe wakes up to go to work) it didn't seem that the night had been long enough!

The children didn't have school yesterday because of the snow that we got overnight. The snow had drifted pretty badly over the roads. Now this morning it is 36 degrees with a cold rain. We've also had a thunder and lightning over the past 24 hours, so we're getting a little bit of everything this January. The children were excited to have the day off, especially since Jacob's children spent the day here. We had some pretty tired children here last night after a day playing together.

The butchering was done in our pole building. It was nice to have the girls home to help care for the little ones. They sure can save us a lot of steps. It's a full-time job just keeping the 2-year-olds (our Joseph and Emma and Jacob's little Benjamin) out of trouble. It seems they can't play with something very long and then they go to something else. Or else they both want the same toy at the same time.

Baby Lovina woke up when Joe and I did this morning at 3:30. After taking her bottle she's sleeping again. Joe leaves for work shortly after 4:30 a.m. He's working at a factory about 40 minutes from here. The hours are better than construction work. He's home by 3:15 or 3:30 in the afternoon. (Editor's note: In the area Lovina lives in, many Amish men who don't farm work in nearby factories. The factories are generally quite good at observing local Amish customs and beliefs).

Today we want to clean up and start processing meat. Jacob's will take theirs home. We also want to bag some more. Jacob's plan is to butcher pork on Saturday. We aren't planning to do pork this year. Joe would like to get a few pigs to raise for next winter. Also we'd like to start raising our own beef. It's so nice to have your own.

Well, I think I'd better bring this pen to a halt and get started on some work around here. Will be glad when this greasy butchering job is done, but I am so glad for the fresh meat.

A reader in Hutchinson, Kan., asked for a recipe for vanilla pie. Try this delicious favorite:

HOMEMADE VANILLA PIE

Cook & cool:
- ½ c. firmly packed brown sugar
- 1 tbsp. flour
- ¼ c. dark corn syrup
- 1 ½ tsp. vanilla
- 1 egg, beaten
- 1 c. water

Crumb Topping:
- 1 c. flour
- ½ c. firmly packed brown sugar
- ½ tsp. cream of tartar
- ½ tsp. baking soda
- 1/8 tsp. salt
- ¼ c. butter

1 unbaked 9-inch pie shell

Combine first five ingredients in two-quart saucepan. Slowly stir in water. Cook over medium heat until mixture comes to a boil, stirring constantly. Let cool. Combine rest of ingredients (except pie shell) and mix until crumbly. Pour cooled mixture into pie shell and top with crumbs. Bake at 350 degrees for 40 minutes or until golden brown.

JANUARY 2005

We had more snow overnight and it is snowing off and on. Yesterday morning was our coldest temperature reading for the winter. A cold 10 below zero!! Brrrrrr!! It's times like that when we could use just a little extra heat. We hope to put in a few gas wall heaters for days like that, but with temperatures in the 20s today it feels comfortable again.

Today, 10 months ago we moved here from Indiana. It's been a short 10 months. Daughter Susan will be 9 years old on Jan. 24, which is also my sister Liz's 36th birthday.

We had a cold day to process Jacob and Emma's pork on Saturday. We are now enjoying the fruits of our labor, though. We made "pon hoss," a pork dish which we often make on butchering day, and it turned out real good. Dad always told us how much flour, salt, and pepper to add to the pork juice. I never thought to write it down as I just thought he would always be here. We took a guess, though, and it turned out good.

A lot of work goes into butchering a hog, with cleaning the intestines, tongue, brains, etc. I don't care for the tongue or brains but Joe does. He likes them rolled in flour, fried to eat with eggs, and potatoes for breakfast.

The intestines are scraped clean to be stuffed with sausage later on. The lard is cut up into small pieces and rendered in the big iron kettle. We also made liver pudding. It's a big job to clean everything up again.

Jacob's came here on Monday night for supper. Joe and Jacob cut up all the pork chops, pork steak, ribs, etc. on our saw. We bagged it and it was ready for their freezer. It's nice to be able to freeze the hams and bacon. Dad and Mom had to always sugar-cure the meat when it warmed up so that it would keep. I always thought it tasted too salty. I fried some fresh ham last night for supper that Jacob's gave us. The children really liked it. Lovina is now 8 months old and has her two bottom teeth now. It looks like her two top teeth might be pushing through.

Her gums look real thick and sore. I told Joe I think I was just as excited again to see that first tooth as I was the first one. We are enjoying watching her grow and do different things.

FEBRUARY 2005

Another week has flown by, and it's already time to get this column written and sent on its way. We are so thankful that my husband Joe's back seems to be improving. He has been treating a badly pulled muscle in his back. The doctor lifted the restrictions on his lifting and twisting, so he is doing his full job at work again, although he's sore by the end of the day. It'll take time to heal. Otherwise, except for colds and coughs, we are all doing well.

Our thoughts and prayers are with my sister Liz and Levi's oldest daughter, Elizabeth. They have scheduled her to have heart surgery in Indianapolis at Riley's Children's Hospital on Feb. 14. She had developed pneumonia, which was why they had been putting off her surgery. We hope and pray the operation will be a great success and that she'll be lots healthier after this.

I wish we could be there with them, but it's just not so easy with the many miles between us now. Elizabeth has missed so many days of school from being sick. We wish them God's blessings in the future. "He" is a great comfort. If we only keep our trust in "Him," God will help us through the hard times.

We had a nice surprise on Sunday afternoon. My brother Albert, his wife, Sarah Irene, and family arrived for a short visit. They had Sarah Irene's mother along; she lives in a nearby community. Albert's oldest son Ben turned 16 on Sunday. Ben used Joe's bike to visit my sisters Verena and Susan, who live nearby. Then, they came over here awhile before going on to the young people's singing. Brother Albert's visit was too short.

Jacob re-shod our horse, Itty Bit, on Saturday. Since Joe's back still isn't strong enough to do it, I was sure glad for Jacob's help.

Today, the children will get their teeth examined and cleaned at their school. Some dentists are coming to the school to do it. It sure will help us out not to have to take them to a dentist's office.

We awoke to a ground covered with snow again, and it's still snowing great big flakes. It's such a pretty scene, especially after the last two rainy, dreary days here in Michigan.

Last week, I took supper "in" to three Amish families who recently had babies. My neighbor lady took me to deliver the meals, so I sent a supper home with her, too. Also, I sent some food over to my sisters Verena and Susan. I know I appreciated all the meals brought in after Lovina was born. It sure is a treat at a time when you are adjusting to a new schedule.

A reader in New Philadelphia, Ohio, requested a recipe for homemade butterscotch pie. Try this one:

BROWNED BUTTERSCOTCH PIE
A 9-inch pie shell, baked
1-1/4 cups brown sugar, divided use
1/3 cup water
2 eggs
1/3 cup all-purpose flour
2 cups milk, scalded
1/2 teaspoon salt
1/4 cup butter
1 tablespoon vanilla extract
Whipped cream or whipped topping to garnish
Yield: 1 pie, 8 servings

Set aside the baked pie shell to cool. In a large, heavy saucepan, combine 1/2 cup of the brown sugar and the water. Bring to a boil over medium heat, and continue cooking for about 3-1/2 minutes, or until mixture is thick and bubbly. Set aside.

In a large mixing bowl, beat both eggs until frothy. Add the flour and blend until smooth. Add the remaining 3/4 cup of brown sugar and blend. Then slowly add the scalded milk, stirring all the time. Over low heat, reheat the sugar-water mixture until liquified again. Then pour the milk-egg mixture into it, stirring with a rubber spatula all the time. Cook over medium-low heat until the mixture bubbles up and is very thick, 3 to 5 minutes. Add salt, butter and vanilla. Let cool for 15 minutes, then pour into the cooled, baked pie shell. Chill. Top the pie with whipped cream or whipped topping.

FEBRUARY 2005

It is a beautiful day with the sun shining, but it is still quite cold: Our thermometer shows 28 degrees on this Feb. 22. We had quite a snowy day on Sunday. It snowed great big flakes most of the day and then turned to rain and ice. Such a slushy mess! My husband Joe, oldest daughter Elizabeth, and Benjamin attended church services Sunday morning while I stayed home with the children that had the flu. I was also still getting over a bout with the flu, so I figured it was best for all of us just to stay home instead of passing around the germs.. I am so thankful that I had the worst of it before the children got it and not at the same time. I could hardly stand being up too long but I managed to pull through during the days until my husband Joe and the school-age children came home. It seemed to me that the children were extra ornery and so much louder, but I think it was only me. It sure isn't fun being sick, but how thankful can we be if it's something curable? There is so much flu going around, it seems.

Now, the younger ones are feeling better, while Elizabeth, 10, and Verena, 8, are home from school today with the flu. Hopefully we'll wipe it out of the house pretty soon. Joe is hoping he can get by without catching it. It'll be nice to see spring and warmer weather arrive soon!

With everyone being sick it seems like I have the house all in a mess. I have started cleaning out closets and am sorting and rearranging again. Baby Lovina is growing out of so many of her clothes so it is time to dig out the next size for her. Loretta and Joseph are also growing out of some of their clothes, so I'll store theirs away for Baby Lovina to use someday. Sometimes I can pass clothes on down to the next one and it's not necessary to put into storage. Verena and Loretta are not too much different in size except Verena's a little taller so it's a good thing Benjamin is a boy or I'd have to have the same size for him. It gets confusing sometimes having seven children with seven different sizes to keep track of!

MARCH 2005

March sure came in like a lion. I hope the old saying is true, and it'll go out like a lamb.

We had quite a bit of snow and wind during the first few days of the new month. It was a winter wonderland. While we live only a few hours away from our old home in northeast Indiana, we really have experienced a lot more snow here in Michigan. I'd be interested in knowing what's the latest date this region of Michigan has experienced snow. That'd be helpful for garden planning, which is just around the corner.

This morning, it's quiet around here for a bit, so I thought I would finish the column. I should've had a column ready for my editor when he came for a visit yesterday (that would be Kevin Williams from Middletown, Ohio), but I just hadn't finished it yet. Then, last night, I was going to sit down and finish writing, but the girls needed help with their homework. Then I thought I'd finish this when Joe left for work at 4:30 a.m., but I was still so tired that I decided to go back to bed until 6 a.m., when the girls have to be awakened for school. That extra 90 minutes of sleep gave me a boost!

Ever since the weekend, it appears that this household is healthy and "flu-free" once again. I hope that Mr. Flu Bug is done at our house for the year. My husband, Joe, and children Joseph, Benjamin and Baby Lovina all escaped getting sick, but the rest of us were laid up with the flu at one time or another over the past month.

Baby Lovina is crawling now, and she gets into everything! I have to keep my floors swept extra-good, as she'll find any little thing to put in her mouth. It seems babies like to put anything into their mouths that they can find. But not my oldest daughter, Elizabeth, almost 11 years old. It was so unusual that she would not put anything into her mouth. She was also very picky about getting even a little dirty. When she turned 1, we made a little cake for her and gave it to her to dig into. She wouldn't touch it. If we gave her a bite with a spoon, she'd eat it, but not with her hands. She always wanted a washcloth beside her when she started eating by herself and, after every bite, she'd wipe her mouth. Then, my next daughter Susan, now age 9, came along and I was so spoiled by Elizabeth that it was a real chore to keep everything out of Susan's mouth. And when Susan got her first birthday cake, she just had a real ball with it. It was a big mess to clean up.

Baby Joseph, who will be 3 years old this summer, keeps an eye on Lovina, but he's just a little too bossy with her. She has so much fun crawling through Joseph's toy fences and animals after he works so hard to set them up.

The children are having a "reading week," and they have to keep track of how many minutes they read. So our last nights of winter have been spent eating supper, doing homework and then reading. Makes for quiet evenings!

It is almost daylight now -- when the children must go to school at 7 a.m. It'll probably be different in a month when the time changes.

MARCH 2005

My husband, Joe, left for work a few minutes ago. So the house is quiet now in the early morning, before the children begin to wake up. I made Joe a breakfast of fried eggs and potatoes, bacon, toast, and cheese. I decided to get this written while everything is quiet.I usually wake the school children up at 6 a.m. Usually the younger ones wake up then too. Sometimes I wish they'd sleep longer, but then I guess I can get breakfast for all seven children fixed at the same time.

I took Susan, 9, and Benjamin, 5, to the doctor yesterday. They both have "strep" throat. So they'll be home for the rest of the week. I thought we were rid of sickness in this house after their bouts with the flu. Hopefully we can prevent the other children from getting strep. It seems if its not one thing it's another.It makes me appreciate the times when they are all healthy.After awhile it can wear a person down tending for the sick, getting meals, and doing the daily duties.I am thankful that I have the health to do it. My three youngest - Loretta, Joseph, and Lovina - haven't been sick yet, but Loretta does her share of faking it around mealtime and I just play along. I always use real nice dishes to take to the ones that are sick to make them get a better appetite. They think it's special to eat out of a nice dish and seems they eat better. So that's why Loretta wants to be sick at mealtime so she gets to eat from the couch out of nice dishes.

We bought another pony named "Stormy" since it was a born on a very stormy night. The children have sure have enjoyed her.Elizabeth can drive it real well. Benjamin loves the pony, but he sure is missing Stormy since he's been sick.Benjamin begged to go out to see it last night so we bundled him up and let him go outside awhile. He likes to lead the pony around although he can't ride horseback on it yet by himself.So instead he rides around on top of our big dog "Yellar." He tried hitching a sled to the Yellar so he'd pull him around in the snow.It was funny because Yellar wouldn't budge until Benjamin unhooked the sled.What little boys don't think up next.

A reader in Gig Harbor, Washington requested a soft pretzel recipe:

SOFT PRETZELS
(Makes 12)
1 cup warm water
1 package dry active yeast
1 12 cups flour
2 tbs. vegetable oil
1/2 tsp. salt
1 1/4 cup flour
4 cups water
2 tbs. baking soda
2 tbs. coarse salt

Dissolve the yeast in the warm water and let stand for 10 minutes. Add the vegetable oil, salt and 112 cups flour. Stir together until thoroughly combined. Add remaining flour and knead dough for 5 minutes. Let the dough rest for 1 hour.

Divide the dough into 12 equal shapes and reform them into small balls. Let them rest for 15 minutes. Roll them into 18" lengths and form them into pretzel shapes or cut each length in half to make sticks. Preheat oven to 475 degrees.

In a large pot, place the baking soda and water to a boil. Let the pretzels rise for a12 hour. Add the pretzels to the boiling water for 1 minute. Remove and place on a greased sheetpan. Sprinkle with coarse salt and bake for 12 minutes

MARCH 2005

I have Benjamin ready for school and need to get this written and in today's mail. I have so much work waiting on me and it would be easy to let this go for now. It's a relief that the children are all back in school now and feeling better. Only Susan and Benjamin ended up with strep throat. I was so afraid more of the children would catch it. I'll keep my fingers crossed.

My husband Joe had a misfortune while training my sister Susan's colt on Friday evening. As Joe was working with him, the colt started kicking while going at a pretty good speed. Joe pulled on the reins and the colt fell, causing Joe to go flying off the cart from the sudden stop. He landed on the horses' head. Joe was in so much pain and we figured he might've broken a rib. After getting it checked out he found it's badly bruised and no breaks. He sure is having a rough time getting through each day at work. Because of the bruised rib, Joe hurts so much when he coughs and he has a bad cough right now. He's using pain relievers, but they don't seen to hold out long. Nights are very miserable for him. Just hope it'll heal up soon. He won't be able to work with the horse for a while so he asked someone else to finish training her. I am so relieved! There'll be plenty of spring work and I know he would be pushing it to try and train horses while getting everything else caught up.

Meanwhile, my daughter Elizabeth was washing eggs last week one night. We are getting plenty of eggs from our hen house these days and it's a chore to wash them all. Elizabeth took a break and joined all of us as we went to the window to watch Joe drive the colt. When we looked back Joseph, 2, was having the time of his life cracking one egg after another onto the countertop. What a mess!

That reminded me of the time when Benjamin was almost 18 months old and Jacob and Emma's Jacob was younger and not walking yet. Verena and I had come back to dad and mom's with quite a few flats of eggs we had just bought. Verena took the eggs inside and set them on the countertop and came back outside to help me with the horse. When she came back in the house, Benjamin had climbed up on the step stool and was tossing eggs down to Jacob on the floor. They were having a real ball! Eggs are such a mess to clean up and what a mess that was. There were close to 100 eggs so luckily Verena seen them before they got too far. We are getting around 20 eggs a day right now from our hens. We are getting stocked up with too many eggs, so I should make homemade noodles soon! Easter is coming up so that'll use up some when the children color eggs.

MARCH 2005

For this week's column I thought I'd share the comings and goings around here in the form of a daily diary. So this will be a list of the activity around this household on this Thursday, March 24:

* 3:45 a.m. Time to wake up and start another day. My husband, Joe, gets ready for work and then goes out to the barn to let the horses out for the day and do the other morning chores. Meanwhile, I pack his lunch and make his breakfast.

* 4:20 a.m. Joe eats his breakfast of a grilled cheese sandwich and eggs. Ten-month-old Lovina wakes up, so Joe gets to hold her before leaving.

* 4:35 a.m. Joe leaves for work. I fix Lovina a bottle and take her to bed with me. I hope that she'll settle down again, and maybe I can catch a little nap before I have to go get the other children up for school.

* 6 a.m. I wake up the girls, so they can get ready for school. They eat breakfast and we pack their lunches. It seems it takes a lot of groceries to pack five lunches each day.

* 7 a.m. The school-age girls are ready to leave. The younger children are still finishing their breakfast. I wish the younger ones would sleep a little longer in the mornings, but it is nice to get breakfast over with all at once. They all take a longer nap later, except Loretta. She doesn't take a nap each day.

* 7:30 a.m. I've started on the dishes. Benjamin and Loretta go out to the barn to play with the dogs and cats. Benjamin rides horseback on our big dog, Yellar.

* 9 a.m. I am finally finished with washing the breakfast dishes. I get interrupted by Joseph and Lovina, so it was taking longer than it should. I miss it when the older girls aren't home to help with dishes. Last week, they were on spring break from school, so their help was nice. Loretta does wipe off for me sometimes, but she doesn't get them dry enough, so I usually check them. But that is how they learn -- by trying.

* 10:30 a.m. I cleaned some windows, and Benjamin is ready for his half-day of school.

* 11 a.m. I fix lunch for Loretta, Joseph and me: eggs and toast. We are well-stocked with eggs from our hens.

* Noon. I rock Joseph and Lovina to sleep for their afternoon nap. I hang some laundry outside that we hung in the shed last night. Then I fold the clothes that were dry already and put them in everyone's drawers.

* 2 p.m. I take the children over to sister Emma's while I go to town with the horse-and-buggy to get groceries. The school children will be ready to come home then, so I will just pick them up on the way back from town.

* 6 p.m. We are finally back home. Meanwhile, Joe has arrived home from work and has the evening chores done and also fixed one of the barn doors that needed repair. He is now frying chicken for our supper. Yum! That sounds good, especially if I don't have to fry it. Ha!

* 7:30 p.m. Supper is over with, and the dishes are washed. Now Joe and I are helping the children with their homework, reading, etc.

* 8:15 p.m. We get the children all in their beds and try to settle them down for the night. Joseph is going through a spell where he thinks he needs to sleep with us instead of with Benjamin. So we usually wait until he falls asleep on the couch and then move him to his bed. He usually sleeps all night then.

* 9 p.m. Everyone is asleep, and I think I'm more than ready to join them. Good night, sweet dreams, and I hope everyone had a happy Easter.

A reader in Hutchinson, Kan., asked for a recipe for homemade cheese pie. Try this one.

HOMEMADE CHEESE PIE

This is a crustless style of cheesecake in pie form.

For the cream cheese mixture, beat 3 eggs to blend in a large mixing bowl. Beat in 1/2 teaspoon lemon extract, a pinch of salt and 16 ounces (2 blocks) of cream cheese, at room temperature and cut into pieces.

Mix thoroughly, using an electric hand mixer, if you have one.

Lightly grease a glass pie plate with oil or shortening. Have the oven heating to 325 degrees, a rack set in the oven's center.

Pour the cheese batter into the oiled pie plate and bake at 325 for 30 minutes.

Prepare a topping by mixing 2 cups dairy sour cream with 6 tablespoons granulated sugar and 1 teaspoon vanilla extract. Mix ingredients and pour over the top of the cheese pie. Return to the 325-degree oven and bake 10 minutes more. Cool or chill the pie thoroughly or overnight before slicing.

APRIL 2005

The last days of March stayed true to the saying this year: March did come in like a lion and leave like a lamb. Such beautiful spring days are here now. The temperature this morning is already 52 at 7:15 a.m. I keep walking around the yard looking for any signs of dandelion greens peeping through. It makes my mouth water to think of a fresh dandelion-green salad. I always think they're a treat, but some of our children don't care for dandelion greens. I think they will learn to like them, though.

I see my rhubarbs are peeping through now, but I still haven't seen a sign of my winter onions. I hope they'll come up. I also planted peppermint tea last fall, and I hope it'll come up again. I would like to start different kinds of tea. Around here, fresh tea is served at the church lunches. They dry it for wintertime use and serve it year round. Mom always made good tea using different kinds of herbs mixed together. I sometimes wish I could've gotten some starts from her garden. Several ladies have offered to give me more starts. I hope I'll have some nice tea plants soon. Tea is so much healthier to drink than coffee, I think.

We had a nice Easter together. It turned out to be a beautiful day, although a little chilly. We spent the day at sister Emma and Jacob's. Jacob's family was here visiting for the day from Indiana. This would also be my husband Joe's uncle, aunt and cousins. Sisters Verena and Susan grilled chicken at home and brought it to Jacob's. It was delicious! They tried out their new gas grill. This was the first time they used one, so it was something different.

The children had fun driving the ponies around the field. We took our pony and cart, too. "Stormy" is proving to be a safe, strong pony and is gentle with the children. They have hours of fun with him.

The children colored around 100 eggs last week one night. They had so much fun, especially little Joseph. By the time they were through, he looked like he colored himself, too. He finally traded his color with someone else's -- as we weren't getting any eggs from him that weren't cracked open. The mess was worthwhile to clean up with all the fun they had. But I'm sure glad we only do it once a year. Although the children really enjoy coloring eggs, we want them to also understand what Easter is about: How our dear Savior died for all our sins. Do we serve Him enough to think what all He went through for us? Prayers are so badly needed in this world.

Next week is spring break for the school children. How nice it'll be to have them home all week. No lunches to pack, no homework, etc.

I hope to get out and start raking up the yard soon. Our younger dog has made a mess, dragging things around this winter. I hope he's over that teething stage.

Meanwhile, Joe is busy outside trimming trees at night, and he has our potatoes cut up to dry before we plant them.

I hope everyone had a happy Easter.

APRIL 2005

It is 9:30 p.m. here in Michigan. We are adjusting to the time change again. It helps, though, that the children don't have school this week. They are enjoying their spring break and what wonderful weather we have had so far!

We are getting a lot of spring work accomplished. Joe has finished trimming the fruit trees and is slowly burning the branches. The trees were really overgrown and looked like it has been years since they were trimmed. We had some windy weather so it's dangerous to burn branches on nights like that.

Tonight was windy also so Joe tilled the garden instead. The dirt looks so smooth - it makes me eager to start planting. I'm afraid we'll get some more cold weather, though. I'll wait and see how next week is and then maybe plant some early things such as potatoes, peas, radishes, lettuce, and onions.

Today I cut out a royal blue dress, apron and cape for me and am almost done with the dress. I still need to sew the cape and apron, which goes pretty fast. I usually think the dress takes the most time. I have enough material to make us all an outfit but don't know if I'll get to it. It seems every time I sew us all the same color outfit then one or the other grows out of it soon.

I'm looking forward to the Amish garage sales that should start soon. A person can't buy the material for the good clothes you can buy at very reasonable prices. I love to sew but keeping clothes up for a family of 9 is almost too much at times.

Another thing that adds up with a big family is laundry. We washed a very big laundry today and had such nice weather for it to dry. And what a good help the girls were to have here to help me with it. Everything is dry and smells so fresh from the outdoors. Joe put up a new bigger wash line for me last summer and now I still want to keep the old one as I can use both when I have a lot of laundry.

We had our first taste of dandelions tonight. Yum! We got a few more of the children to try them and they were surprised they liked them. I spent quite a while finding them outside. There are a lot of small ones and surely in another week we should have all we want.

Joe and all the children, except Elizabeth and Susan, have now gone to bed. The girls are reading the "Little House" books by Laura Ingalls Wilder and they really enjoy them. I am letting them stay up later at night since they don't have to go to school this week.

Friday we plan to attend a friend's wedding in Indiana in the community we moved here from. We plan to stay until Saturday and then come home. Sister Susan is a witness at this wedding so they will leave Thursday night . My daughters Elizabeth and Susan will go with them, and also Jacob's oldest daughter. Hopefully the weather will hold out and stay so beautiful for the wedding.

This is a good time of year to repeat a recipe that readers continue to request:

WEDDING NOTHINGS
1 egg, beaten well
three big cookspoons of milnot or other cream
pinch of salt
enough flour to make a stiff dough (don't use bread flour)

Mix all of the above ingredients well and make into 6 or 7 balls and roll out each ball very, very thin. Make three two-inch slits on each piece. Have a kettle of hot lard or Crisco ready. Put one piece at a time in the kettle. Turn over with two forks when you see a slight gold and again till slight gold. Take out and put on a plate of paper toweling (2 sheets) to drip off rest of lard. Put on a plate and sprinkle with sugar. Stack all, 6 or 7, on top of each other on a plate. These are made to eat at weddings.

APRIL 2005

We had a cold reading of 39 degrees on this very beautiful April morning. A brisk wind made it feel even colder outside. We are having a lot of windy days lately and are having a hard time getting the branches burned that Joe trimmed from our fruit trees. The house felt chilly this morning so I started coal in the stove again and it feels good. Hopefully one of these days we'll be done with coal for the summer.

Joe has planted quite a few rows of potatoes, lettuce, and peas in our garden. I want to get some more seeds sown and also some onion sets. We're hoping the mercury doesn't; dip too low. So far I haven't been helping Joe very much in the garden. We used to plant all of our seeds by hand, but two years ago we bought a seeder and planting now goes so much quicker. Although potatoes and onions still have to be planted by hand.

Joe also planted marigolds all around the outside of the garden. This helps keep the moles from digging through the garden. The dogs are also starting to hunt for them. Those moles sure can tear up the yard, but God must've put them on this earth for a reason.

We attended the wedding of friends in Bryant, Indiana last Friday, April 8. We got to visit with sister Liz, Levi, and family at the wedding. Also we stopped in for a short visit with brother Albert, Sarah Irene, and family. We wanted to go there as they will be moving in a few months. I am not sure but I think that they will only be around 25 miles from here. They are moving to a nearby community. I know exactly what they are experiencing with all of the packing that goes with moving.

My sister Emma, her husband Jacob, and their children, plus my sisters, Susan, and Verena, also went to the wedding. Susan was a witness at the wedding. We stayed until Saturday and then headed back. There's no place like home!

Uncle Joe and Betty gave us a visit on Saturday evening, it was nice seeing them again. Then we all got together at Emma and Jacob's on Sunday for a "brunch." It was a nice warm day so Joe and some of the children decided to bike there, while Elizabeth, Joseph, Lovina and I went with the pony and cart. I was surprised that the younger children could bike the four miles. Benjamin and Loretta were so proud that they could bike on the road as we always make them bike in the driveway.

Emma had a very delicious meal of eggs, fried potatoes, bacon, sausage gravy, biscuits, tomatoes, hot peppers, cheese, pie, cookies, juice, milk, and coffee.

I must get busy. I would like to mop all the floors and then bake a big batch of oatmeal cookies. I told the lady who has church that I would bring some cookies. Would like to do the laundry also, but I don't think I'll get to it. Lovina is being fussy as I think she is pushing more teeth.

APRIL 2005

It looks like rain outside today. I am hoping we will get some as it has been a bit dry lately. Because it has been so dry, my husband, Joe, has been watering the garden every night. There sure have been quite a few fires around here because of the dryness. We still have branches to burn from trimming our trees, but it remains too dry. The hay field would certainly get a good boost from rain.

Our asparagus is really coming along, and I would like to start using some as we have a big patch.

The dandelion flowers are popping up. That makes the dandelion greens turn bitter, so much so that we won't use them for salads anymore. Dandelion greens taste best when they are very young. We have had our share of them the past few weeks. Three of our children eat them now, but the others don't care for them yet. I think we've had our fill for another year.

Now that the asparagus is starting in, the rhubarb will be ready to use before long. There are so many homegrown, good spring treats.

My winter onions came up but not too many. We aren't using them this year, so that their roots will get stronger. We had a taste of them over at Jacob's. They got a lot of onions from their neighbors. It is so nice to have good neighbors.

Speaking of neighbors, I can see our 77-year-old neighbor lady hauling wood from her woods with her tractor. She is such a wonderful neighbor.

Tomorrow Loretta, 4, Joseph, 2, and Lovina, 11 months, and I will go with Jacob and Emma to a wedding in this community. A boy in our church district is getting married. Joe can't have off work too often for weddings that aren't relations, but he told me to still go.

On Saturday, Elizabeth, 10, and Susan, 9, and I baked around 160 peanut butter cookies. The girls are learning fast how to measure out ingredients, etc. It'll be nice to hand that job over to them. We took some of the cookies to church on Sunday. This is a very delicious cookie. It was the first time I had tried this recipe, which I got from Aunt Mary Coblentz. I'll probably make them a lot, as we loved them.

I'll share the recipe if you readers would like to give it a try. If anyone has any asparagus recipes, I'd appreciate them. Also, does anyone know if asparagus can be frozen?

PEANUT BUTTER COOKIES
1 cup shortening (or margarine)
1 cup peanut butter, chunky or smooth
1 cup white sugar
1 cup brown sugar
2 eggs
*1 teaspoon vanilla
2 to 3 cups all-purpose flour
2 teaspoons baking soda
1/2 teaspoon salt
1 package of chocolate chips or M&Ms, optional
Yield: About 5 dozen

In a large mixing bowl, thoroughly beat together the shortening, peanut butter and both sugars. Beat in the eggs and vanilla. In a smaller mixing bowl, stir together 2 1/2 cups of the flour, the baking soda and salt. Add the dry ingredients to the bigger bowl and make a stiff dough, adding a little more flour as necessary.

If using chocolate chips, opt for mini-chips or roughly chop larger chips or the M&M candies to make better-looking cookies.

Drop the dough by large spoonfuls onto an ungreased cookie sheet, allowing enough space to flatten each cookie by pressing twice with the back of a floured fork to make a crisscross pattern.

Bake in preheated 350-degree oven for 8 to 10 minutes or until light brown at the edges, lighter in the centers. Remove from the oven and let cookie sheet stand for a few minutes before transferring the cookies to a cooling rack. Once cool, store airtight.

MAY 2005

This is a shorter than usual column as my husband Joe and I are here at the local hospital where we've been since Friday evening with our baby daughter Lovina. She was badly dehydrated from having diarrhea and vomiting. There

seems to be a virus affecting a lot of babies in this community. The doctor thought that having her on an IV for a day or two would help get her hydrated again. She'll be a year old already on May 18th.

It was good that Joe and I could both be here as she would've been a handful for one. She keeps trying to pull out her IV. We had a hard time getting her to settle down but after that she slept real good. She's a little fighter and tries to fight the nurses when they come in to take her temperature, etc.

I am trying to help keep her entertained while Joe goes after some breakfast. At the same time I thought I could write a few lines but it doesn't seem to be working too well. I'm afraid my editor will have a hard time reading my writing. It's so hard to have a child beg to eat or drink when they aren't allowed to. The doctor said we could try food this morning and see if it'll stay down. If it does, hopefully we can go back home by tonight.

Meanwhile my sisters Verena and Susan have our other six children at their house since last night. What a blessing to have family to help. Jacob will go do our chores.

This is now later and we were allowed to feed Lovina some bananas and applesauce. So far she has kept it down. Joe is trying to settle her down for a nap. I think she misses the other children and all the noise she's used to at home. The doctor hasn't been in yet so don't know if we'll have to stay or not.

Last week my sister Emma and I spent the day at Joe's sister Carol's house making noodles from almost 100 eggs. Joe's sisters MaryAnn, Loretta, and Susan were also there and MaryAnn's married daughter. MaryAnn and her daughter babysit for three children so all in all there were seven 2-year-olds there. The children were all very tired by evening. Mine fell asleep in the buggy on the way home.

It's still asparagus season around here and lots of readers have shared their favorite asparagus recipes. Try this delicious one!

ASPARAGUS BREAD
3 eggs
1 cup oil
1-2/3 cups sugar
1 cup brown sugar
2 teaspoons vanilla
2 cups (3/4 pound) asparagus, cleaned and grated
In separate bowl mix:
3 cups flour
1/4 teaspoon baking powder
1 teaspoon salt
1 teaspoon soda
3 teaspoons cinnamon
1/2 cup chopped nuts (optional)

Beat eggs until light and foamy. Add oil, sugar, brown sugar, vanilla and asparagus; mix lightly. Add flour mixture and blend. Add nuts. Bake in greased loaf pan 325 degrees F for 1 hour or until done. Yield: 2 (5 x 9-inch) loaves.

MAY 2005

It is a cool May morning as I write this. The temperature dipped down to 45 degrees last night. Yesterday we had a thunderstorm that gave us a good, soaking rain. It's been cool ever since.

Today is my sister Emma and husband Jacob's youngest child Benjamin's 3rd birthday. My sister Susan turned 29 on May 10, and my daughter Lovina will be a year old on the 18th. Then my birthday will be May 22, making me 34 years old.

My little daughter Lovina was in danger of being dehydrated, which I mentioned last week. She ended up being in the hospital for two days and two nights. I ended up taking her to the doctor again as her fever went up to 105. The doctor thinks it's a viral infection. He gave her some medicine, and she seems to be feeling herself again. I'm so glad all the other children stayed healthy.

Lovina is back to crawling around and getting into everything, which is a good sign that she is feeling better. The other children really missed her while she was away.

Our older girls have left for school now, and my four youngest are still sleeping -- nice for a change. We got to bed later than usual last night, as Joe and I took our oldest daughter Elizabeth to the fifth-grade orientation at the school. It is so hard to believe she will be in middle school. The children all read their portfolios to us parents.

We left the other children at Jacob and Emma's, and they gave them supper. That sure helped me out to not have to fix supper for everyone.

Jacob re-shod all of our horses while we were gone. They live within walking distance from the school, so we walked, which was nice exercise.

Elizabeth put a vase of fresh lilacs on my desk, and they smell so good. I love the fragrance of lilacs. We have both the purple and white in bloom now, but fading fast. I'd like to get more started.

I made some coffee and am enjoying a cup while I savor this rare moment of peace and quiet. The birds are singing gaily outside my window. Spring is such a lovely time of the year. Our Creator has given us so many blessings.

Joe is being kept busy taking care of the yard at night. He's feeding our horses the grass clippings, which they really like. As soon as we get a fence up around our pasture field, they will have a lot of good pasture to eat.

I am hoping to finish planting the rest of the garden soon. The corn we planted is finally peeping through, the potatoes are coming up nicely and, oh my, asparagus is shooting up so fast. I'm sharing asparagus with others, as it's way too much for us. I would like to freeze some.

Thanks so much to all the readers who sent recipes for different ways to fix asparagus. I have more recipes now than I'll have time to use. I told Emma she'll have to try some for me. May God bless you all! Here's one more unusual asparagus recipe that a reader in Pontiac, Ill., sent me:

ASPARAGUS PANCAKES
2 cans drained asparagus or equivalent of fresh cuts, cooked and drained
1 egg
1 cup finely shredded Parmesan cheese
1 cup seasoned bread crumbs, or as needed
2 tablespoons vegetable oil

Mash the cooked and drained asparagus cuts. Blend in the egg, shredded (not grated) Parmesan and bread crumbs. Mix well and shape into patties. Brown on both sides by frying over medium heat on a griddle or in a large skillet. When golden brown, serve hot as a side dish to scrambled eggs or grilled chicken.

MAY 2005

Another week has flown by! Where does the time go? Our baby Lovina turned one on May 18th. We gave her a little chocolate cake with chocolate frosting to eat. She really looked a sight when she got done, making quite a mess! She looked at us like she couldn't believe we let her make such a big mess. She smiled when we sang "Happy Birthday" to her and put up one finger to show us how old she was. We were always doing that before saying "you're going to be one." Such a sweet age!

Daughter Loretta will get to go to school for about three hours today to prepare for school for the first time this fall. She's very excited about going. I imagine her little brother Joseph will seem lost without her, although he and baby Lovina do have times where they play together real nicely. The children have only 9 1/2 days of school left this term and they are counting the days. It will be nice to have them home for the summer.

The factory where my husband Joe works is down to operating just four days a week, we hope not for too long. Joe's been real busy here in the evenings, though, mowing the yard, cutting wood, etc. It seems I hardly get out to help him much anymore. It's a full time job getting meals, cleaning, washing dishes, doing laundry, mending, sewing and all that comes with raising children. The school-age girls are a big help at nights, though. But it seems that once they get their homework done and supper eaten, dishes, washed and dried, it's time for bed. The nights just aren't long enough. What I dislike most about the time change is getting the children to bed at the right time. They seem to think as long as it's daylight outside, it's too early to go to bed. (Editor's note: for those new to the column, Lovina and her family recently moved to Michigan from Indiana where daylight savings time is not observed)

We're getting some rain this morning. I'm hoping it'll clear up soon so I can do laundry. If not I have plenty of other things to do. I want to bake a couple rhubarb pies. Joe has been asking if I'm going to make some. I always thought Mom could make the best rhubarb custard pie.

Saturday we plan to attend the Eicher reunion in Berne, Indiana. We want to start out at 6 a.m. We would like to go visit Mom and Dad's graves. Tomorrow it will be five years since dear father passed to that Great Beyond. In April it was 10 years that Joe's Mom died. And in September it'll be 3 years since my dear Mother left us. Oh how we still needed them here, but it wasn't God's plan. We must go on, even though we miss them so very much.

A year ago I was in the hospital for a week after baby Lovina was born. I am so thankful for better health. God has been so good to us!

JUNE 2005

Last night we finally put more of our garden out. We planted tomatoes, hot peppers, green peppers, cabbage, some more lettuce, onions and peas. In addition, we also planted pickles, watermelons, muskmelons and zucchini. My husband, Joe, tilled me a separate patch of garden to put in spearmint, tea, dill, chives, etc. Hopefully it'll all grow well this summer. I hope to finish getting the rest of the garden planted today. And my flower beds are still empty, so I need to get those worked up and filled. It is a busy, busy springtime! Yesterday was the first warm day for a while and I hope it's here to stay. That cold weather we had after that nice week in April sure was surprising.

Another reason I am hoping it'll warm up is that we got 57 little baby chicks that we ordered. Twenty-five are fryers and the rest are layers. The fryers we want to butcher when they get big enough. That makes for the best-tasting chicken! I still remember Mom going to the chicken coop and getting a chicken, chopping off the head and getting it ready for supper. I've never been brave enough to do that. I'm hoping I can get my Benjamin to do that part. We had the chicks in the house for a few days until my husband, Joe, heated a place for them outside. I am glad they're out now as baby Lovina was bad about always going to the boxes and trying to grab a chicken. Our hen has hatched one of her eggs but it died and the rest haven't hatched yet.

Saturday we attended the Eicher reunion in Berne, Ind. It was a large attendance. We had supper at my sister Liz's. My sister Emma, husband Jacob and children were also out there at his parents and then at Levi's for supper. My brother Amos and Nancy and children came when they heard we'd all be at Levi's. And then we saw our brother Albert in town. So we got to catch up with most of our siblings.

While in Indiana, Jacob's and us went to Mom and Dad's graves. I don't really care to go as I think it just brings back too many memories. We thought we should, though, for our children's sake, so that they keep remembering their grandparents. We also went to the other cemetery where Joe's Mom was buried 10 years ago. It was five years on May 20 that Dad passed away and it'll be three years on Sept. 17 that Mom died. Oh how we still need them here but God knows best "He" sees things we don't always see. It's surprising how the children's memories have started dimming about their grandparents.

I turned 34 on Saturday, May 22. Joe took us all to a nearby "breakfast buffet." What a treat! Then he cooked supper outside on the grill and I got out of cooking all day. I really felt like I was having a birthday.

I was almost done with this letter when I received very shocking news. My aunt Betty Yoder from Geneva, Ind. (Dad's youngest sister), age 62, died unexpectedly from a heart attack. Oh, I can just imagine what that family is going through. So it looks like I should start getting things ready to leave for the funeral. It brings back memories of losing my own dear parents. God knows the future and let us trust in Him to lead the way.

Talking about chicken earlier, try this recipe. Using fresh chicken will make a big taste difference:

Chicken loaf
1 (5 lb.) chicken, cooked and cubed
2 cups chicken broth
2 cups uncooked rice

2 cups milk
2 cups bread cubes
4 eggs
Salt and pepper to taste
2 cups diced celery

Stir and mix all ingredients. Spoon into a greased baking dish. Bake at 350 degrees for 1 hour or until a knife comes out clean when inserted in the center of the loaf. Serve in slices. Feeds about 20.

JUNE 2005

This is a nice, cool June morning after quite a few 90-degree days. We had a lot of rain yesterday and it has finally cooled off. We have hay down so hopefully it'll dry enough so that it can be put in this week. The hay was rained on a little.

On Saturday, my brother Albert, Sarah Irene and family will move to their new home. It will be nice to have them closer. They bought Sarah Irene's mom's farm and will build a little house for her mom and sister to live in. We want to go help them unpack and unload. My husband Joe isn't sure if he can go because of taking care of the hay here, but he told me to still go. It will be nice to be able to go to Albert's with horse and buggy again. I'm not quite sure but I think it's around 18 to 20 miles, which probably will take around 90 minutes to drive with horse and buggy. I wish them God's blessings in their new home. I am sure they will like it, we have never regretted our move.

Everyone is enjoying their early garden goodies, especially green onions, lettuce and radishes. My radishes are over with now for the season. I kept wanting to plant more and just didn't get around to it.

Today my sisters Emma and Verena will come to help finish washing walls and ceilings. Church will be held here on Sunday, June 26, so there is still much to do to get ready. I also want to wash some more curtains. We have the living room, kitchen and entrance area left to clean still. Verena has a week off from her job at the sewing factory, so she's been an extra help to me. The basement and upstairs are cleaned and so are the three bedrooms and two bathrooms. Everything now looks a little more hopeful of getting done!

I want to get a breakfast casserole in the oven as I told Verena and Emma to eat breakfast here.

My sons Benjamin and Joseph are awake already as they went to bed earlier than usual last night. Meanwhile, baby Lovina woke up before Joe left for work, so I rocked her back to sleep. I should wake up the girls soon. I hope to have the girls wash out my kitchen cabinets today. They sure have been a help since school is out for the summer. My oldest, Elizabeth, turned 11 on the 14th. Jacob and Emma were married 10 years on the 15th. These years fly by so fast.

My new dinner table comes today. I'm excited to have a new and bigger table. Joe gave it to me for my 34th birthday.

Speaking earlier of radishes, try this delicious summer salad to use up those radishes.

GARDEN RADISH SALAD
4 cups radishes, washed and sliced
1/2 cup thinly sliced onion
1 cup diced fresh tomato
1 1/4 teaspoons salt
1 small clove garlic, minced
1/8 teaspoon pepper
1 teaspoon finely chopped fresh basil or fresh mint
2 Tablespoons lemon juice
2 Tablespoons vegetable oil
fresh chopped parsley for garnish

Combine sliced radishes, onion, and tomato. Whisk together the salt, garlic, pepper, basil or mint, lemon juice, and vegetable oil. Toss with salad then garnish with parsley.

JUNE 2005

With the month of July here, it puts us over halfway through 2005. It is hard to believe. Time is just going too fast.

We are having very hot weather right now, even here in Michigan. This morning we got a much-needed rain, but could use more. Our grass is turning brown from the dry spell. We've been keeping our garden watered each day, so with the rain this morning, that will be one chore off the list for today.

Our children have been kept busy giving water to the 40 new chicks that were delivered two days ago. They've also been caring for the last batch we ordered. They're now 5 weeks old and soon to be used for feeding our family. We would like to have some cooler days to do that or for any other type of butchering that needs to be done.

The children and I spent yesterday at sister Emma's. Sister Verena was there, too, as she has this week off from work at the sewing factory. While at Emma's, we washed off walls and ceilings in all three of their bedrooms, the bathroom and living room. Before beginning work, we all enjoyed a homemade breakfast. Emma prepared a delicious meal of scrambled eggs, fried potatoes, homemade biscuits with sausage gravy, sliced cheese, coffee and orange juice. So it was a delicious way to start the day. Emma and Jacob have church coming up at their house next weekend. They plan to hold the church services outside under the big church tent, which should make it cooler on a hot day.

My husband, Joe, will be home from work for a 10-day vacation this month. We sure will be glad for the break, although I imagine we'll still be kept busy with gardening and other summer chores. I also want to help Jacob and Emma some more in getting prepared for church services.

Before we know it, school will be back in swing. The summer is flying by too quickly. I need to sew Benjamin pants for school. He is sure getting taller.

Loretta will be 5 tomorrow. She just can't wait to go to bed, as she said when she wakes up it'll be her birthday.

On Monday, Verena helped us do a big laundry, sweep and mop all the floors and freshen everything. We also washed out the pole building floor. It was so nice to have church services out of the house and in the pole building. We had church services at our house on Sunday, June 26. We also served lunch in the pole barn. We served coffee, tea, homemade white and wheat breads, bologna, cheese, the traditional Amish peanut butter mixture consisting of peanut butter, marshmallow creme and corn syrup, pickles, red beets, hot peppers, rhubarb jam, etc.

For supper that day, we had only family back for the evening meal. The men cooked outside to keep the house cooler from not having to have the wood cook stoves going. Try this delicious, light, cool recipe on these hot summer days:

SEVEN-LAYER SALAD
1 medium head of iceberg lettuce, torn into bite-size pieces
1 cup sliced celery
4 hard-cooked eggs, sliced
1 (10-oz.) box frozen peas, at least partially thawed, uncooked and separated
1/2 cup diced green bell pepper
1 sweet onion, thinly sliced
1-1/2 cups mayonnaise
2 tablespoons sugar
4 ounces grated Cheddar cheese (at least 1 cup), or aged Swiss cheese can be used
8 slices bacon, fried and crumbled
Fresh chopped parsley, as much as desired
Yield: About 10 servings

In a large serving bowl, layer the chopped iceberg lettuce, followed by the celery, then the hard-cooked eggs, the thawed peas (young, tiny peas are best in salads), the bell pepper and mild, sweet onion.

For dressing, combine the mayonnaise with sugar, stirring well, and spread it over the layered vegetables. Sprinkle with the grated cheese. Cover tightly and refrigerate the entire salad for eight to 12 hours.

Just before serving, uncover the salad and sprinkle the top with crumbled bacon and fresh parsley. To serve, toss the salad or place it as prepared on a buffet table.

JULY 2005

6 a.m. It is time to begin another day. My husband Joe is on his one-week vacation from the factory where he works. For us, 6 a.m. feels like sleeping in. Joe normally goes out and does the morning chores and harnesses up our horse, Itty Bit, while I wake up the children, which is difficult to get them up. So we get up much earlier on workdays. Today, we plan to go help my sister Emma and her husband Jacob prepare for church services which are to be held at their place on Sunday, July 10.

7:15 a.m. Joe hitches our horse to the buggy and we load up to go to Jacob's. The four miles to their house takes 15-20 minutes depending on how peppy the horse is. On hot days we let the horse take its time. Our mornings have been pretty cool lately, though.

8:15 a.m. We all enjoy a good breakfast of fried potatoes, eggs, bacon, hot peppers (which are fresh from the garden), homemade wheat bread, butter, Colby and hot pepper cheeses, coffee, and orange juice.

9:15 a.m. Jacob's girls and our girls wash and dry dishes while the rest of us do other chores: Joe and Jacob haul manure, Susan works in the garden, and Emma, Verena, and I do a big laundry. Verena and Susan were at Jacob's when we got there, arriving shortly before us. After doing laundry we started cleaning the small summer house which Emma and Jacob have on their property. They plan to have church services in a big tent beside the summer house. They will use the summer house to prepare the food and also have a place for mothers who have babies or small children that need to be tended to.

12:30 p.m. Lunch is ready and we all gather to eat. Lunch consists of hamburger-potato casserole, fresh pickle salad (from Emma's garden), cheese, ham, and ice cream

1:30 p.m. The girls again do dishes while we all go back to work. Joe and Jacob are back to hauling manure. Joe and Jacob also clean out the barn, mow, till the garden and some more last-minute jobs. The ladies finish up the summer house, more weeds are pulled, and laundry brought in. We also do some odd and end jobs which fill up the afternoon.

5:45 p.m. We head for home. The children are tired from a long day. After two big meals they aren't too hungry, so we have sandwiches for supper for whoever is hungry. Most of us are ready to wash up for bed.

8 p.m. Most of the children are sleeping. Some are still reading books. It has been a full day but it is nice to be able to help each other out with work. It makes the load lighter for everyone.

9 p.m. Rest of us head to bed. We want to go to town tomorrow morning early to get groceries. We told the children they can all go along which makes them excited. It takes more time but it's nice to all go. Good night and God's blessings to all. We hope you had a wonderful July 4. We enjoyed the day, taking it easy, fishing, etc. Fireworks from a nearby town could be seen from here which the children enjoyed watching.

Earlier I mentioned the pickle salad we had at Emma's. Here is a recipe for it:

PICKLE SALAD
6 cucumbers, peeled and sliced
1 large onion, sliced and diced
1 1/2 cups mayonnaise
1/2 cup sugar
1/4 teaspoon salt
dash of pepper
3 tablespoons vinegar

Put cucumbers and onion into large bowl. In a smaller bowl, stir mayonnaise, sugar, salt, pepper, and vinegar. Stir well and pour over vegetables. Toss and stir well. Refrigerate or chill in a cellar for several hours before eating.

We are butchering more chickens this week. Hopefully we'll finish up with our batch this week. I will be so glad once we are done with this messy job. Before she was married, Mom used to work at a place where they'd butcher chickens all day long. Wish Mom could be here to help us, she was an expert at butchering chickens.

Last night we went to Jacob's for supper in honor of Emma's 32nd birthday. She had a delicious supper of homemade zucchini pizza, fresh green beans (with diced potatoes and bacon), cucumber salad, and hot green peppers and ice cream and cake. These garden goodies sure make a meal easy to prepare.

On Sunday, our little Joseph will be age 3, which is hard to believe. And little Lovina, who is over a year old, is walking everywhere now. It seems so exciting when they start walking. She's also starting to do a lot of climbing. Lovina will push a foot stool up to something else and climb onto the stool and on up. She's at an age that you have to keep a constant watch on her.

Joe's Dad gave us a short visit on Saturday afternoon. He hasn't been feeling too good lately. He found out he has skin cancer and is receiving doctoring for that. Our little Benjamin was so excited to show Grandpa his birthday gifts.

Our grass is turning greener now from the recent rains. It is also helping our garden grow. We had fresh potatoes out of the garden this week. Those taste so much better than store bought.

It is 5 a.m. and I need to get this finished. I didn't get it done yesterday. Joe left for work about 15 minutes ago. Baby Lovina woke up when we did this morning so she wanted to eat with Joe. I made scrambled eggs with bacon, toast, and coffee for breakfast.

We had a pretty bad thunderstorm around midnight. I had a hard time going back to sleep. Some of the children woke up scared. Storms seems to bother them more since that bad one went through one recent Sunday causing a lot of damage. It seems to be taking an extra cup of coffee for me to get going this morning.

Before our midnight storm, one also went through last evening around 5:30 p.m. Joe had started on his way home from Jacob's with our pony, Cheeko. It was so bad that he decided to turn around and go back to Jacob's and wait until it passed through. He had the open pony cart, which would have made for a wet ride. Joe had someone work with Cheeko for a week and now he's taking over to finish training her. She still needs worked on to not shy off trucks and certain things along the road.

We lost some more of the roof off the old corncrib shed from the wind. We are planning to just tear it down anyway as the foundation isn't too good. We hope to get that done before too long but it seems we always have too many other things to do.

Joe sure doesn't get down to the lake to fish as often as he'd like to. Jacob has a boat and they go together to fish most of the time, whenever they get some time that is free, which isn't often.

Lovina has now fallen asleep again so hopefully she'll sleep until the other children get up.

Try the zucchini pizza that Emma fixed us the other night.

ZUCCHINI PIZZA
4 cups grated zucchini
2 eggs, slightly beaten
3 tablespoons Bisquick
1 teaspoon salt
1 cup mozzarella cheese, shredded (reserve 1/2)
1 cup cheddar cheese, shredded (reserve 1/2)

Mix together thoroughly and press into a greased 11 x 15 pan. Bake at 400 for 15-20 minutes or until set. Put on your favorite pizza toppings and add rest of cheese. Bake at 375 for 15 more minutes until cheese is melted.

AUGUST 2005

It is hard to believe that we are halfway through the eighth month of the year, August. Where is this year going?

On Saturday, Jacob's family and our family spent the day at sisters Verena and Susan's place. So many things add up to be done that takes a man to do. Joe and Jacob finished a lot of jobs for them: Putting up a hitching rack, installing a new storm door, etc. We also cleaned out their barn and buggy shed. After hanging up a lot of their garden tools and supplies, they now have a lot more room in there.

Verena and Susan told us all to come over for a "haystack breakfast," which was very delicious. Ideas that can be used for the meal could be: Sausage, bacon, ham, scrambled or diced hard-boiled eggs, fried potatoes, mushrooms, green and hot peppers, tomatoes, onions. Just layer them on top of each other in whatever order you prefer. Then top with cheese sauce, salsa or gravy. In addition to the haystack, we had watermelon, peaches, strawberries, cookies, zucchini bread, coffee, milk and juice. It was a delicious breakfast and a day well-spent together.

Today, my daughter Elizabeth, 11, baked zucchini bread for the first time. She did a good job with it. She also baked over 100 peanut butter cookies. Daughter Susan helped her with the cookies. It sure helps me out to have them do things like that. I trust them more to bake with a gas stove than I did with a kerosene stove. Sometimes the breeze through the window would make the kerosene stove's flames go up and start smoking. Also lighting the burner took a match, which made it harder.

Elizabeth and Susan had over half of the yard mowed when my husband Joe came home from work. Joe and Elizabeth finished it up then. Daughter Susan mopped all the floors after I swept them. This seems to cool the house off more on these hot days. Verena washed and dried the dishes from lunch. Son Benjamin, 5, wiped off the breakfast dishes for me. He didn't think he should have to do a girl's job but he did a pretty good job. I told him I had to help milk cows when I was a little girl.

We had sweet corn again for supper. I also cooked green beans and potatoes together until they were almost soft. Then I made a thickening with flour and milk and added it to the potatoes and green beans. After simmering for awhile I added crumbled bacon and cheese. The children really like this dish. They don't care for green beans fixed plain but in something like that they like them.

Try this recipe for homemade zucchini bread. It's a great way to use the garden goodies at this time of year.

HOMEMADE ZUCCHINI BREAD
3 eggs
2 c. sugar
2 c. zucchini, shredded
1 c. cooking oil
2 tsp. vanilla
3 c. flour
1 tsp. salt
1 tsp. baking soda
1 tsp. baking powder
2 tsp. cinnamon
1/2 tsp. nutmeg
1/4 tsp. cloves
1/2 c. chopped nuts
1/2 c. raisins

Beat eggs until foamy. Stir in sugar, zucchini, oil and vanilla. Gradually add dry ingredients and spices. Stir in nuts. Pour into bread pans which have been greased only on the bottoms. Bake at 325 degrees for 60 to 80 minutes. Cool 10 minutes. Remove from pans and cool completely. Makes 2 loaves.

AUGUST 2005

We are doing a lot of outside work today, so we came in for a quick lunch. I thought I'd better get this written before the mail lady comes.

Susan, Verena and I cleaned out our pole building this morning. It doesn't take much for that building to get disorganized again after cleaning, so we have to stay on top of that.

We also weeded flower beds while my daughter Elizabeth, 11, was mowing. After lunch we want to get the small building beside the house cleaned out. I am glad to get everything organized before schools starts, which is Monday already. Hard to believe the summer went so fast. The basement is almost all cleaned, also, which will be nice to have done.

Joe didn't work yesterday, as the factory shut down for a funeral. Our community was deeply saddened by the passing away of a 19-year-old Amish boy. The cause of death was ruled an aneurysm. He was with some friends fishing when it happened. What a shock to friends, relatives and his special friend. Joe worked with him at the factory sometimes. Such a young age! It once again reminds us that God chooses from all ages, and we don't have to be old to die.

The community gathered last Saturday (and some on Friday, also, to prepare) for a "sub-drive" to help a young Amish couple with their hospital bills. It is so nice to help each other in time of need. Volunteers started making submarine sandwiches at

3 a.m., and they were ready to start delivering to surrounding communities by 7:30 a.m. They made over 4,000 subs, so it took a lot of willing workers just to deliver them.

Saturday, we are looking forward to having my oldest sister Leah, her husband, Paul, and their family come here to see for the first time where we four Coblentz sisters moved to (from the Berne, Ind., area to lower Michigan). My sisters Verena and Susan plan to make a taco dinner for us all before Paul's family heads on to visit with his parents in a nearby community. Leah turned 46 on the 15th, and my sister Verena will be 39 on the 22nd.

Joe's family from this area enjoyed a good Sunday dinner at his sister Esther's house. His sister Ruth, her husband, Chris, and their family from Berne, Ind., came to visit Joe's Dad. It was nice to get to visit with them again.

Joe's 91-year-old grandmother plans to have a sale to get rid of a lot of her belongings. It doesn't look like we'll be able to go, but it sure would be interesting to go. Joe doesn't see his uncles, aunts and cousins often.

A reader in Oxford, Ohio, asked for a peach pie recipe. Try this one:

AMISH CRUMB-TOP PEACH PIE
1 unbaked pie shell
6 sliced fresh peaches, at least partially peeled
1/4 cup all-purpose flour
3/4 cup granulated sugar
1 cup cream
Streusel topping:
1/3 cup all-purpose flour, additional
1/3 cup granulated sugar
3 tablespoons butter, softened

Arrange sliced peaches in the prepared pie shell, unbaked. Mix the flour, 3/4 cup sugar and cream and pour over peaches. For the streusel-crumb topping, mix flour, 1/3 cup sugar and butter until crumb-like and sprinkle evenly over the pie. Bake in a preheated oven at 425 degrees for 10 minutes, then reduce oven temperature to 350 degrees. Continue baking until the peach custard is set, about 30 minutes.

AUGUST 2005

I thought I'd write this column before I have to wake the children to get ready for school. It is now 5:25 a.m. and my husband, Joe, left a half-hour ago for work. I let the children sleep until 6 a.m. because they don't have to leave for school until around 7. It's been hectic this week, easing back into a schedule and getting five children ready, feeding them breakfast, and getting them off to school on time.

Daughter Elizabeth, 11, is now in fifth grade. Susan, 9, is in third grade. Verena, 7, is in the first grade. Benjamin, 6, and Loretta, 5, are both in kindergarten. Loretta seems to be adjusting to school, although she's tired by evening. We were going to send her to half-day preschool, but she seems to be adjusting to a full day. Benjamin likes to remind everyone that, even if Loretta is in the same grade, he is still older than her.

Our youngest, Joseph and Lovina, seem lost when the others all go to school. They like to get into everything they can. My sister Emma watched them for me one day this week while I went to get groceries. They had fun playing with her 3-year-old Benjamin. Emma's son Jacob Jr. is also starting kindergarten this fall, so her Benjamin misses his brother and playmate during the day.

It is quieter around the house during the day with the children at school, so Joseph and Lovina usually take a nap at the same time, which is a nice quiet time for me.

Our hay is cut and raked and ready to be baled today, so Joe has hay to put in tonight. Jacob plans to come help him tomorrow after work.

Joe has some cement work to do here and there. He's been busy evenings, getting things formed up and ready for cement.

I want to make a batch of salsa today. I have so many garden tomatoes, green peppers and hot peppers that need to be used up. I still have enough tomato juice and our version of homemade V-8 from last year's garden and canning season, so I'd rather wait until next year to do more.

We spent part of the day Saturday visiting with my sister Leah, Paul, and their four children. Two of their older children, Benjamin and Elizabeth, brought special friends with them. They came to see where we live now.

Jacob's, Paul's and our family all had a taco dinner at sisters Verena and Susan's house, plus lots of other goodies. That day -- Aug. 20 -- would've been Paul and Leah's daughter Mary's 14th birthday. She died when she was 5 years old. She was a sweet little girl and is still greatly missed

SEPTEMBER 2005

Hi! I'm Lovina's oldest daughter, Elizabeth. I'm 11 years old. I told Mom I would write for her this week, as she's very busy taking care of my new baby brother.

Baby Kevin was born Sept. 2 at 7:27 a.m. He weighed 8 pounds, 4 ounces and was 21 inches long. We are very excited to have a new baby again, but we try to give my little sister Lovina extra attention, so she doesn't get jealous.

Aunts Susan and Verena took care of us seven children while Mom and Dad were in the hospital. They were there two nights and two days. We were glad when they came back home. Baby Kevin has yellow jaundice and was supposed to stay at the hospital, but they let Dad and Mom bring him home for treatment. We have to keep a light, which they call a biliblanket, on him. Mom has to switch (the baby) from (its) back to front every two hours. It keeps her busy. We try to help Mom at nights, when we're home from school.

Aunts Verena and Susan came last night to help, and Aunt Emma and Benjamin stayed with Mom, Joseph, Lovina and Baby Kevin while we were in school. Emma will come again today. Our neighbors brought supper in one night, which we really enjoyed.

Mom has to take Kevin to the hospital every day to get a biliruben test on his yellow jaundice. When it gets under "10," Kevin can have the light taken off.

I have to go to bed now so I can get up earlier to help Mom pack Dad's lunch and get his breakfast. It is hard to believe Kevin is already six days old. We really enjoy him. I hope I wrote enough! Try this recipe!

AFTER-SCHOOL NO-BAKE COOKIES
1/2 cup sugar
1/2 cup corn syrup
1 cup peanut butter
5 tablespoons unsweetened cocoa powder
5 cups corn flakes

Heat sugar, corn syrup and cocoa powder in a medium saucepan just to boiling. Remove from heat and stir in the peanut butter. Have the corn flakes in a large mixing bowl. Pour on the hot cocoa mixture and stir. Turn the coated cereal into an oblong pan. Press into an even layer. Let stand until cool before cutting into bars.

SEPTEMBER 2005

Hello to all you wonderful readers once again. I need to take time this evening to get a column written. It is almost 9:30 p.m. on Wednesday, Sept. 21. My husband, Joe, and all the children, except Joseph and Elizabeth, are in bed.

Three-year-old Joseph is having a hard time settling down for the night in his older brother Benjamin's bedroom. He is going through a stage where he gets scared once it is dark.

Most of you have read by now about the welcome addition of baby Kevin to our family. He is doing good and eats and sleeps most of the time, but he is beginning to be more alert and smiles at us. Such a sweet baby! I had Kevin by C-section at the hospital, where they also repaired a hernia. I am feeling as good as can be expected after surgery. Although, I'm taking care of eight children now, and it's hard to get enough rest.

Every morning, our five school-age children have to be ready by 7 a.m., which can make for a rushy morning, especially if Kevin decides he wants to eat right then. We are thankful, though, for all the children's good health, and that the surgery went well. Life has so many blessings.

Lovina turned 16 months on Sunday. She's still a baby yet, also, but she loves Kevin. I try to give her extra attention, and so does everyone else. The last few nights, her older sisters Elizabeth and Susan have taken her upstairs with them to bed. She sleeps real good with them.

I want to put 2 1/2 bushels of Concord grapes into juice yet this week. What a big canning job, but I am so glad for the homemade juice on hand all winter. The store-bought grape juice is just too sweet.

Kevin will be 3 weeks on Friday. He usually wakes up once during the night for his feeding and diaper change -- although there have been a few nights when he didn't think Mom needed sleep at all. I can't complain, though. On Sunday, Joe took Elizabeth, Benjamin, Loretta, Joseph and Lovina along to church. My daughters Susan and Verena stayed home with Baby Kevin and me, so I got to rest quite a bit. I hope, next time, we can all go together once again.

On Saturday, Sept. 17, it was three long and lonely years that dear mother was laid to rest. (She was the original Amish Cook columnist, Elizabeth Coblentz.) It is at times like now with a newborn that I miss her even more. She was there for my first six children's births, doing all she could to help me along. And she was always there to turn to with questions. We must not question why, as we know God makes no mistakes. That is a great help knowing that. And it would be nice to have Mom and Dad here for the news of brother Albert's oldest daughter Elizabeth's wedding, coming up in October. This would be my parents' first grandchild getting married.

My 11-year-old daughter Elizabeth recently made this cake for Joe to take to work for some of his co-workers:

CHOCOLATE SHEET CAKE
2 cups all-purpose flour
2 cups sugar
1 teaspoon baking soda
1 teaspoon salt
1 stick of butter or margarine
1 cup water
1/4 cup unsweetened cocoa powder
2 eggs
1/2 cup sour cream
1 teaspoon vanilla
Yield: 1 sheet cake (About 16 pieces)

Have oven heating to 350 degrees. In a large mixing bowl, stir together the flour, sugar, baking soda and salt. In a medium saucepan over medium-high heat, combine the stick of butter (sliced into pats), the water and cocoa powder. Bring to a boil. Add this hot mixture to the bowl of dry ingredients and stir well. Add eggs and beat well. Then beat in the sour cream and vanilla extract.

Turn the cake batter into a greased jelly roll pan, spreading the batter evenly. Bake at 350 degrees in the center of the oven for 25-30 minutes. Cool cake in the pan on a rack and then spread on this chocolate frosting:

CHOCOLATE FROSTING
1/2 cup butter or margarine
6 teaspoons milk
1/4 cup unsweetened cocoa powder
1 teaspoon vanilla
Chopped nuts, optional

In a medium saucepan, heat the butter, milk and cocoa powder, stirring well. Remove from heat and cool. Add the vanilla and chopped nuts, if using. Stir until the frosting is well combined. Frost the sheet cake when it's completely cool.

OCTOBER 2005

It is now 10 a.m. on Thursday, Sept. 29, and I am holding Baby Kevin as I write this. He seems a little fussy this morning, so my dishes are still stacked, waiting to be washed. My precious children come first and then the work, which I'm sure will still be there when I get to it.

Joseph and Lovina are having a snack of cereal and juice. They eat with the school-age children at 6:30 a.m., so they usually get hungry about mid-morning.

Mornings have been cool lately, but the afternoons warm up. Sister Emma and her son Benjamin came yesterday to help me do my very big batch of laundry. The perfect autumn afternoon allowed it to dry nicely on the line.

Leaves are already starting to fall, but we're still getting tomatoes, green and hot peppers and cabbage from the garden. My husband, Joe, has tilled half of the garden.

Last Thursday and Friday found us processing nearly 3 bushels of grapes into juice. We processed 143 quarts. It's a lot of work, but I think it's worth it. The children did well in helping take grapes off the stems and washing them.

Sister Verena came Friday, as she didn't have to work. She helped me finish canning the grape juice. Then, while I went into town to the doctor and to get groceries, she stayed with my three youngest children, Joseph, Lovina and baby Kevin, and they kept her pretty busy. She also did laundry while I was gone.

I appreciated my sisters' assistance over the past few weeks, following Kevin's birth, especially with the heavier work. This has just been a busy time of helping one another with chores. But that is what family is for.

On Friday night, Emma and Jacob and family and we all went to Verena and Susan's house to help them process their grapes into juice. And then on Saturday, Jacob's family, Verena and Susan spent the day here helping butcher chickens, do cleaning, etc. We also processed 14 quarts of broth and cut up the rest of the chickens. My 143 quarts of grape juice also got wiped off and carried down to the basement. I sure was glad what all got done. Then a neighbor lady brought supper in for us, which was another nice treat.

On Sunday, we were just home all day, which was nice to catch up on resting after a busy week. In the afternoon, we had visitors from our church to come see our precious new baby. I fixed a "haystack supper" for us then, which is a favorite of Joe's. A "haystack supper" is a layered dish of cooked and crumbled ground beef, shredded cheese, chopped tomatoes, potatoes or noodles and any other favorite topping.

Joe has started putting in more hours at work, so it's hard for him to keep up with everything that needs to be done here.

Recently, we had a nice surprise when our good friend Jim from Huntington, Ind., came to see where we moved to here in Michigan. He stopped to pick up Joe's Dad and bring him along, so we made them stay to eat with us. We had fresh fried chicken along with all the trimmings. We were sorry that Jim's wife, Marias, couldn't come along, but it was a great visit.

Daughter Elizabeth, 11, wants me to thank everyone who took time to write to her after she wrote this column a couple of weeks ago. May God bless you. I don't know what I'd do without the girls' help. They do a good job.

Well, until next week, try this simple but delicious salad. The second recipe is one I saw, and I'm including it here just for fun.

BROCCOLI CAULIFLOWER SALAD
1 bunch broccoli, stalks diced, the top cut into small florets
1 head of cauliflower, trimmed, cut small
1/2 cup crisp bacon crumbles
2 cups grated cheese
1 small onion, finely diced

Dressing:
1 cup sour cream
1 cup salad dressing or mayonnaise
1/2 cup sugar
1/2 teaspoon salt

In a large salad bowl, combine the finely cut broccoli and cauliflower. Add the crisp bacon, grated cheese and the onion. For the dressing, mix the sour cream with mayonnaise, sugar, salt. Add lemon juice or vinegar to taste, maybe some ground pepper. Mix well and then pour over the vegetables and cheese mixture. Stir well, cover and keep chilled until time to serve.

ELEPHANT STEW
1 small elephant
Salt
Pepper
2 rabbits

Cut elephant into bite-sized pieces. Add enough water to cover. Cook at 465 degrees for 4 weeks. Yield: 3,800 servings. If unexpected company arrives, add the rabbits. Only add rabbits if necessary since most people don't care for "hare" in their stew.

OCTOBER 2005

It is 6 p.m. on Wednesday, Oct. 12, and I'm holding baby Kevin while trying to get this column written. Days fly by so fast and, before I know it, it is time to get this out again. I'm not feeling too good this week, battling allergies and I have a bad cold. My coughing has been keeping me awake at night.

My husband Joe is getting supper on the grill, which I'm glad for. I think I just needed a break from cooking. Last night I made a vegetable soup the children call it "Grandma's Soup," as Mom used to make it quite often and it was a favorite of theirs. Speaking of the kids, they are outside now horseback riding our pony Stormy. They ride bareback but we should get a saddle for them. That pony sure has been a pastime for the children.

We are having cooler weather so a little heat in the house feels good. Joe got our stove going for the winter on Saturday. We will burn coal for heat once the weather turns colder.

Sister Verena didn't have to work today so she came over and helped me do my laundry. What a relief that was for me. With the little ones to take care of doing laundry seems like such a big job. With Verena's help it was quickly done and on the lines. I left most of the clothes hanging on the lines as it wasn't a very good drying day outside. I'll see if they'll dry better tomorrow. It's been dreary all week, but I needed to get the laundry done.

Deer hunting season has opened here in Michigan. A neighbor brought us a taste of deer meat. He got one with a bow and arrow on opening day.

Joe says that supper is ready and I have Kevin sleeping, so I'll write more later.

This is now after 11 a.m. already on Thursday, Oct. 13. I didn't get this column finished last night. Joe is trying to get to bed earlier with longer hours at the factory. When Kevin decided to go to sleep early I decided to go to bed also and get some sleep. I feel better this morning. Kevin slept until Joe got up at 4 a.m.

Joseph, age 3, and Lovina, 16.5 months, seem to be wanting the same toy today. Then after awhile the toy just lays there on the floor and nobody wants it. Lovina just likes to pull Joseph's curly hair when they get into a quarrel. For her age she sure can keep up her end. It takes so much patience raising children.

It seems when I don't feel well everything seems worse than it is. But children are such a blessing and prayers are badly needed so that we will lead them in the way God wants us to. We need to keep all our trust in God and he will help lead the way. Try this recipe for the vegetable soup.

GRANDMA'S SOUP (VEGETABLE SOUP)
2 tablespoons of butter
1 cup of potatoes, diced
2 cups of tomato juice
2 cups of milk
1/4 cup of flour
1 onion, chopped
1/2 cup of celery, chopped
1 cup of diced carrots
1 1/2 teaspoons of salt
1 pound of hamburger

Brown meat and onion in butter. Drain grease. Add remaining ingredients, but reserve the milk and flour. Cook vegetables over medium heat until they are nice, soft and done. Mix the milk and flour and stir until smooth. Add to soup and cook until thickened.

OCTOBER 2005

It is Wednesday, Oct. 26, a little after noon. Joseph and I are here at the local hospital. Little Joseph was admitted last evening after running up a 105-degree fever. The doctor is having tests done to see what seems to be wrong. I hope and pray it's nothing serious. It is hard for a 3-year-old to understand what's going on. He hates the IV in his hand. When they draw blood, you just hurt right with them. (Editor's note: Use of modern medicine is not prohibited among the Old Order Amish. Views about modern medicine vary greatly among Amish communities and from person to person. Some Amish are quite comfortable using hospitals and doctors. Others are more reticent to seek treatment.) My husband Joe was here all night with us and left a little before 5 a.m. for his job. I'm sure he was worn out. I told him to go home, but he thought he should stay as Joseph wanted him to hold him.

Our seven other children are staying with my sisters, Verena and Susan. It was hard to leave our children, but I know they're in good hands.

Verena is off from work for a few weeks, so this worked out very well. Baby Lovina, 17 months, and Kevin, 8 weeks, are practically a full-time job. I miss them all already, but I feel Joseph needs me here with him.

I don't know what a person would do if we wouldn't have a great God to turn to for help. Do we thank him enough when everything goes well? Bad things happen sometimes to strengthen our faith in "Him." If everything would always go well, we might soon forget that we need "Him." He won't give us more than we can handle.

Joseph is starting to eat a few bites and drink some juice, which he wouldn't do yesterday. His fever has gone down to normal now. The doctor wants him to stay another night, as he wants him on an IV yet and to do a few more tests. Joseph seems to want me to hold him most of the day. The nurse gave him a little toy, and he won't let go of it.

Verena said baby Kevin slept "good" until 3 a.m., and then he was very hungry to eat and eat. He will be 8 weeks old on Friday. I really miss taking care of him, but I'd hate to have him here at the hospital where he might catch some flu. It really helps to know they are in good care. Sister Emma and her Benjamin were going to spend the day with Verena and help her along with my dear little ones.

PUMPKIN COOKIES
1 cup shortening or margarine
2 cups sugar
2 cups fresh-cooked pumpkin puree
2 teaspoons baking soda
2 teaspoons baking powder

2 teaspoons cinnamon
4 cups all-purpose flour
1/2 teaspoon salt or less, optional

In a large mixing bowl, beat together the shortening and sugar. Stir in the pumpkin (canned puree can be substituted, though it may be more concentrated than fresh-cooked).

In another mixing bowl, stir together the dry ingredients: flour, salt, cinnamon, baking powder and baking soda. Stir into the pumpkin mixture. Drop cookies onto a lightly greased baking sheet. Bake in a preheated 350-degree oven for 8 to 10 minutes. Repeat until dough is gone. Drizzle the cookies with white frosting after they cool.

NOVEMBER 2005

Our Master Artist has once again painted such wonderful scenery. The colorful array of leaves are in their autumn splendor as the covered buggies in this area make their way down the roads.

We are already into the 3rd day of November and we have lots and lots of leaves that need to be raked up. The wind is helping to blow some of them away. We have around 20 trees in our yard, so we get our share of leaves. I'd like to get a few more rakes so that the job would go faster when we all go rake. Meanwhile, the temperature is already at 60 degrees at 9:30 a.m., so it looks like a wonderful day to rake up those leaves. It doesn't look like I'll get out there, though, as I am still getting caught up with indoor work after being gone most of last week.

We are thankful that two of our children who spent last week in the hospital are now home. Little Joseph was hospitalized for 5 days and baby Lovina for 3 days. They both had pneumonia, but Joseph had it the worst, with a temperature that at one point was as high as 105 degrees. We took Lovina to the hospital after her temperature hit 102. We had them both in the same room, which was quite a task when I was there alone. My husband Joe spent every night there with us, coming straight from work to the hospital. Both children had IVs hooked up to them so it was hard to keep them from pulling it out. Joseph pulled his out of his hand so they had to start it on his foot. We came home around 5 p.m. on Saturday with both children. It was so nice to all be together again as a family. I missed the other children so much.

We sure appreciated the help from my sisters Verena and Susan, and sister Emma, husband Jacob, and their children. What would we do without family?

Since the time change, Joe has had to leave for work around 3:45 a.m., which makes us have to get up around 3 a.m. This will change after they quit working overtime. They are still working on orders from the hurricanes. We try to get to bed an hour earlier if we can. I usually go back to bed for awhile after Joe leaves. (Editor's Note: The Old Order Amish, once primarily an agrarian society, have been gradually seeking employment in other areas. In the rural Indiana-Michigan border region, some estimates have over 20 percent of the Amish men employed in the area's numerous RV factories. Such non-Amish owned businesses often have to make special accommodations for their Amish employees, such as observation of certain holidays and a strict observance of the Sabbath. Many of these RV factories have seen a significant uptick in business with FEMA contracts for emergency housing trailers in the aftermath of Hurricanes Katrina and Rita.)

NOVEMBER 2005

3 a.m. - It's time to get up and start another day. My husband Joe goes out to do the morning chores, then comes in and washes up for work. He reminds me to let the chickens out later. We are averaging 25 eggs a day. We sell what we don't use for ourselves. I fix Joe's breakfast, pack his lunch, and fill his water jug with ice and water. We had a non-electric water softener installed and also a drinking water purifier. We have to regenerate the softener every week or more often depending on how much water we use. It has made a tremendous difference in our water quality.

3:45 a.m. - Joe leaves for another day of work at the trailer factory. I stay up this morning as Joseph and Lovina have a doctor appointment in the forenoon. I know the morning hours will go fast. Baby Kevin wakes up and needs his diaper changed. He eats and I rock him and doze off a few minutes myself, then put him back to bed. Kevin really coos and laughs out loud and I just love to play with him.

6 a.m. - I get the children up to get ready for school. They all get dressed while I start breakfast. I make grilled cheese sandwiches and fried eggs, milk, and grape juice for their morning meal.

7:05 a.m. - The older children leave for school. Joseph and Lovina are still finishing their breakfast. I start washing dishes and get halfway through when Kevin wakes up again. I put him in the baby swing and finish washing the dishes. Then I feed Kevin and get him happy again. I dry and put away the dishes. Time is going way too fast.

9 a.m. - Joseph and Lovina are in the tub taking a bath while I give Kevin his bath. I get all three dressed and contented as I quickly wash up before they get into too much trouble.

10:30 a.m. - I leave for the doctor. Sister Verena goes along with me to help with the children.

2:30 p.m. - We're back home from town. I got a few groceries while we were in town so I'm working on putting those away.

3:20 p.m. - The children are home from school and husband Joe from work. Joe puts back on a shoe that came off our horse Diamond and does the evening chores. We are burning hard coal now so the ash pan has to be emptied every night.

The girls and I fix supper and it's ready to eat when Joe, Benjamin, Loretta and Joseph come in from the barn

6 p.m. - We eat supper

7:30 p.m. - We are all done with our evening meal and Joe and the younger children go to bed. The school children do homework, read or whatever they need to practice for their lessons.

8 p.m. - The rest of us head for bed. It's been a long, rushy day. Hopefully tomorrow I won't have to leave again.

We hope you all had a safe and happy Thanksgiving. We had our Thanksgiving dinner here with Emma and Jacob's and Verena and Susan. It is so nice to spend a day with family. We have so much to be thankful for and it doesn't have to be Thanksgiving to thank our Heavenly Father for everything. With Christmas coming up, try this recipe for old-fashioned homemade Christmas cookies:

CHRISTMAS COOKIES
3 cups of flour
1 cup of sugar
1 teaspoon of baking soda
1 teaspoon of cream of tartar
1/2 teaspoon of salt
3 tablespoons of milk
2 eggs
1 teaspoon of vanilla
1 1/4 cup of margarine

Mix dry ingredients. Add remaining ingredients and stir. Roll out thinly. Cut in any shape desired. Bake at 375 for about 10 minutes, or until golden around the edges. Let cool and decorate as you wish. They taste better after setting for several days.

DECEMBER 2005

Our extended family has grown by one member, so we are all excited. My brother Albert and his wife, Sarah Irene, were blessed with their 11th child. They had a daughter named Sylvia on Sunday, Dec. 4. This makes six girls and five boys for them, although their oldest child Elizabeth has moved to her new home with her husband Amos. Elizabeth and Amos will spend a few weeks at Albert's, however, helping mom with the new addition. I'm sure the family is excited to have Elizabeth back home for awhile.

Sylvia would make grandchild number 42 for my dear (late) parents, although my niece Mary went to her heavenly home eight years ago, when she was just a small child.

My husband, Joe, is still leaving for work every morning at 3:45 a.m. It is a very cold morning today, with the mercury still sitting at 1 below zero at 5 a.m., as I write this. I have fixed Joe his breakfast and gotten him on his way, so it is quiet around here now as I wait for the children to wake up.

We received the sad news yesterday of the death of Joe's Uncle LeRoy, age 67, of Milroy, Ind. He died after a struggle with that dreadful disease, cancer. Our understanding and sympathy go out to the family. We have plans to start out Friday night for Milroy and stay for the funeral on Saturday. Joe's dad and some of his sisters, their husbands, and my sister Emma and husband Jacob (LeRoy was also Jacob's uncle) will set off for Milroy with a hired van driver. It's around a four- to five-hour drive from here in Michigan.

Sisters Verena and Susan will keep our eight children and Jacob's four children at their house while we're gone. I'm so glad they are so willing to put up with 12 children. I'd like to take them along, but with it being so cold and that many hours riding in a van, it'll be better for them to not go. I will miss them and hope and pray we will have a safe trip.

Our daughter Verena will turn 8 years old while we are away. We will have to celebrate her birthday another day. I am sure she'll enjoy her birthday at her aunt's house, especially with all her cousins there. Meanwhile, Joe's grandmother will be 92 tomorrow. She has been a widow for 17 years. This is her son-in-law who died.

I need to bake some cookies for our neighbors who will hold church services at their house on Sunday. I baked two loaves of Amish cinnamon bread this past weekend, and it's all gone already. The children really liked the sourdough bread with cinnamon. I got the starter from my sister Emma. Her neighbor lady gave it to her. It takes 10 days until it's ready to mix and bake. Daughter Elizabeth takes care of it or else I'd probably forget about it on some days.

I must get busy now because I have floors to mop and laundry to fold and put away.

Tonight, we plan to attend the children's Christmas program at school. It should be cute to see all the young children.

Here is the recipe for Amish cinnamon bread. The amounts of sugar, flour and milk (noted as "divided use") are to be used gradually over time to feed the starter. Then, the remaining amounts of sugar and flour are used in the sweet bread batter. The bread recipe instructions are followed by a sourdough starter recipe.

AMISH CINNAMON BREAD
1 container sourdough starter
1 cup vegetable oil
1 teaspoon baking soda
3 cups sugar, divided use
1/2 teaspoon salt
4 eggs
3 to 4 teaspoons cinnamon
4 cups flour, divided use
1 small box instant vanilla pudding
1 cup chopped nuts, optional
1 cup raisins, optional
2 cups milk, divided use
Yield: 2 loaves

Directions:

Day 1: Receive sourdough starter and cover loosely. Do not chill.

Days 2, 3, 4: Stir starter.

Day 5: Add 1 cup sugar, 1 cup milk and 1 cup flour. Stir.

Day 6 and 7: Stir.

Day 8 and 9: Do nothing. Do not feed the starter. Do not stir.

Day 10: Add 1 cup sugar, 1 cup flour, 1 cup milk and stir. Remove 3 cups of the mixture and place in three separate containers. Give two of the starter containers away, but keep one container for yourself.

To the remaining starter, add vegetable oil, baking soda, 1 cup sugar, salt, eggs, cinnamon, 2 cups of the flour, the dry pudding mix, nuts and raisins. Beat by hand. Pour into two greased loaf pans (editor's note: pan size is not specified, nor is any rise time or proofing indicated here, but you might want to let the loaf pans stand at room temperature to increase volume).

When ready to bake the loaves, have oven heated to 350. Bake the bread 1 hour. For those who want to make their own starter, here's a simple starter recipe:

HOMEMADE SOURDOUGH STARTER
1 package active dry yeast (not Rapid Rise style)
2 cups warm water (105 to 110 degrees F.)
2 cups flour
1 tablespoon sugar

Directions: Dissolve the yeast in the warm water in a large bowl. Add the 2 cups flour and 1 tablespoon sugar and beat until smooth. Cover with cheesecloth and let stand at room temperature five to 10 days, stirring two to three times per day. The time required to ferment depends upon the temperature of the room. A warmer room will cause it to take less time than a cooler room. Cover the starter bowl and refrigerate until ready to use in three to five days.

DECEMBER 2005

This snowy December morning is rushing by way too fast. Today is the deadline to get this column in the mail to my editor. It has to be out in my roadside mailbox by Thursday each week.

Oh my, life is sometimes just way too busy. Little children take a lot of care, but the joys they bring to us! Each one is so very precious. Do we take enough time for our children, to teach them and pray for them in these troubled times?

We had some sleet earlier this morning, and now it is snowing, making such a beautiful winter wonderland.

I want to bake cinnamon rolls today. The children would like to take some to school for their teachers. Tomorrow is already their last day before Christmas break. They will have two weeks off.

In those two weeks, I hope we can find time to start washing walls and ceilings and get started cleaning for the upcoming church services that will be held here sometime in January, Lord willing. A reader wrote to ask why we Amish wash off our walls and ceilings so often. It just refreshes everything to have the walls and ceilings clean. The coal stove seems to dull things up in the house, not to mention the many little dirty handprints on the walls from the children.

With young ones, there are so many spills and messes, that it just seems to freshen everything up to do a good cleaning. So often we don't take time to clean the extras, and that is one good thing about having church services twice a year. It makes you get it done.

We left at 4 p.m. last Friday to go to Milroy, Ind., with some of my husband Joe's family and Jacob and Emma. My sisters Verena and Susan kept our children and also Jacob's four children until we arrived home later Saturday evening. The children enjoyed their stay at their aunts' house. It was nice to know they were in good care.

We attended the funeral on Saturday in Milroy of Joe's Uncle LeRoy, age 67. Cancer is such a horrible disease. It brought back memories of when we laid our dear parents to rest. It was nice to have a short visit with sister Liz, as they were there also.

Sunday morning came around before we knew it. We attended church in another district. Visiting other church districts is a good way to meet more people from the Amish community. We moved here to Michigan two years ago this spring (from Indiana). I still don't know everyone yet, but I am slowly learning.

I am holding Baby Kevin while I write this column. I sure can tell he is growing. He's a lot more active. He is so interested in watching my pen move. He is 3 1/2 months old now. Peace on Earth and God's blessings to all through this holy season

2006

This was a year that saw the Eichers settling into their newly-built house, which they built on the same property. The newer house is more spacious and allows for much more room for the growing Eicher family.

In the rest of the world the Associated Press named the continuing war in Iraq and the success of Democrats in recapturing Congress as the big news stories of the year.

JANUARY 2006

It is hard to believe we are a couple of weeks into 2006 now. What does the unknown future hold for us? Only God knows. Isn't it good that we don't know our future and take only one day at a time?

Everything has gone back to normal in this household since the busy holiday season. Seems quiet with only Joseph, Lovina, Kevin, and I here at home. The rest of the children are back at school. Although a few minutes ago it didn't sound too quiet. Joseph and Lovina were having a little disagreement which resulted in some hair pulling. So I settled their disagreement and now they are enjoying a snack of homemade party mix and grape juice. They are sitting side by side now. If adults could forgive each other as fast as these innocent children I doubt there would be so much turmoil in this world.

My husband Joe will have a day off on Friday, Jan. 6. Most of the factories around here honor this Amish holiday known as "Old Christmas." It is a day we take off from our busy life to honor dear Savior who died for our sins.

If possible, I'd like to get started washing walls and ceilings as church services will be held here in 2 1/2 weeks. Then again 2 weeks later, as Jacob and Emma will take their turn here. I didn't do much fall cleaning as I knew we'd be hosting church services.

It's another dreary day and raining. Yesterday I did the laundry and just hung it in our tool shed to dry. Also I filled the clothes racks here in the house. With all the clothes hanging around it makes one look forward to those good ol summer days when doing laundry only takes a day. But I still like the changing of the seasons. There is something good and bad about every season.

Brother Amos and his wife Nancy will have our family Christmas gathering on January 28. I am glad that one of the church services here will be over with. The next time isn't so bad to prepare. We are over 60 in my family when we all get together. Our dear parents will be greatly missed. There always will be something missing from family gatherings.

We spent New Year's Day at Jacob and Emma's. Sisters Verena and Susan joined us. Our family here in Michigan exchanged names, so we had our gift exchange which was an excitement for the children to see who had their name and what they got.

For New Year's Day, we enjoyed a big dinner consisting of turkey, dressing, scalloped potatoes, mixed vegetables, veggies and dip, homemade cheeseball and crackers, apple crumb and apple pies, chocolate chip cookies, jello cake, oranges and grapefruits, etc.

My mother's side of the family used to always gather at my grandparents house on New Year's Day. The family would usually all gather down the road at our house and then we'd all go together. We would sing the New Year's Song outside grandpa's door. After that each of us 81 grandchildren would line up and greet grandpa and grandma and wish them a happy new year.

Try this recipe for apple crumb pie. Have a happy new year!

APPLE CRUMB PIE
2/3 c. sugar
1/4 tsp. cinnamon
1/4 tsp. nutmeg
6 to 8 green or baking apples, pared and sliced
1 unbaked 9 inch pie shell

Blend sugar and spices; toss with apples. Arrange mixture in pie shell.

SUGAR CRUMB TOPPING:
3/4 c. packed brown sugar
1/4 c. sugar
3/4 c. flour

1/4 tsp. salt
1/2 c. butter

Blend sugars, flour and salt. Cut in butter until mixture is crumbly. Spoon crumb topping over apples. Bake at 425 degrees for 15 minutes. Reset temperature to 350 degrees and continue baking for 35 to 40 more minutes.

JANUARY 2006

We are constantly cleaning this week, as we prepare to hold church services at our place this Sunday. Walls and ceilings are being washed, and we're making time for all the other chores that come with preparing a house to hold church services. Usually, each member of our church takes a turn holding Sunday services about twice a year.

My sister Emma, her husband Jacob and their 3-year-old son Benjamin came here yesterday to lend us a hand. Jacob is off work this week yet. He built two more horse stalls in our barn that my husband Joe has always wanted to do but has never found the time. Joe is really happy to have those new stalls.

While Jacob was hard at work, Emma and I did a very big laundry and hung it outside to dry. I guess we took advantage of the warmer weather. We sure haven't had much of a winter yet. But I wouldn't write Old Man Winter off too soon -- February's still to come. Emma washed off the walls and ceilings in the kitchen, which is usually the worst room.

In between feeding Kevin and changing diapers, I helped Emma with these chores. Our 3-year-olds -- Joseph and Benjamin -- sure put in a hard day playing. They enjoyed being outside with Jacob. Twenty-month old Lovina waddled behind them and tried to keep up with the two older ones. Jacob's scholars came off the bus here with ours, making a total of eight children coming off the bus, so it grew busier around here during after-school hours.

Yesterday, my good friend Patricia and her son Ben came for a short visit. She came to give all our children a Christmas gift of new books. What a treat for the children!

Tomorrow, we will send our pony Cheeko to the horse auction. It has just been taking too much hay to feed three horses and two ponies. We figured we have to sell one of our horses, and Cheeko is only "green broke" (partially trained). Everyone in our family voted to keep Stormy, so Cheeko was picked to go to auction.

This spring, we will get someone to train Ginger, Itty Bit's colt. She was born six days after we moved to Michigan, so she'll be 2 in March. (Editor's note: Itty Bit's Ginger would properly be called a filly.)

We will then have to make a big decision on which of the three horses we will sell. We raised Diamond from the time he was born almost 12 years ago. I just can't get used to the idea of selling him. Although he's not the fastest traveler, he's safe and sound, which means a lot, especially when I take him into town. Itty Bit is also a safe horse, but a faster traveler, and she's younger, so she's Joe's pick to keep. I guess we will have to wait and see how Ginger turns out. It's so easy to get attached to a horse.

The land here in Michigan is more rolling, unlike the flat land of Indiana, our former home state. Our horses have had to toughen up to pull the buggies uphill. Also, the covered buggies used by the Amish here weigh more than an open buggy, required by our Amish community in our part of southeast-central Indiana. It took some time for our horses to get used to that change, but every time we drive in the rain I am so thankful for a covered buggy. I don't miss always washing our winter coats after riding in an open buggy. The horses and passing cars would splatter mud up into the buggy. We had to hold up umbrellas the whole time, too.

Try this delicious recipe.

COLD-DAY SOUP (no meat or broth)
1 large carrot, diced
2 cups water
2 large onions, peeled
1 quart peeled, diced potatoes
2 tablespoons uncooked regular rice
1/3 cup uncooked elbow macaroni
1 teaspoon salt

1/4 teaspoon milled pepper
2 cups milk
2 tablespoons butter

Chop the carrot and cook it in 2 cups water. Meanwhile, chop the two onions. When the carrots are partially cooked, add the onions, diced potatoes, rice, macaroni, salt/pepper. Add enough water to cover; cook until tender. Add milk, butter; heat thoroughly.

FEBRUARY 2006

It is now into February as I write this. Another month has started in this still young year already.

We are again in the process of cleaning whatever needs to be cleaned around this house. Church services will be held here again on Sunday, Feb. 5. We are holding the services for Jacob and Emma's turn.

The weather early February weather is making for some nice spring-like days, which makes it easier to wash windows and do laundry.

I am afraid our winter has been too mild. We will get winter weather when it's time to start planting the garden. Only God knows as He alone controls the weather.

We attended the Coblentz gathering at my brother Amos and Nancy's in Berne, Ind. This was a late Christmas gathering. We had a perfect attendance which was nice. Dad and Mom's presence will always be missed, especially when we sing the New Year's Song in German. There will always seem to be something missing, not hearing their voices. Amos's had barbecued chicken, turkey, dressing, mashed potatoes, gravy, mixed vegetables with the rest of the family bringing the salads, fruit, desserts, vegetables, dip, etc. All the food adds up and there was plenty for everyone.

It was a nice day with no snow to travel. The children enjoyed playing outside. After dinner we spent the afternoon singing and visiting. Before we knew it we were ready to start our 2.5 hour drive home. Most of the children slept on the way home, being tired from a long day.

Today the temperature soared up over 60 for awhile. I regretted that I didn't do the laundry.

Joe and the children have all retired for the night. We finally got Kevin to settle down. I think he's pushing teeth but it seems they can bother them quite awhile before they get their first tooth. Tomorrow he will be 5 months old.

It's been a long day so I will probably call it a day and get some rest while I can. It sounds like everyone has settled down. Sometimes it takes awhile to get everyone settled. They have just a little too much energy when bedtime comes.

Good night to everyone and mayGod keep you in his care tonight and always.

FEBRUARY 2006

I will attempt to write this as I hold 5 1/2-month-old baby Kevin. He's so active, and right now I think he just wants attention. When I lay him on his activity blanket, he doesn't stay there for very long anymore. Kevin pushes himself forward on his tummy, and he also rolls from back to stomach and stomach to back. Doing all that, he hardly stays in one place too long. Also, when I put him in his baby swing, he goes back and forth with his body to make the swing move itself.

On Monday evening we received the shocking news that sister Liz's father-in-law died from a heart attack. This would be her husband Levi's father. He was only 58. Once again, we are reminded that God is in control and that He determines our stay here on Earth. Our hearts go out to the grieving wife and family. I know the pain they are experiencing and wish them God's guidance through this very difficult time.

The viewing and funeral services will be held at Levi and Liz's place. They built a big pole barn last year, which is where the funeral will be held. My husband Joe had just talked to Levi's dad two weeks ago about ordering a covered wagon for our pony.

Tomorrow morning at 5 a.m. we will start out to attend the funeral service at Levi and Liz's. Our children don't have school tomorrow because of a midwinter break (and also not on Monday), so we will take all the children with us to Indiana. Our oldest daughter Elizabeth, age 11, will leave tonight with my sisters Susan and Verena. I will miss her help, but I hope she'll be able to assist Liz in the morning. Tomorrow would also be my dear father's 75th birthday. And on May 20th, it will be six, long-and-lonely years since Dad left this earthly home.

Tonight, Joe has to take our buggy over to the buggy shop to get the rubber on a wheel fixed. When we lived in Indiana, we had steel-rimmed buggy wheels. Here in Michigan, we have hard-rubber wheels. They are so much quieter than the steel, which make quite a noise crunching over gravel roads.

MARCH 2006

Joseph and Kevin have both been taking a nap since lunchtime. While they are sleeping, Lovina is playing "mommy" to her little doll that she calls "Ken." She doesn't pronounce the "v" in Kevin, so she calls all babies "Kens." Her eyes are looking droopy, so it probably won't be long before she'll fall asleep, too. I decided to take this moment of peace and quiet to write this.

I have laundry that needs to be folded and put away, dishes that should be washed. So many things waiting to get done that go with raising a family. Time is just so limited; do we use it wisely? I must remember that when my work gets overwhelming, we have a Father up above to turn to with our struggles.

We attended the funeral at sister Liz and Levi's place for Levi's dad. The funeral services were held in their new pole barn and in the house. Both places were really packed. A lot of friends and family from other communities were there, plus the locals, which made for quite a large group. Our thoughts and prayers are with the loved ones who are struggling through this trying time of sorrow.

I saw all of my brothers and sisters at the funeral, except Leah. In the afternoon, we went to visit with Leah, her husband Paul, and children Elizabeth and Paul Jr. Their boys Ben and Levi weren't home from work yet. Leah set out some good snacks for us. After leaving Paul and Leah's, we went back to Levi's where the last people were leaving. I wanted to give Levi's family plenty of time to visit with their guests before we returned to say goodbye. We left Liz and Levi's in the evening, so it was after 11 p.m. when we arrived back home in Michigan. We had a lot of sleepy children to get off to bed.

This coming Sunday my brother's family -- Amos, Nancy and their children -- have plans to travel to Michigan to see where we four sisters moved to two years ago. They have never been here yet. They wanted to come in September when I had come home from the hospital. I told them I would enjoy a visit better once I regained my health. Having three surgeries at once and two the year before left me quite weak for awhile.

I am so thankful for my health now. And baby Kevin had the struggle with yellow jaundice in his first few weeks of life, which we treated here at home. He is such a happy, healthy little boy now, and such a joy to have around, as are all our children. Each one is special.

A reader in East Chicago, Ill., requested a recipe for pot roast. Try this delicious, juicy recipe.

AMISH SUNDAY POT ROAST
3 pounds Swiss steak, trimmed of fat
1 tablespoon vegetable oil
1/4 cup soy sauce
1 cup coffee
2 bay leaves, crumbled
1 garlic clove, minced
1/2 teaspoon dried oregano
2 onions, sliced
Yield: 10 servings

Preheat oven to 300 degrees. Do not pound or flour the beef. Heat oil in a heavy skillet over high heat, then sear meat on both sides. Meanwhile, in a large roasting pan, combine soy sauce, coffee, bay leaves, garlic, oregano and one of the sliced onions. Transfer the browned meat to the roasting pan. Top with the second sliced onion. Cover and bake at 300 degrees for 3 1/2 hours, basting every hour with pan juices. If the liquid begins to boil away, add another cup of coffee and a splash of soy sauce. You may need to repeat this procedure; there should be quite a bit of liquid.

To serve, let the meat rest and then cut it in thin slices and serve with pan juices.

MARCH 2006

Here's a diary of a day in this household:

* 6:30 a.m. Sister Emma and I are preparing breakfast now. It will be nice to eat breakfast together. Emma, her husband, Jacob, and their four children came over last night to assist us with work around here. Since they were planning to be here today to help again, I told them to stay overnight. So last night was a full house.

We are in the process of tearing down some older outbuildings on our property to make way for our new house. Our plans this summer are to build a new house behind the one we live in now. But these buildings have to be cleared away first to get ready to have a basement dug.

* 7 a.m. Breakfast is almost ready to serve. We are waiting for the menfolk to come in to eat. Joe, Jacob and the four boys all went out as soon as daylight arrived to start cutting up a big tree that Joe chopped down last night. It was a large maple tree, and the sap was really running out. This tree was also in the way of the new house, so it had to be taken down.

* 7:30 a.m. Sisters Verena and Susan walked down here (from their nearby house) to have breakfast with us and pitch in with the work today. They assisted us last night also, but decided to go home to sleep. Our breakfast menu consists of fried eggs and potatoes, bacon, Swiss and Colby cheese, toast, garden-grown and canned hot peppers, bananas, oatmeal pie, homemade cinnamon rolls, milk, home-canned grape juice, coffee and tea.

* 8:15 a.m. The men and boys have gone back outside to continue cutting up the maple tree. The women and girls all pitch in and get the dishes washed, floors swept and beds made while the men are working outside.

* 9:15 a.m. Verena and Susan and the girls go outside to help pull branches from the maple tree to the fire, and help carry wood away. Emma and I gather laundry and wash it. We hang it all outside, and it looks like it will dry nicely today. After we're done, we join in helping the rest. We carry boards from the old buildings to burn.

* Noon. It's lunch time already! I set out ham, cheese and bread for sandwiches, hard-boiled eggs and horseradish, pickles, lettuce, chips. We just eat sandwiches for lunch, but I'll make a bigger supper.

* 12:30 p.m. Everyone is back to work after lunch. Things are really getting cleared out to make way for the basement to be dug.

* 3 p.m. Everyone is coming in for a snack, and I'm fixing a pizza casserole to put into the oven so that everyone can eat supper before heading home. Next, I'll go outside to get the laundry in. It all dried very nice.

* 4 p.m. Verena, Susan and Emma come in and sweep and mop my floors. Sure refreshes everything. We get the rest of our supper ready.

* 4:45 p.m. Time to eat and call it a day. We have everything cleared away where the new house will be built. We have an old corncrib building out by

the road that still needs to be picked

up. But we will call it quits for today. We will all eat supper together, and then everyone will get ready to go home.

* 5:45 p.m. Everyone has left for home, and I give the younger children their baths while Joe does the evening chores. After being outside all day, the children are really dirty.

* 8 p.m. Everyone is cleaned up, and we're all ready to go to bed early. We sure appreciate all the good help we had today.

Here is the recipe for "pizza casserole" that we served. Everyone enjoyed it!

EASY PIZZA CASSEROLE
8 ounces of noodles, cooked
1 pound ground beef, browned and crumbled
1 cup diced onion
1 cup fresh sour cream
1 cup homemade or store-bought pizza sauce
1 cup homemade or store-bought cottage cheese
1 cup diced or shredded Colby cheese for topping
Yield: 8 servings

Cook noodles in a Dutch oven with lots of salted, boiling water and then drain well when noodles are almost tender. Set aside with noodles returned to the large pot. Meanwhile, brown the beef in a large skillet, adding the diced onion near the end. Drain off the drippings and add beef and onion to the noodles in the large pot. Stir in the sour cream, pizza sauce and cottage cheese. Turn into a 13-by-9-inch baking dish. Sprinkle the Colby cheese on top and bake at 350 degrees for about 1 hour.

APRIL 2006

The children had a nice spring break last week and are now back to school.

There was never a quiet moment from dawn 'til dusk all week. And then it rained for several days, which was a little nerve-racking on Mom. Oh, but how thankful can I be that my children are all healthy and full of energy!

We passed some time by baking several batches of different kinds of cookies. My daughter Susan, 10, made the frosting for the first time for the sugar cookies. She did a great job. A reader asked how I make my frosting. I take two heaping tablespoons of shortening and blend that together with three-fourths cup of powdered sugar. After it is smooth, I add a tablespoon of vanilla. Then I gradually add milk and additional powdered sugar, making it smooth enough for frosting -- as thick or thin as you want it.

If you want a bigger batch, just add more milk and powdered sugar. For different colors, gradually blend in tiny drops of the food coloring preferred. For chocolate frosting, I add a bit of cocoa powder. I hope I explained it good enough. I like this frosting for cookies, as it sets nice, so you can stack the cookies with waxed paper in between.

We received the sad news this morning of the death of my husband Joe's 88-year-old grandmother from the Sugarcreek, Ohio, area. We are planning to leave tomorrow sometime for the funeral, which will probably be a four- to five-hour ride by rented van. The trip will probably take longer since we plan to take all eight of our children along. The funeral is on Thursday.

I have so much packing to do, even if we'll only be gone two days and one night. Packing for 10 people is no picnic. I know, though, that the children will be glad to be with us and see the beautiful hills of Holmes County, Ohio (northeast of Columbus). A person just doesn't know from one day to the next what God has in store.

We are having very beautiful, 70-degree days. Sure am anxious to get some garden planted, but this week looks too busy. We have to put our garden somewhere else as our new house is being built where the garden was. After the basement is poured, we can work up our new garden in a different spot. In the meantime, Joe will work up a little patch somewhere to get a few of the early things out in time. We need to transplant our rhubarb, winter onions, and some asparagus because they are also in the way of the new house.

Our plans are to have the basement dug this week. We finally have our building permits.

On Good Friday, sister Leah and Paul and family came here to Michigan for a visit. We all got together at Jacob and Emma's. On Sunday, Paul and Leah were married 25 years. And on April 15th, their oldest son Ben was 23. He is my parents' oldest grandchild. How these years fly by!

Talking earlier of cookies, I will share a cookie recipe with you. These are delicious and moist.

SOUR CREAM COOKIES
2 cups white sugar
1/2 cup butter

1/2 cup shortening
2 eggs
1 cup sour cream
1-1/2 teaspoons vanilla extract
2 teaspoons baking powder
1 teaspoon baking soda
1/4 teaspoon grated nutmeg
1/4 teaspoon salt, optional
About 4 cups all-purpose flour
Yield: 6 dozen cookies

Beat together the sugar, butter and shortening until fluffy. Add eggs, vanilla and sour cream, beating well. Sift dry ingredients and stir into the butter mixture until blended.

Have oven heating to 375 degrees. Drop cookie dough by tablespoonfuls onto a greased cookie sheet, spacing them well apart to allow for the cookies to spread during baking. Bake at 375 degrees for 10 to 12 minutes.

APRIL 2006

We have been having beautiful spring days, with chilly mornings, but warm afternoons in the 60s and 70s. Our basement for the new house has now been dug out. And in a few days they will begin to pour the basement walls and floor. It is excitingto see when another step has been accomplished.

The older children have left for school, while Joseph and Lovina are still sleeping, which is unusual. But we went to Jacob's last night for supper and got to bed later than usual, which is why they are still sleeping. Last night my husband Joe, brother-in-law Jacob, and some of the children went mushroom hunting. They didn't have too much luck, though.

I decided to take advantage of the peace and quiet and get this column written. My dishes aren't washed, floors need to be swept and the laundry to be folded. All that will be easier to do once the children are awake and I can keep an eye on them. It seems like I sweep the floors so much more often since the basement has been dug. The children drag in clumps of dirt on their shoes, in their pockets, etc. I can imagine the fun I'll have once it rains.

As I write this, and the others sleep, little Kevin (8 months) is in his walker. He gets around everywhere. He's already trying to open my cabinet doors. So he needs to be watched more and more.

We started out for Ohio on Wednesday morning. It took us six and a half hours to get to the tiny town of Walhonding, where the viewing was held for Joe's grandmother. She doesn't have to suffer anymore, although she will be greatly missed by all her friends and family.

We then headed for the Sugarcreek, Ohio, area as the funeral was to be near there the next day. While in the area, we stopped in to visit my Aunt Lovina and her husband, Abe Raber. She was surprised to see us and we had a nice, but too short visit. I hadn't seen Aunt Lovina for almost three years. She is my Mom's sister and resembles her a lot. I was named after her. We lived in the same church district while we both lived in Berne, Ind. My uncle Toby passed away seven years ago from cancer. Lovina remarried to Abe about three years ago. I wished that the time hadn't been too short to visit Lovina's daughters (my cousins) Elizabeth and Lovina and their families and Lovina's son Amos and family, who all live close by her.

Thursday was the funeral in the Sugarcreek area on the place where Joe's grandmother grew up. The funeral was largely attended. We saw a lot of Joe's family, uncles, aunts, cousins. I also saw my brother Amos and sister-in-law Nancy there. Joe's grandmother would also have been Nancy's grandmother. I also met a lot of Holmes County readers of this column. It seemed like a very friendly community

APRIL 2006

On April 30, we had communion services, which are held twice a year. Our communion services start at 9 a.m. and end at 3:30 p.m, which is three or four hours longer than a usual Sunday. It makes for a long day for the children. A lunch is always served during the services. A few rows of people leave the room at a time to eat until everyone has been fed. They served chicken noodle soup yesterday, homemade bread, bologna, pickles, pickled beets, peanut butter spread, jellies, cookie, coffee and tea. The tea was made fresh from the garden. The children are really beginning to like the tea, which is healthy for them.

We are still enjoying dandelion greens. The flowers are popping up fast. Once the flower blooms, the greens taste too bitter to eat.

Even though Easter is over, the children colored 130 eggs on Saturday, which was a good way to use up these hard-boiled eggs. We diced them into the dandelion greens. Then I made a sour cream dressing and poured it over them. The dressing is made with a salad dressing, vinegar, salt and milk. Others also add a little sugar, but I don't. We also like eating hard-boiled eggs with horseradish.

Asparagus should be popping up by now. I was very disappointed when we arrived home from Ohio to discover our basement had been dug and my rhubarb winter onions, tea and asparagus were covered up with dirt.

We were going to have the man doing the excavating dig all this up with his scoop on his Bobcat. With us being gone, he forgot all about it. He dug up some of the asparagus roots and we replanted in hopes they'll take off.

MAY 2006

Our new house is coming right along. The basement is done, and plans are to start framing this week. It is rainy outside and doesn't look like they will be able to work on it. We had a light rain all day yesterday.

That should really boost up the gardens, though, for those who have a garden out already. I am still waiting until we have a space worked up. We plan to make a small garden where the old corn crib building was. We tore it down this spring. Once we have its foundation leveled and cleared away, Joe will be able to till the area. Right now, the ground is too wet.

We have planned a "frolic" for Saturday. Don't know how many people will show up, as we gave everyone short notice, but we hope to get a lot done on the house then.

(Editor's note: "Frolic" is a term the Amish use to describe any all-volunteer gathering for the purpose of completing a task. The term is used most commonly for barn-raisings, but also for other events, such as, in this case, helping construct a house).

Our community was shocked to hear of the tragic news of the death of 16-year-old Ada Eicher. She was in an accident and killed instantly. She was on her way home with her sister and her sister's special friend. Ada's sister has a broken pelvis and lots of scratches and bruises. Her sister's friend is in critical condition at the hospital and isn't in very good shape the last we heard. Our hearts go out to the grieving parents and her family.

I cannot imagine the pain of receiving such terrible news of one of your dear children killed. But God is in control, and He never makes a mistake. Once again, we are reminded of how "undetermined" our stay here on Earth is. May we always serve Him as though it would be our last day.

On a brighter note, we received a wedding invitation from Joe's nephew, Clarence, from the Berne, Ind., area. Clarence and Marie have picked May 12 for their special day. I am to be one of the cooks that day.

My almost 12-year-old daughter, Elizabeth, sure has been excited with the books and all the nice letters and recipes you readers sent her after she wrote a recent column. May God bless you richly for taking the time to send them to her. I am not sure if I mentioned it yet, but she did win a book in the March reading contest that her school sponsored. Also, a thank you for the encouragement to me.

Baby Kevin is 8 months old now. He has pushed through two teeth in the last week. His top teeth are also trying to push through, so he is fussy.

I am going to make these bars with the rhubarb a friend brought me. My rhubarb plants were ruined by the recent digging for our house construction. (Editor's note: Hothouse rhubarb stalks are now in supermarket produce departments.)

RHUBARB DREAM BARS
Pat-in crust:
1-1/2 cups all-purpose flour
2/3 cup powdered sugar
3/4 cup regular stick margarine (or part butter)

Filling:
3 eggs, beaten to blend
2 cups sugar
1/2 cup additional flour
1/2 teaspoon salt
3 cups rhubarb, the stems chopped into small pieces
Yield: 15-18 bars

Mix the first three ingredients, the flour, powdered sugar and margarine like a pie crust, that is stir together the flour and sugar; cut in the margarine with a wire pastry blender to form small crumbs. No liquid should be necessary because this is a very rich mixture, high in fat. Have oven heating to 350 degrees.

Press the crumbly mixture over the bottom and partway up the sides of a 9x13-inch baking pan. Bake 15 minutes at 350. Meanwhile, in a large mixing bowl, whisk together the eggs, sugar, additional flour and salt. Stir in the chopped rhubarb. Pour onto the hot, partially baked crust. Return pan to oven and continue baking at 350 degrees for 35 minutes. Cool on a wire rack and then cut into bars.

MAY 2006

As I write this, my sister Susan will celebrate her 30th birthday tomorrow. To mark the occasion, Susan invited us and some others over to her house on Sunday. She served a homemade pizza and ice cream dinner. In addition to having a good meal, it was also a beautiful day, so the adults did some bicycling and the children were taking pony rides.

My husband Joe gave me a new tri-bike for my upcoming birthday. I didn't expect a gift with the expense building our new house is taking. We grew up in a community where the Amish didn't allow bikes. The Amish here in Michigan do allow them. At almost 35 years old and after having eight children, I am scared to try a two-wheel bike. I'm afraid I might fall and break a bone. What Joe got me, though, has two wheels in the back and one in front. It really is a smooth riding bike. We have had lots of fun biking together as a family. It's so relaxing to go for a bike ride after a hard day's work. A person doesn't notice the rolling land until you bike.

On Saturday, we had our frolic (Editor's Note: "Frolic" is a term the Amish use to describe a gathering of volunteers that meet to complete a task, often a barn-raising, in this case, the Eicher's house) Most of the second floor has now been framed. Also, the 20-by-20-foot added on utility room was framed in.

Now the rafters should be going up this week and maybe the windows. The crew hasn't been here yet this week but they plan to come tomorrow and the rest of the week.

Sister Emma brought us some rhubarb and winter onions, so I need to use the rhubarb up. And lo and behold, asparagus is now popping up here and there on the dirt piles around the house. We thought they had been buried by the construction work. So I might still have asparagus. I fixed a meal of fresh asparagus, creamed and added bacon pieces and cheese. Joe likes it served that way. Try it!

ASPARAGUS WITH BACON-CHEESE SAUCE
1 to 1/2 pounds fresh asparagus, cooked and drained
2 tablespoons butter
2 tablespoons flour
1 cup milk
1/4 teaspoon salt
1 cup shredded American or mild Cheddar cheese
4 to 6 slices crisp cooked bacon

Melt butter in saucepan; stir in flour until smooth and bubbly. Gradually add milk. Cook, stirring constantly, until thickened. Add salt and cheese; stir until cheese is melted. Pour sauce over hot drained asparagus, then sprinkle with crumbled bacon. Serve hot. Serves 4-6 people.

MAY 2006

It is so good to see the sun shining once again after having rainy and dreary weather the last week. Yesterday we had only a few sprinkles, but I managed to get most of my laundry dry. I have a basketful that needs to be hung out to finish drying.

Joe and I and our two oldest children, Elizabeth and Susan, went to the wedding of my nephew Clarence and Marie's wedding. Lovina and Kevin were sick, so we left our six youngest with my sisters Verena and Susan.

It rained most of the day, so I was glad I didn't take Lovina and Kevin to the wedding. We started out about 5 a.m. on Friday morning and we arrived back home around 11:45 p.m. We stayed at Verena and Susan's for the night since the children were all asleep by the time we got there to pick them up.

It was still rainy on Saturday and Sunday. I stayed home from church with Lovina and Kevin so that they could continue to recover. They seem better now, with only a small cold.

But as soon as they began feeling better, I began to feel worse. I think I caught a touch of the flu. I feel a lot better today though. Since I was not feeling well last night, Joe and the girls made supper for us all. It's just harder when mother gets sick. Hopefully, no one else in the family will. We went to bed at 8:45 p.m, which is earlier than usual for us. The children asked why we were going to bed when it was still daylight. But I think we all needed a good night's rest.

Once the ground dries up I need to get out into the garden and the grass needs mowed again. Busy, busy springtime!

Our new house is ready for shingles and siding. The windows and doors should be here by next week. The decking is also being put on. Everything takes time and money — nothing is cheap anymore,

Tomorrow will be Lovina's second birthday. I want to make a cake for her. I'll never forget how sick I was when she was born. Do I thank God enough for good health? It's so easy to take our good health for granted until we don't have it anymore.

I will also soon have my 35th birthday. Time has such a way of slipping by too fast. At this time of year we are once again reminded of Dad's passing six years ago. We still treasure the precious memories we have of him in our hearts. I know if he'd be living he'd be here helping us all he could on our new house. He put a lot of labor in helping his children as did Mother.

Precious memories and how they linger. Our daily wish is to all be reunited in that great Kingdom in heaven. How beautiful heaven must be!

I'll share a rhubarb recipe since the rhubarb is growing fast.

RHUBARB BREAD PUDDING
2 cups diced fresh rhubarb
3 /4 cup sugar
1 tablespoon grated lemon rind
11 /2 tablespoons lemon juice
1 cup bread crumbs
1 cup milk
1 egg, beaten

Mix all together and put into a buttered casserole. Dot with butter. Bake covered for 1 hour at 375. Serves 6.

JUNE 2006

This is the first day of June already. The children only have 2 1/2 days of this school term left. It will be a relief to have them home with me. Yesterday, Benjamin's class went to the zoo. Then, tomorrow, Loretta's class will go. Benjamin really enjoyed his day, and I'm sure Loretta will, too. The trip was a real treat after the kids worked hard all year at school.

Our new house is having the siding put on today. We also have someone lined up to do the chimney. Everything takes time and money. Getting the house built has been stressful, but it'll be worth it once the work is done, and we are enjoying "the fruits of our labor."

On Saturday, my husband Joe and my brother-in-law Jacob put 31 windows into our new house. Installing the windows took them only five hours, which I thought was pretty good, especially on such a hot day. The house sure looks nice with the windows set now.

Next week, we will have a septic system installed. After that, we can start getting our yard leveled back out. I hope we'll get some grass planted soon.

My garden is up and growing, except my cabbage plants, which aren't in yet. I also am going to plant a few more hot pepper plants and radishes. Then, later on, I'll put in some endive and winter radishes. Everything is growing "good."

It's been a very nice spring for growing garden goodies. The corn is coming up real nice. We've also had a few good rains, so that saved us from watering the garden. For a few days, though, our temperatures were in the 90s. Elizabeth and I mowed the grass, but it was a hot job.

After a long weekend of work on the house, Joe and Jacob went fishing on Memorial Day. They were out at the lake by 6:30 a.m. They spent most of the morning and early afternoon fishing. They caught a lot of fish, a lot of nice bluegill. By the time they left the lake around 1:30 or 2 p.m., they had a 5-gallon bucket full of fish.

When they went up to our friend's house to start cleaning fish, they saw smoke coming out of the house. Someone called the fire department, which arrived quickly. Only two rooms were burned, but there was a lot of smoke damage. They had just had their house painted. I sure felt sorry for them.

Joe and Jacob left their fish sitting in the bucket while they ran to check on the fire. By the time they got back to the bucket the fish had been sitting in the hot sun for awhile, so they didn't think we should eat the fish. So it was disappointing to not have fish to eat, but Joe said it was still fun and relaxing just to be out on the lake.

Baby Kevin will be 9 months old tomorrow. His two top teeth are showing through his gums. He's an active little boy. He's trying to crawl, but just kind of scoots instead.

Tonight, we want to attend the kindergarten graduation at the school. Last night, we went to the school for the academic-honors recognition and dessert banquet. My daughter Elizabeth won the language-arts award for her grade. Joe thinks he should be home working on the house instead of going to school, but it is good for him to take a break once in awhile.

Try this recipe to use some of the garden goodies that will be coming up over the weeks ahead:

SIMPLE SUMMER SALAD
2 cups fresh green peas, uncooked
2 green bell peppers, chopped
2 carrots, slivered
2 young cucumbers, thinly sliced
1/2 cup minced fresh parsley
2 tablespoons olive oil
1 tablespoon fresh lemon juice
Lettuce leaves

Place the peas, green pepper, carrots, cucumbers, and parsley in a bowl. Toss well with the olive oil and lemon juice until the vegetables are well-coated. Serve on lettuce leaves.

JUNE 2006

We are having rain off and on today, which makes it difficult to hang the wash out on the lines. So in between the showers, the clothes have been drying. I don't like to have clothes that are almost dry get wet again. I should've maybe waited to wash the clothes until tomorrow.

With the storms and all the rain we had last night I thought it might be nicer outside today, but it's still showery. The children and I picked up my sisters Verena and Susan yesterday morning and then headed over to sister Emma's house to help clean. Emma's will be holding church services at their house in the near future. We cleaned out closets and washed walls, ceilings, and windows in several bedrooms. Closets are time-consuming to clean.

Around 4:30 p.m. we decided to start home, but saw that a storm was brewing in the northwest. We waited at Emma's awhile longer and the storm seemed to just blow over so we started for home. But we were wrong. Almost halfway home it started getting very windy and large chunks of hail started hitting our buggy. We put our lights on and I could hardly see where we were going. The horse struggled to keep going. Rain pelted the buggy and we just all tried to remain calm and hoped our steady horse would get us home. The children were scared. How thankful we were for having a covered buggy, but it was still scary to realize what could happen. We sure were relieved once we arrived home. My husband Joe had been worried that we might be in the storm and opened the pole barn door for us to pull into. When we arrived home several branches were off our trees and my corn was flattened. It is starting to stand up again today. The rest of the garden also looks battered up some.

Sunday we were surprised to see Joe's Dad and his uncle Solomon from Sugarcreek, Ohio drive in to visit. We made them stay and have dinner with us.

Solomon stayed a couple of days and him and Joe's Dad came here each day to hang siding on our new house. We sure appreciated their help. There is a little more siding still to do, but that that will be a big job to have completed and over with. The boys sure enjoyed being outside with grandpa and Uncle Solomon.

Our blocks came for our chimney on Saturday. Joe, Elizabeth, and I carried some to every level in the house. What a tiring job! Our porch railing should come this week. I'll be relieved once the railing is on. The children like to play on the porch and I am always afraid they'll fall off. Our porch goes out over our walk-out basement so it's a little higher. We ate quite a few meals out there on the new porch already. It is so nice and breezy under there. I can't wait until we can get a porch swing to hang up.

JULY 2006

We are really enjoying having my husband, Joe, home from the factory this week. It's nice not to have a schedule and not worry about getting up quite so early. Although it hasn't been too relaxing of a vacation for him, with all the work that needs to be done on our new house. Joe is outside working on the house now. There is a little section under the deck going over the walk-out basement that needs siding still.

Tomorrow and Saturday, a few men will come help Joe hook up our gas lines into the new house. (Editor's note: Some Amish churches allow gas-lights, others do not. The church district where Lovina lives in Michigan allows gas lights). Our lights will be piped in. That will be so easy not have to fill lanterns, plus they will have self-igniters on them. When we lived in Berne, Ind., we just had the kerosene lamps. Our next step with the house is to start insulating.

Yesterday, Joe and our two boys, Joseph and Benjamin, hauled quite a few loads of manure. It sure makes it a lot easier with the new manure spreader. Manure makes the best fertilizer. Joe said little Joseph sure tries to get manure into the spreader even if he doesn't quite get it in. Benjamin does pretty well with it. He sure is excited about turning seven soon.

Joe and Jacob plan to go fishing Friday night in Jacob's rowboat. That will at least be one relaxing activity for him on his vacation. Hopefully, he can relax more next year when we should be enjoying our new house.

Meanwhile, I am trying to get some mending done. I cut out and sewed me a new dress and hope to get another one sewn soon. A lady from our community gave me a box of clothes her children had outgrown. It sure helped me out for her children. I really appreciated her thoughtfulness.

My sisters Verena and Susan are on an eight-day trip to the Smokey Mountains with a group of Amish from here. Sounds like they are enjoying their trip. Yesterday I went over to their garden and picked green beans, peas, and cucumbers. We brought their horse over here to take care of while they are gone.

Earlier this week, Jacob, Emma, and family and our family enjoyed a day at the park. The children enjoyed the swings, slides, merry-go-rounds, etc. We also spent some time with our friends that had the recent house fire. They are still not back in their house.

Brother Amos and Nancy's second oldest daughter is getting married this month. So we'll probably be attending their wedding in Indiana in a couple of weeks. A reader in Harmony, Minn., requested a recipe to use homegrown green beans. Try this one:

DELICIOUS GREEN BEANS
6 bacon slices
1 small onion, sliced
3 teaspoons cornstarch
1/2 teaspoon salt
1/2 teaspoon dry mustard
homegrown green beans or the equivalent: 2 cans (141/2 ounce size) green beans — drained; half the liquid reserved
2 tablespoons brown sugar
2 tablespoons white vinegar

Fry bacon until quite crisp; crumble. Reserve 11/2 tablespoons of bacon drippings. Add the onion to remaining drippings in pan and saute until lightly browned. Stir in cornstarch, salt and mustard. Stir in reserved green bean liquid and bring to a boil. Stir constantly. Blend in brown sugar and vinegar; add drained green beans and heat through. At serving time, garnish with crumbled bacon.

JULY 2006

My husband, Joe, is back to work after having a 10-day vacation. Time went too fast! We are now once again getting up around 3 a.m. on his work days.

The last three nights, Joe has been helping Jacob build a wall between their tool shed and barn, so that has kept him busy. Church services are set to be at Jacob's for Sunday in a week. Next week, we'll be back helping Jacob and attending the wedding on Friday, July 21, at my brother Amos's and wife Nancy Jean's. The wedding is for their daughter Elizabeth and her groom, Paul Graber.

Our garden is doing real good. My corn is tasseling, and we've picked our first tomatoes and green peppers. My second batch of radishes is ready, and cucumbers are really starting in. It is so easy to make a meal with fresh garden goodies. Looks like green beans are going to be a good crop. We have been having nice rains so that we don't have to water the garden too often.

I went to an Amish garage sale early this morning. Had some luck finding some clothes. What a help it is not to have to sew all the clothes. Prices of material are so high, and it is a real bargain to get a sewed outfit for cheap.

Tomorrow, July 14th, is Benjamin's 7th birthday. He sure has looked forward to that.

On Saturday, July 15, Joe and I will be married 13 years. Daughter Verena, age 8, remarked when she heard about our anniversary: "Mom, I wish I could have been at your wedding. It would have been fun to see you and Dad get married." I thought that was cute: such innocent children!

Joe and Jacob took our Benjamin and Jacob Jr. along fishing in the rowboat out on the lake one night last week. The boys were really excited to pull in their first fish. And it is good to have sisters Verena and Susan home. They enjoyed their trip to the Smoky Mountains. It would be a great trip to take, but not with as many little ones as we have.

The Coblentz reunion was in Berne, Ind., on July 1. We couldn't go with all the work on our house here, but I heard our Uncle Melvin was there. It was probably hard for him to go alone since our Aunt Esther passed away.

The girls are helping weed the garden now, which makes a difference. Loretta wanted to help, but she didn't last long since she started pulling the "good weeds" (the vegetables). I imagine she thought it would be faster just to start pulling everything up. I hope to get more weeding done and also get the grass mowed. It is a hot, muggy day.

JULY 2006

The girls and I have been busy weeding the garden and picking vegetables during this hot week in July. Yesterday we processed 44 quarts of pickles, from dill to banana, sweet to bread and butter. I like to make a variety of pickles. The pickles will come in handy when church services will be held here the future, as people seem to like homemade pickles.

Today we picked green beans, which will need to be canned soon. We also are enjoying sweet corn, tomatoes, green and hot peppers, and all those other garden goodies. Even 11-month-old Kevin likes chewing corn on the cob.

On Friday, we attended the wedding of Elizabeth and Paul Graber in Indiana. We arrived home shortly after midnight. While there we saw my family and Joe's sister Ruth and family. We also visited with uncles, aunts and cousins that we have hardly seen since our move. It was a long day, and the children slept on the way home. Once we arrived home, it took a while to carry all the sleeping little ones in and to remove five car seats and booster seats. By the time we had everyone in bed it was 1:45 a.m.

Sunday morning church services were at Jacob and Emma's house. Joe and I biked and the children took our pony, Stormy, and the wagon. They had services and lunch in their tool shed.

I imagine Emma is relieved because she was busy sewing and cleaning for church services all last week. Monday and Tuesday Jacob was laid up with a pinched nerve. He had quite a bit of back pain, but now he has returned to work. He went to a chiropractor for X-rays. I hope he continues to recover.

Monday I went to town to get groceries. I needed vinegar and sugar for the pickles. The highway into town is getting repaved, and our horse didn't get spooked by all the construction trucks. It pays to have a horse that is safe in town and also one that readily stands by it when you wait on a red light.

I'm always relieved once I get off the busy highway. Seems like the four lane roads here in Michigan are easier for cars to get around a buggy than a two-lane, which I was used to in Indiana.

We are almost ready for our mechanical inspection on our new house. We had to move the water heater, which was a job. Since we burn a solid fuel for our heat — hard coal — we could not vent it through the chimney according to Michigan building code.

Monday night a man from our church helped Joe construct a vent so the smoke will go up through the roof. Joe needs to do some fireproof caulking around the gas line and then hopefully it will pass inspection. Until then we are at a standstill on the new house.

AUGUST 2006

It is hay-making time again. Last night, we put 243 bales of second-cutting hay up in our haymow. It was a very hot day with the temperature still more than 100 degrees at 9 p.m. It sure was hot up in the haymow. We don't have an elevator so it helped to have two guys throwing the bales up in the haymow while us girls stacked it. My husband, Joe, was out in the field stacking the bales on the wagon. Everyone washed up to cool off before we ate supper. We made a haystack supper and sweet corn.

The temperature this forenoon is already 90, but with a better breeze than yesterday. Rain would be welcome, which might help to cool things off.

We finished our first patch of sweet corn, which was "early sunglow." We really liked that kind. Now my next patch of "Seneca sweet corn" is ready. I also have a patch of 95-day corn called "tender treat" out for later use. I've never tried this variety so we'll find out if we like it. I like to try different varieties to see which we like better. So far we haven't had a problem with raccoons getting the corn. We have two rat terriers that help keep them away. The dogs have caught quite a few moles for us in the garden and yard. Our female rat terrier is going to have her first litter of puppies, so the children are really excited. We've had her for two years now.

I have hot peppers, pickles, green beans and red beets that should be put up this week yet. We pulled the stalks from the first batch of corn and fed them to the horse. Now we have a few spaces that should be tilled. My tomatoes are really starting in, so once I get enough, I'd like to make salsa. We have watermelon out so hopefully that will make it before the growing season is over with.

School doesn't start until Sept. 5 this year. That will be after Labor Day, so the children have another month at home yet. I will really miss their help once they go back to school. We need to mow some more today. We mowed some yesterday. Elizabeth and I took turns so that we wouldn't overheat. I overheated once when I was younger and it still bothers me to work in the hot sun too long.

AUGUST 2006

We continue through the "dog days" of August. Hopefully cooler weather will soon come.

On Monday, my school-age children planned to go canoeing down the river that runs behind the school. This was a school-sponsored event for students that wanted to go. I decided to take the children, but we didn't get very far. We had just turned out of our driveway and on to the road when a buggy brace snapped by the shaft. This left the one end loose from the buggy. I was just ready to urge the horse into a run when I happened to see the shaft coming loose. I tried to get the horse stopped and then jumped off the buggy.

Our horse, Itty Bit, was shook up as I imagine she knew something wasn't right. I helped her while the children all got off the buggy. Elizabeth and I unhitched her from the buggy and Elizabeth led her to the barn while the other children and I pulled the buggy off the road. It wasn't too easy pulling the buggy with only one side attached. We were all shook up to think what could've happened had we been going down a hill or out on a busy road. If that had happened on a hill, that could make a horse start kicking and also to have the buggy ramming into their back. My husband, Joe, will take our buggy to the buggy shop to have it fixed. He's also going to have brakes put on right away. That will help — if something like that happens again we will be able to brake the buggy.

On Friday, the school is taking any student who wants to go to the zoo. Ours are going, and I am going as a chaperone. I asked if I could bring 4-year-old Joseph along, and they said "yes." My youngest, Lovina and Kevin, will stay at my sister's that day. Joseph is so excited to get to ride in a school bus and go to the zoo. Every day he asks me if he can still go and asks if he can wear his new pants and shirt. Sister Emma and her children are going along also. That makes Joseph more excited to have Emma's 4-year-old, Benjamin, along. The two cousins get along so well.

Joseph is such a neat little boy. He won't wear a shirt if a button is missing. He doesn't like it if his pants have a hole in them either. I guess that way I get my mending done sooner. Seven-year-old Benjamin is exactly the opposite. He doesn't care what I give him to wear. It's surprising how siblings can be so different.

Two-year-old Lovina is going through a stage where she repeats everything she hears. Joseph gets so annoyed when she always repeats what he says and does. Now Lovina is starting to complain about her dress when Joseph does about his shirt.

I managed to process 14 pints of salsa yesterday. I also did 12 quarts of pickles and 10 pints of jalapeño peppers this week.

Try this recipe for a good, easy lasagna.

LAZY DAY LASAGNA
12 ounces of cottage cheese
1 quart spaghetti sauce
1 teaspoon parsley flakes
9 uncooked lasagna noodles
2 cups mozzarella
1/2 teaspoon dry basil leaves

1 pound ground beef, fried and seasoned

Mix cottage cheese with sauce and spices. Layer sauce, ground beef, and uncooked lasagna noodles in 9-by-13-inch pan. Add 1/2 cup water around edges of pan. Seal tightly with foil. Bake at 350 for 45 minutes. Uncover and add 2 cups mozzarella on top and bake15 minutes longer.

AUGUST 2006

We have been having beautiful weather this week. The cooler evenings and mornings makes sleeping a lot better and also makes canning vegetables not such a hot chore.

We canned our red beets and 10 quarts of bread and butter pickles. This makes a total of 66 quarts of pickles of different varieties that we have canned. I think we have enough now. I picked quite a few more from our garden this week, but gave them to my sister Emma.

We did 14 pints of homemade thick and chunky salsa also. I hope to make pizza sauce yet, but have enough tomato juice and V-8 from last year. I also have enough green beans from last year, but could use more corn. I still have some corn left from last year, but we don't like it as much as what we have this year. We are now eating from our last patch of sweet corn. We like this new variety called "tender treat." It has really big cobs. I also have some pretty nice size watermelon coming along.

My husband, Joe, and I recently went with a vanload from this community to Bryant, Ind., which is a little farther south from Berne. We went to the viewing of my great-aunt Lovina Neuenschwander — age 87. I will always remember her as having a smile for everyone. She was a sister to my grandmother Graber (my mother's mother) who died at age 92. I was named after my aunt Lovina, and she was named after my great-aunt Lovina. If I'm not mistaken, my great-aunt Lovina also was named after her aunt Lovina. The name has been passed down for generations.

Friday evening and Saturday we and Jacob's family were at sisters Verena and Susan's. Joe and Jacob did some minor remodeling in their kitchen and also installed some new kitchen cabinets. They need to lay the new flooring yet.

The children really enjoyed their trip to the zoo last Friday. Little Joseph fell asleep on the way home. Emma's son Benjamin and my Joseph really thought it was neat to ride the school bus. They also enjoyed riding the train and the tram at the zoo.

Joe took our buggy to the buggy shop to get it fixed. Now it's ready to use again, plus he also had brakes put on it. When Joe gets home, we plan to go to town to get groceries and some things Joe needs for the new house. He's been coming home earlier this week. It's good that it's a cooler day, which makes it easier for the horse to travel.

SEPTEMBER 2006

This week we did some more canning with the plentiful garden vegetables. We canned more red beets and 24 more pints of homemade salsa. We now have 38 pints of salsa, which should last us a while. I have had extra garden vegetables to share with friends and neighbors. I sure am thankful for such a good yield. We didn't have to water the garden more than a few times this year. It seemed the rains were timed just right. I also think we picked a good spot for a garden. The soil is sandy and it drains really well.

We will probably have our framing inspection done tomorrow on our new house. We will also get our insulation in the coming days. If the framing inspection passes, we should be able to start insulating by Saturday. What a relief it will be once we get that final inspection.

Today, my sisters Verena and Susan came over to help sweep and clean up all the messes in the new house. We burned the scrap wood and other debris, which was a good way to get rid of it. I know my husband Joe will be glad to have everything organized before we start insulating.

Tonight we all are invited to Loretta's teacher's house for a picnic supper in their backyard. This will be a great way for Loretta and her classmates to meet one another before the school year begins. The children still have next week here at home, and then they will start another school term. It sure will seem quiet with five less children around. I sure will miss the girls' help. Joseph, 4, and Lovina, 2, will seem lost until they get used to having them gone through the day. Baby Kevin will be a year old already next week. He will miss his babysitters once they are off to school. It makes me wonder if he will attempt to walk sooner when there's not always someone around to pick him up. He does walk by holding onto furniture or with help, but not alone yet.

On Tuesday, sister Verena had her 40th birthday. She sure doesn't seem 40 already. I guess she's young at heart. We were there for a pizza and ice cream supper. My oldest sibling sister, Leah, turned 47 on Aug. 15.

We had thunderstorms throughout the night, which brought a few of the children to our bed. We have a few that do not take well to thunderstorms. We had a half inch of rain during the night, which we were in need of.

I read another batch of letters and cards from readers from various states. I appreciate the kind words, and I am sorry if I don't get to answer all of them. Some day I hope to have a few extra moments to do that. Thank you and God bless you all.

Try this delicious casserole for a hungry family.

PIZZA NOODLE BAKE
1 pound hamburger
4 ounces of noodles
1 cup water
1/4 teaspoon garlic powder
4 slices mozzarella cheese
1/2 cup chopped onion
15 ounces of tomato sauce, homemade or store bought
1 teaspoon salt
1/2 teaspoon oregano

Brown hamburger and onions. Combine uncooked noodles, hamburger and onion in casserole. Mix all liquids and spices and pour over noodle and meat mixture. Bake at 350 for one hour. Top with cheese during the last 10 minutes

SEPTEMBER 2006

It is a nice sunny morning, a pleasant change from the rainy days this week. This week did, however, bring our first hint of winter. One morning this week the mercury dipped down into the mid-30s and it looks like Mr. Jack Frost nipped a few things in the garden. We don't have the coal stove going yet, but this is a sign that colder days are just ahead.

The first floor in our new house is all drywalled except the back entrance room. My husband, Joe, is working on the drywall in the evenings and is almost done with the second coat. Once the final coat is on and sanding done I'd like to get started painting. It looks like I'll have to wait to paint the upstairs bedrooms until next spring. We still hope to move in once the first floor is painted and the floors are down. Joe can work on the upstairs and put trim on this winter when he'll have more time. Everything takes time.

Jacob, Emma and family, and sisters Verena and Susan have been here most Saturdays this summer. I imagine they will be about as relieved as we will be once we get moved in. We sure appreciate their willing help.

Tonight, Uncle Jake and Mary Coblentz from Wisconsin will be at sisters Verena and Susan's for supper. Brother Albert and sister Emma and Jacob and their families and our family also will go. They haven't seen where we live in Michigan.

I want to put up some more jalapeño peppers today. We picked a lot of things in the garden last night in case it would frost. Among the goodies we picked were 16 watermelons. We had a few already, but I wanted to send some home with Albert's and Jacob's tonight as we won't be able to eat them all.

Baby Kevin had a bad cold earlier this week but is a lot better this morning. He's pushing teeth and is fussier than usual. He weighs 24 pounds already.

Sept. 17 once again arrived, taking our minds back four long and lonely years when dear Mother took her final breath. We loved her and miss her. Shortly after she died my sisters found this verse in her diary:

Somewhere there is no sunset
Somewhere it's always dawn
Somewhere no clouds obscure the blue,
Somewhere there is no parting,
Or sorrow, tears, or pain,
And there your loved one waits the day when you will meet again!

May God bless her and grant her that wish!

OCTOBER 2006

Foremost on our minds is the Pennsylvania Amish community that experienced the tragic school shooting. Our hearts ache for the parents and families of these children. As with everything, God had a purpose for this. We know He makes no mistakes so we must trust Him to lead the way. We question "why" sometimes, and we don't always see His purpose right away. But let us keep praying and follow His great words in our Holy Bible. This community needs our prayers to find the strength to go on. May God be with them as they go through this awful trial. My "mother heart" cannot grasp the feeling if my child would've been involved. It makes me want to never let them out of sight. God promised to never give us more than we can handle if we keep our trust in Him.
(Editor's note: Two funds, including one for the wife and three children of the gunman, have been established by a bank in Paradise, Pa., where many Amish do business. Coatesville Savings Bank has established the Nickel Mines Children's Fund and the Roberts Family Fund. The bank can be contacted at (717) 886-8800.)

Our sympathy also goes to the family of Joe's Uncle Menno, age 70, who passed away Saturday. He battled that dreadful cancer for six weeks. He was often in pain and may he rest in peace now. Joe and 4-year-old Joseph and I went to the funeral on Tuesday, which was in Berne, Ind. Sisters Verena and Susan also went along. Jacob and Emma kept our other seven children until we were home. Emma had her hands full sending eight children off to school before 7 a.m. Joseph felt pretty special having all of Dad and Mom's attention for the day.

While in Berne, we visited Levi and Liz and brother Amos and Nancy at the funeral. We also visited Dad and Mom's graves, as it was in the same cemetery as Uncle Menno was buried. We then drove past the old homeplace. It brought back memories, but a lot has changed. There are two more sets of buildings on the farm now. Life goes on and changes are made. Home is where the heart is. May we all meet again in that Heavenly home where there will be no more sorrow, pain or partings.
After leaving the funeral we made a quick stop at Joe's sister Ruth and Chris. From there we went to sister Leah and Paul's. Paul fixed a part on our harness that Joe brought along. Leah and niece Elizabeth quickly made a good supper so we could eat before starting home. They have their own little cider press to make their own cider. They have a lot of different kinds of apple trees, so the cider had a good, fresh taste. We arrived back here in Michigan around 9 p.m. and picked up the children at Jacob's. By the time we got back home and had every one settled for bed it was past 10 p.m. It was nice to be back home and all together again.

A reader in Canon City, Colo., asked about a bread pie. Try this:

WET BREAD PIE
8-inch baked pie shell
1 cup crumbled bread (moistened in water)
1 cup granulated sugar
3 eggs, separated
juice of 1 large lemon
2 tbs butter
3 tbs sugar

On top of double boiler mix wet bread, sugar, egg yolks, lemon juice and butter. Cook until thick, stirring occasionally. Pour into baked crust. Top with meringue made with the egg whites and 3 tablespoons sugar. Bake in 350-degree oven for 15-20 minutes, until browned.

OCTOBER 2006

It is evident that autumn has officially arrived with trees gradually losing their leaves. It was windy yesterday, helping blow some of the leaves away. We mowed the grass, which got away from us with all the recent rain. I wonder how many times we still have to mow before we are done for the winter? We sure had some bumpy places to mow with all the construction equipment that has pulled through the yard this year to build our new house.

It is still early as I write this, 4 a.m., and my husband Joe has left for work. I know I have to get this letter out in today's mail. The days have a way of slipping by, and I realized this morning that today is Thursday, the deadline for me to get this column in the mail. I put it in our roadside mailbox.

We are once again in a routine of having the children come home with homework, so we are settling into our "school-year routine." Evenings seem so short with the children doing their homework, getting supper, doing chores, taking baths, brushing teeth and then getting settled down for bed earlier than in the summer. A good way to make the younger ones sleepy is to read to them once they are in bed. I enjoy doing that.

The children's school had an open house and supper one night this week to welcome in the new school year. Our children were disappointed that we were not able to go. It's just been so busy around here in the evenings, with working on the new house. It would be nice if we could get moved in this fall yet. That is our hope. Joe continues to work on the drywall. Some places are now ready to start sanding.

Later today, my brother-in-law Jacob and sister Emma and their 4-year-old Benjamin will come here to help with our new house once again. Jacob has a few days off work this week, so Joe is grateful for his assistance. My 4-year-old Joseph is so excited to have his cousin Benjamin coming today. Those two never get tired of each other.

On Saturday, Jacob took our Joseph and 2-year-old Lovina home with them for the night. They sure were tickled to be able to go. It is a treat for them to spend the night at their aunts' and uncles' houses. We then went there Sunday evening for a good fried chicken dinner and to bring the children back home.

When Joe comes home this afternoon, Jacob and he plan to hang more drywall upstairs. There's not too much more to go, and then we can put insulation into the attic. It will be easier to keep heat in once we have the insulation.
I neglected some exciting news around this homestead. Our rat terrier Frisco had four little puppies recently, although she lost one. Joe came home from work in time to save the other three. This was her first litter. She is a good mother and very protective of her young ones.

With this being apple season, I've had readers asking for apple recipes. Try this delicious one for apple brownies.

AMISH APPLE BROWNIES
1 cup butter, softened (2 sticks)
1-3/4 cup sugar
2 eggs, well beaten
1 teaspoon vanilla
2 cup all-purpose flour
1 teaspoon baking power
1 teaspoon baking soda
1 teaspoon cinnamon
1/2 teaspoon salt
2 cups cooking apples (most any besides Red Delicious), peeled and chopped
1/2 cup chopped pecans or walnuts
Yield: At least a dozen brownies

In a large mixing bowl, beat together the softened butter, sugar, eggs and vanilla until smooth. Combine dry ingredients in another bowl or large measure and stir into the butter mixture. Mix until flour is just moistened. Fold in the chopped apples and nuts. (There is no chocolate content.)

Spread in a greased 9 x 9-inch baking pan and bake in preheated 350-degree oven 45 minutes or until done. Do not overbake and dry out the brownies. They should still be rather moist in the middle, when tested with a toothpick. Best served warm with a drizzle of vanilla glaze using 1/2 cup powdered sugar, 1 tablespoon hot water and 1/4 teaspoon vanilla.

OCTOBER 2006

On Oct. 12, we awoke to our first snow. The children were out of bed pretty quickly when they noticed the snow swirling outside. This was a very early snow. My garden had not even experienced a killing frost yet, but I imagine it's now history for this year. So, instead of gardening, I'm planning to do laundry if it quits snowing. The sun was out a while this morning, so I'm hoping maybe the snow will quit and I can make it out to the laundry lines.

Meanwhile, the snow didn't stop sister Emma from running some errands into town. She left her Benjamin here while she went to town. So Joseph and Benjamin are outside playing. They said they're going to make a snowman, but I doubt they'll get too far. There is only a thin layer of snow. Looks like maybe our leaves will get covered, but it isn't sticking to too much else.

We haven't started our coal stove yet, but we probably will now with the arrival of this wintery weather. Our hard coal was delivered on Saturday so the timing was good. Joe still needs to check the chimney before we use it. We always like to clean it out before we start the stove in the fall — we always want to prevent chimney fires. In our new house, we plan to heat the house from a coal stove in the basement. That will be nice to have the coal and ashes mess down there away from everything. My husband, Joe, is now only working four days a week, so he has extra time to work on the house. We are still hoping to be moved in before the real winter weather arrives.

On Sunday, we took the buggy for a 12-mile ride to visit Joe's dad. We took a dinner along with us. This visit was in honor of his 68th birthday, which was on Oct. 9. He is losing a lot of weight. Joe's dad is battling skin cancer and is also diabetic. He has a lot of pain. Joe's sister Carol, her husband, Pete, and their family also were there and brought some food. We started home around 4 p.m. It was a very beautiful fall day to go for a long ride, past the turning trees and apple orchards.

Apple pies, apple crisps and apple dumplings are finding their way onto our table. Our children all like apples, which is great, because they are such a healthy snack. We've also been enjoying fresh apple cider. A family in our church has an apple farm. They told us to bring containers and fill them with fresh cider. We sure were glad for it. Popcorn and cider tastes good together as a snack in the evening.

Well, now I'm not sure if I want to do laundry today after all. It's really blowing snow again. Brrrrr.
I must go get the children a snack. Kevin is begging to be held. It's almost naptime for him. He is taking a few steps once in awhile. He has plenty of teachers but he still thinks crawling is faster for now.

Nothing tastes better this time of year than a homemade apple pie with fresh apples. Try this favorite of ours:

FRENCH APPLE PIE
3/4 cup sugar
1 tsp cinnamon
6-7 cups sliced apples
1/2 cup butter or margarine
1/2 cup brown sugar
1 cup flour

Mix sugar and cinnamon with apples and put into an unbaked 9-inch pie shell. Make a topping of butter or margarine, brown sugar, flour and sprinkle over pie. Bake 15 minutes at 425 degrees and then 30-35 minutes at 350 degrees.

OCTOBER 2006

It is another rainy, dreary day here in Michigan. Seems we've had our share of those lately, but that is typical of autumn. Yesterday, however, was nice, and it was the only day we didn't have rain this week. I took advantage of the opportunity to do a lot of laundry, which piles up quickly in a few days around this household of eight children. I still have clothes that are finishing drying beside the stove. We have our coal stove going now, as the weather gets colder. In our new house, I'll have wash lines in the basement to hang clothes on during the winter months. With the stove being down there, the clothes will dry faster.

We have the coal stove hooked up in our new house already. We have a big register on the first floor, which is right above the stove in the basement. So the warm air from the stove will rise from the basement and heat the whole house. Then, alongside the outside walls we have smaller registers for the cold-air return. This helps the heat circulate better. We have the stove going, and the system is really heating well. We need to finish insulating the attic yet, which will help keep the heat in.

The children enjoy playing over in the new basement. With it being heated, it makes it nice for them to play over there. Joseph and Lovina like to ride their tricycles in there. We'll also hold church services in our basement.
My husband, Joe, has tomorrow off from work again. It sounds like work will slow down even more next month. Work seems to be slow at a lot of places around here. It's going to be a struggle, but God doesn't give us more than we can handle. He will see us through if we put our whole trust in "Him." Why worry when we can pray?

Joe wants to finish up with the drywall this weekend. The heat will help dry up the mudding faster. On these cold, damp days, it didn't want to dry without heat. Joe hasn't been able to work in the house much the last couple of weeks. There are just too many other chores to complete before the long winter arrives.

We have our garden cleared out now. Joe tilled it on Monday evening before it rained. We picked the rest of the peppers and the last of the green tomatoes. I'll wrap the green tomatoes in newspaper and put them in the basement. This keeps them from turning red as quickly and makes for a better-tasting tomato.

We also picked the seeds from the marigold and zinnia flowers, which takes time, but will come in handy again next year. The garden for 2006 is now history.

Some of our top soil has been spread, but it has rained, so now it has to dry off. Leaves are everywhere and need to be raked. With so many trees, it's hard to keep up.

This morning, I read some more letters from you readers. Thanks so much for the encouragement. May God bless you all! With this still being apple season, try this delicious recipe.

APPLE PIE CAKE
1/2 cup margarine
3/4 cup sugar
1 egg, slightly beaten
1 cup flour
1 teaspoon baking powder
1 teaspoon ground cinnamon
1/2 teaspoon salt
1/2 teaspoon ground nutmeg (less if grating it fresh)
1/2 teaspoon ground cloves
1/8 teaspoon vanilla
2 cups peeled, chopped apples
Yield: 8 servings

Thoroughly grease a 9-inch pie pan by preheating the oven to 350 degrees with the margarine in the pie pan. When melted, swirl around the pan and pour into a large mixing bowl. Blend in the sugar and egg. Mix in flour, baking powder, cinnamon, salt, nutmeg, cloves, vanilla and chopped apples. Spread into the greased pie pan. Bake at 350 degrees for 40 to 45 minutes. Best served warm or at room temperature.

NOVEMBER 2006

We entered the month of November today, and with it celebrated the 34th birthday of my brother-in-law Jacob (sister Emma's husband). We will wait to go over to their house to celebrate his birthday supper until Thursday night, since Joe and Jacob don't have to work on Friday. Also the children don't have school on Friday because of a teacher workshop, so it'll work better to go when everyone doesn't have to get up so early the next day.

For Jacob's birthday, Emma prepared a delicious dinner of mashed potatoes and gravy, grilled pork chops, corn, peas and salad. Then Emma surprised him with an ice cream cake, complete with candles. Sisters Susan and Verena joined us. Since it was so cold outside, the children mainly played in their basement. As always, the cousins have a great time playing together.

Before leaving for Jacob's, I went after some rhubarb at the home of one of the families from our church. They dug some rhubarb roots for us and we went to pick up them up. Then we planted about eight starts of rhubarb on Thursday night before we left for Jacob's. It was cold work on the hands planting the rhubarb.

It was really cold that night on the 15- to 20-minute ride to and from Jacob's. Even with the covered buggy, it felt cold. We had snow flurries swirling, and the wind was really cold. In the covered buggy, at least we can all just wear one coat. In the uncovered buggies that we had back in Indiana, we'd have to wear several coats, a shawl and maybe had the umbrellas open to hold off the wind. We'd have to dress a lot warmer. The wind moves the buggy box more back and forth when it is windy, but it beats an open buggy.

Today, I cut out a hunter-green dress, cape and apron for me. I hope to get started sewing on it tomorrow. First I need to go to town, though. I'm out of so many baking supplies. I want to make cookies, but I don't even have enough flour.

On Friday someone will come look about hooking up our water to the new house. We need to dig a new water line from the well to the pole building, then from there to the house. Joe and the boys have been working in the pole building at night, trying to make room for the water pump. The corner he wants it in is where his work bench is now. He's moving his work bench to the other side now. He wants to build a wall to separate the pump room from the rest. We had such a beautiful fall day on Sunday and Monday with temperatures going up into the lower 70s. I took advantage of the weather and did extra laundry: coats, quilts, mattress pads, blankets, etc. Everything dried in one day.

With the warmer weather we had earlier in the week, we had to let the coal stove go out. Now with the temperature in the upper 20s, Joe started it again. It felt cozy since the house had really cooled off.

My baby Kevin will be 14 months old tomorrow. He had strep throat. He sure was a sick little boy, but is back to being ornery again. I am thankful that none of the other children had strep throat. Kevin loves to climb. He'll crawl on a step stool and onto a chair or a bed. It's scary to see that they don't see the danger of falling. He loves to clean out my cabinets and unroll rolls of toilet tissue. I usually keep the bathroom door shut, but when one of the children forgets to close it, he's the first to notice. I am just so glad he's better though. Kevin stands alone for awhile and has taken a few steps, but other than that, he'd much rather crawl. I had a few children that didn't walk until they were 14 or 15 months.

Try this delicious, easy pie for the holiday season:

MARSHMALLOW PIE
½ c. milk
¼ c. butter
1 10-oz. package mini marshmallows
1 c. whipped topping
Chopped chocolate pieces or chocolate syrup
1 graham cracker pie crust

Melt marshmallows in pan over low heat with milk and butter. Let cool, then mix in whipped topping. Spoon into pie crust and top with chocolate pieces or syrup to your taste. Let cool until set. Pie is a no-bake pie.

NOVEMBER 2006

This column is a little shorter than usual maybe, because it was an unexpectedly rough week. We had baby Kevin in the hospital over the weekend. He had a respiratory infection and something like an asthma attack. He started sounded raspy and he cried when he coughed. This continued for awhile, so I called the doctor. The doctor heard how fast he was breathing and told us to take him to the emergency room at the local hospital. At first they tested him for RSV, but the test came back negative, which was a relief. So he must have just been congested. Poor little boy had his share of sicknesses this last while. After we brought him home we had to give him mist treatments every six hours. Now I can only do it twice a day. He is feeling much better now.

Joe and I stayed at the hospital all night with Kevin, while sisters Verena and Susan kept our seven other children at their house. Joe came home early Sunday morning to take the children home since Verena, Susan, Jacob, Emma and the children had plans to attend church services in an Amish community about one and a half hours from here. The services were held at the home of one of Susan's friends. Verena and Susan had a breakfast casserole ready for Joe and the children to take home for breakfast.

About lunch time my Uncle and Aunt Joe and Betty Coblentz from Indiana came to our house for a visit on Sunday. Joe made them and our children a light lunch of sandwiches. Joe and Betty then came to the hospital to visit with me. While they were there the doctor came and dismissed Kevin. Joe and Betty brought us home from the hospital. We had to wait on a prescription and arrived home around 4:30 p.m. It was a long, tiring weekend. It was so good to be home again. Uncle Joe and Betty are now headed for home after a short visit with Verena and Susan. They arrived home shortly before we did.

Since it was such a long day, we all went to bed earlier than usual. We hardly had any sleep at the hospital as Kevin had to have care every so often. I am so thankful to be back home again.

On a happier note, our biggest thrill lately was to see Kevin taking his first steps and walking short distances. I think he enjoys the attention when everyone in the family oohs and ahhs when he stands up.

Now it is a very beautiful day after a few rainy days and it has warmed up into the 60s. Last night Jacob and Emma brought us supper which was nice after the stressful weekend. They brought us spaghetti and meatballs, fresh homemade applesauce and just-baked banana bread. It was such a treat to not have to cook supper. It seems I got behind with my work while Kevin was sick. It could have been worse and I'm thankful for good health and to just be able to take care of our dear children.

Speaking of banana bread earlier, try this delicious recipe:

BANANA BREAD
1 ¾ cups all-purpose flour
2/3 c. sugar
2 t. baking powder
1/2 t. salt
2 c. mashed ripe bananas
1/3 c. butter
2 T. milk
2 eggs
1/4 t. nutmeg (or more to taste)
1/4 t. cinnamon (or more to taste)

Combine 1 c. of the flour, the sugar, baking powder, salt, nutmeg, and cinnamon. Add mashed bananas, butter, and milk. Beat with mixer in low to blend, then high for 2 min. Add eggs and remaining flour, stir til blended. Pour batter into greased 8x4x2" loaf pan. Bake in 350°F oven for 55-60 min. or til toothpick inserted in center comes out clean.

NOVEMBER 2006

Tomorrow morning, Joe and I will travel with some others from this community to Berne, Ind., where I grew up and lived with my husband until we moved to Michigan. In Indiana, we will attend the funeral for Joe's 41-year-old cousin. What a shock it was to the family and everyone. Her husband awoke the next morning to see his wife had passed away in bed during the night. We didn't hear yet what happened or all the details, although they suspect an aneurysm could be the cause. Our sympathy goes to her husband and four children and also to the extended family. One of her sons is getting married next week. Once again, our Dear Lord has shown us that we never know when our stay here on earth is up. Joe's cousin was only three years older than my husband. It makes us stop to think about how we should appreciate every day our Heavenly Father gives us together. So often we take life for granted, but the most important part is to be ready to meet our Dear Savior when our time comes.

Along with the sad news, we also received some exciting news. Joe and I are now a great-aunt and great-uncle for the first time. My niece Elizabeth and husband Amos were blessed with a baby girl named Sarah. This puts brother Albert and Sarah Irene on the grandparents' list. Congratulations. And we look forward to seeing our great-niece. We recently had a chance to travel to Kansas and Missouri with my editor Kevin Williams and his friend, Rachel. Also, our eight children and my sisters Verena and Susan were along with us. It was great to meet some of the readers of this column in Kansas. I want to thank you for all your kind words of encouragement. May God Bless you dearly.

Our highlight on the trip was to go up to the top of the Gateway Arch in St. Louis on the way back home. Four-year-old Joseph thought the whole surrounding city looked like a toy set, and he even asked if he could play with the "little cars and trucks" that he saw when we looked down from the top. It sounded so cute. I had to explain that they were all real, that the cars and trucks just looked smaller from so far.

Another thing that meant a lot to me was to pass through the town in Missouri (Blue Springs) where my dear mother passed away. It gave me a peaceful feeling to finally see where she was when she died. Kevin was a very good and safe driver, and I think he did very well to put up with having eight children along. (Kevin says these eight children were amazingly well-behaved.) Rachel was also helpful to have along.

My husband, Joe, is now off from work for two weeks, due to fewer jobs to do. Meanwhile, he's finding plenty to do here at home -- with construction continuing on our new house. The insulation for the attic will come tomorrow. On Saturday, several men will come to help blow it into the attic. That will really help heat the house better.
Tonight, we plan to go to Verena and Susan's for supper. After supper, we will leave our eight children there overnight, as we have to leave at 4:30 a.m. for the funeral. Jacob and Emma will take their four children to Verena and Susan's, also, so they will have a total of 12 children for the night. Eight of them will have to be ready for school by 7 a.m. Susan and Verena will have their hands full. I do appreciate all that they do.

DECEMBER 2006

We are almost all done painting our new house. Jacob, Emma, Verena and Susan assisted us in getting it all painted. I still need to give one bathroom and the staircase walls another coat today. We gave the walls and ceilings a total of four coats of white paint. It takes a lot of time when you do a 32-by-56-foot house. I won't do the upstairs bedrooms until next spring, though. Painting is not my favorite thing to do, but it has to be done. Next week, the floors will be completed downstairs.

We had some bad news when we had someone come dig up our old well. They found everything all rusted out, so we will have to get a new well dug after all. Now we are waiting for that to be done. It will be a relief to know that we have our water taken care of for the new house. My husband, Joe, is home from work sick today. He is very congested and has a bad cough. He was running a fever through the night. I hope he'll get better soon.

On Saturday, my sister Leah, Paul and family came out to Michigan to bring sister Susan's horse that she is buying from their son, Ben. Paul's family, my sisters Susan and Verena, and Jacob and Emma and their family were all here for lunch and supper. I did laundry in the forenoon before they came. That wind was so cold that I didn't hang everything outside. I put some on the clotheslines in the basement in the new house. That way, I could just let them hang until Monday.

On Saturday night, while everyone was here, Jacob and Emma's 10-year-old daughter Elizabeth fell. She hit her head on the edge of a doorjamb. She ended up having five stitches put in right by her eyebrow. Luckily, her eye is OK.

On Tuesday night, we attended the Christmas program at school for our children -- Verena, Benjamin and Loretta . It was so cute to see them sing Christmas songs.

This past Saturday, Dec. 16, we had the Christmas gathering for my family. Next weekend is Joe's family. On Saturday, we all gathered at Albert and Sarah Irene's house by 10 a.m. We ate around 12:30 p.m. Everyone brought a dish, and it was a big feast of barbecued chicken, mashed potatoes, gravy, salad, corn puddings, and other foods. Dessert consisted of three kinds of pies, plus cakes and cookies.

In the afternoon, we sat around tables and sang songs and had snacks (deer sausage, cheese, vegetables, etc). Every year we sing the New Year's Song in German. This song is not sung by the Amish in this part of Michigan, but the tradition was passed down through our family. I'm not sure how far back the New Year's Song goes. Everyone was at Albert's except for Leah's son, Ben, who traveled with a vanload to Wisconsin to visit his girlfriend's family.

Everyone left for home by 4 p.m. The year after Mom died we did not have a Christmas gathering. But the next year, in 2004, Leah had it. Then, in 2005, it was Amos' turn, and this year it was Albert's. Next year, it will be at Liz's, and then Joe and I will take our turn in 2008. In 2009, it will be at Emma and Jacob's. Susan and Verena will take their turn together in 2010.

Meanwhile, some readers have requested a Christmas cookie recipe. This dough calls for molasses and lots of spices. It's ideal for shaping with cookie cutters, but don't substitute corn syrup for molasses or the cookies will bake up too hard.

CHRISTMAS COOKIES
1/2 cup butter, at room temperature
1 cup brown sugar, firmly packed
1 cup light molasses
1 egg, beaten to blend
4 cups all-purpose flour
1/4 teaspoon salt
1 teaspoon baking soda
1 teaspoon cinnamon
1 teaspoon ground cloves
1/2 teaspoon ground nutmeg

Preheat oven to 350 degrees. Grease cookie sheets with shortening. Beat together the butter and brown sugar. Blend in molasses and eggs. Sift dry ingredients together (the flour, salt, baking soda, cinnamon, cloves and nutmeg), and stir into molasses-egg mixture. Roll out dough on lightly floured board and cut into shapes with cookie cutters. Bake for 10 to 12 minutes

2007

Life goes on for the Eichers in Michigan. No new family additions, but the children keep getting older, with 12-year-old Elizabeth leading the way.

In the rest of the US, the housing market began its nosedive and the nation fell into recession by the end of the year. And on the normally tranquil campus of Virginia Tech, the worst campus shooting in US history killed 33 people.

JANUARY 2007

It is hard to believe that we have entered the year 2007. We hope everyone enjoyed the holidays. For us it was a time of celebration, but also of missing our loved ones that have gone on before us to that great unknown. Our holidays would be even more fun with them, but God knows best.

We ended up spending Christmas Day at my sisters' house. The day was just spent together, enjoying each other's company, relaxing and observing the birth of our savior, Jesus Christ. We played various games, but shuffleboard was our favorite. It was a new game for Joe and me, but we enjoyed it very much.

On New Year's Eve, Jacob, Emma and their four children, plus sisters Verena and Susan spent the evening and stayed all night. We had some supper and then played games until midnight. After 2007 arrived, the children had fun listening to the fireworks going off from the nearby town. Jacob and Emma's two boys and our Benjamin and Joseph fell asleep around 11 p.m. I had made them a bed on the living room floor so they could go to sleep in case they got too tired before midnight.

Around 5:30 a.m., the boys woke up and were having fun playing "hide and seek" in the dark. We finally managed to get them to sleep a few more hours. The children are always excited to be together all night, but with 12 children (Emma and Jacob's and ours combined), there's never a moment of peace.

As the New Year dawns, we wonder what 2007 has a in store for us. It's so good we can't look into the future. If we could, would we be able to go on? I'm reflecting on the year ahead extra, as Susan recently gave us a book about the November 2005 tornado that ripped through the heart of an Amish community in Daviess County, Ind. Reading the stories and seeing the pictures shows us what a high power our dear God has. (For more information about this book, please go to amishcookonline.com) We showed our children the book and they have been so shocked at how much damage a tornado can do. The tornado went 13 miles without ever lifting. How hard it would be to see our earthly possessions scattered and lost. The most precious thing was that no one was killed. Someday our earthly material belongings will have no value, but to lose everything would still be hard.

An Amish family had a new house almost ready to move into when the tornado hit. The house was damaged and had to be fixed up again. I cannot image that happening when so much goes into getting one built. But God makes no mistakes; remember that as we progress into 2007.

Today our cabinets in our new home are being installed. How exciting! It is hard for me to concentrate because it is just so hard to believe we are getting closer and closer to having our new home ready to move into.
Joe is helping the Amish man that built our cabinets install them. Earlier Joe helped me get some laundry done. It sure gives me a lift to have his help and to see those new cabinets. I think the new cabinets are the most exciting thing since we started building the house. I am anxious to fill them. They are nice solid oak. I usually had older cabinets in my houses.

Meanwhile, I baked three loaves of sourdough bread this morning. Joe's sister, MaryAnn, gave me a starter that needs to be "fed" every three to five days. MaryAnn got the starter when she lived in Holmes County, Ohio six years ago. I am wondering if any of you readers would have a recipe for starter to share?

I appreciate all of the nice Christmas cards and words of encouragement and wish everyone a blessed and happy new year!

Several readers have written over the past few months asking for a repeat of the recipe that is sometimes served after church services — an easy, sweet peanut butter spread. Some eat it on sandwiches, others just on a slice of homemade bread.

AMISH PEANUT BUTTER SPREAD
1/2 c. creamy peanut butter
1/4 c. marshmallow crème
1 c. light corn syrup

In a mixing bowl, stir all the ingredients together until combined. Place in a covered container. Store in cool place or a refrigerator overnight. Remove and bring to room temperature to serve as a bread spread or ice cream topper. Amounts of each ingredient can be adjusted to suit your taste.

This is an account of our day, just a regular day around here, on Jan. 18:

3:15 a.m. Time to get up. I pack my husband Joe's lunch (usually a sandwich and snack) while he gets ready for work. Another short night! Joe isn't hungry for breakfast since it's still early. Usually he waits to eat until his first break at the factory.

3:45 a.m. Joe leaves for work and I go back to bed to get a little more sleep.

5:30 a.m. I get up and wash up for the day. I then wake up the school-age children to get them ready for school.

6:30 a.m. Everyone eats a breakfast of scrambled eggs, cheese, toast, milk and juice. All the children are up and awake now. Four-year-old Joseph thinks he should be all dressed before the bus comes even though he doesn't go to school yet. (Editor's note: Many Amish children attend public schools. Those who do will often ride a bus to school. Often their only way of finding out about a "public school snow day" is when the bus doesn't come by.)

7 a.m. Elizabeth, Susan, Verena, Benjamin and Loretta leave for school. Joseph, Lovina and Kevin finish up their breakfast. I sit down and eat a little something myself. After a rushed morning it is nice to sit down awhile and relax before starting another day's work. Sixteen-and-a-half-month old Kevin is getting better at eating by himself. He usually ends up holding the spoon and using his hands to eat.

7:45 a.m. I go out and do the barn chores. Then add coal to both stoves, the one at the new house and the one here. It's a cold morning at 18 degrees, after a late start, winter has finally arrived. Our trees are still loaded with ice. A lot of branches and trees are down from the recent ice storm we had. The trees have been sparkling in the sun, like crystal. It is such a beautiful scene created by our master artist.

8:15 a.m. I start washing dishes. Dishes accumulate in a hurry in this household!

9:45 a.m. I'm finally done with dishes and ready to sweep the floors. Kevin likes to put everything in his mouth so it makes me keep my floors swept.

10:45 a.m. I gather laundry and start washing clothes. I hang some clothes on the rack by the stove and the rest in the basement of the new house.

Noon. I'm not quite done with the laundry, but stop and get the children some lunch. While they eat, I hang the rest of the laundry.

1 p.m. I rock Kevin and get him sleeping. Then I rock 2-year-old Lovina, but decide to give up after she doesn't seem to want a nap. I even caught a little nap myself while rocking them.

2 p.m. I empty a few drawers and move the contents over to the new house.

3:20 p.m. Everyone is back home again. The children do their homework. Then we change the bed sheets and clean up here and there. Jacob, Emma and their children are coming for supper and for the night. Also sisters Verena and Susan. Tomorrow we will cut up 1,100 pounds of beef. Jacob's family will take half and we will take half. We have a full day's work tomorrow. Jacob doesn't have to work and that'll help.

5:30 p.m. We start supper. We'll have creamed potatoes, macaroni and cheese, peppers and steak. Should be a good meal to conclude our day.

9:30 p.m. We finally get the school-age children to go to sleep. After getting the younger ones to bed, we all go to sleep. It's been a long day and another one is in store for tomorrow. Good night and God's blessings.

Try this recipe for a good start.

COFFEE-FLAVORED COFFEECAKE
2 c. flour
2 c. sugar
3/4 c. cocoa
2 t. baking soda
1 T. baking powder
2 eggs, beaten
1 c. milk

1 c. hot coffee, strong or weak as you prefer

Mix all ingredients except hot coffee. Add hot coffee and beat slowly. Mixture will be thin. Pour into greased nine-by-nine-inch square pan. Bake at 350° degrees for 30 to 35 minutes.

JANUARY 2007

This is another busy day as we continue to put the finishing touches on our new home. But before beginning work, I wanted to write this column and make a few loaves of bread. Right now I have sourdough bread rising. We really like this bread a lot. Whenever the children see me mixing the bread dough before going to school they ask if I will have it baked by the time they get home. They love to spread butter on it while it is still warm. I almost like best the sourdough bread better than just homemade white bread, which was always a favorite of our family.

I also just completed letting the horses out and a few other morning chores. Joe leaves for work these days around 3:45 a.m. At that hour, he has to light a lantern to do the chores. It is so much easier to do them when its daylight, so sometimes I tell him to just let me do the chores after sunrise. Makes for not quite as rushy of a morning for him.
I also go over every morning to the new house and put more coal in the stove. Joe was off work for two weeks over the holidays, so he took care of both stoves (the one in this house and the one in our new house) which really helped me out. (Editor's note, the new house is being built on the same land as their current house, only about a 150-foot walk away)

The fire in the stove in the new house had died down quite a bit and really needed some coaxing to get it to take off again. I have been enjoying going over there and getting my kitchen in order. The cabinets are now installed in the kitchen and the bathrooms, which really makes a difference in how it looks and feels over there. I have been moving a lot of dishes over already and both my cupboards here are empty now. Sisters Verena and Susan and my daughters helped rewash all the dishes before taking them over there. These are my nicer dishes that I hardly use so they tend to get dusty. I am so happy to have the extra space to store these dishes.

Tomorrow, Friday, Joe will be home as he is only working four days for now. We plan to hang the drywall in the back entrance area and get that completed. We also plan to finish the upstairs, but we ran out of drywall so we have to wait and order more.

Jacob and Emma came to help us on Friday. That is when we got the cupboards moved over. We really appreciate their help.

On Sunday, we took a break from the work and went over to Jacob's for a noon dinner. We got all of the children settled into the buggy for the ride over. It was raining on the way. For our meal we had mashed potatoes and gravy, homemade dressing, meatloaf, and corn. We also enjoyed homemade bread, cake, and ice cream. After the meal, us women and girls just visited while Joe and Jacob and the boys played games. It was a relaxing way to spend the day. On the way back home, around 5:30 p.m., it was dark and the rain had started to change to sleet. This morning it is really icy.

Baby Kevin was breathing hard again this past week, but he is feeling a lot better now. The doctors told us to give him another mist treatment. If he keeps getting attacks like this he might have a touch of asthma. I hope not, but he takes the treatments well. He grabs the mask and holds it over his face. Kevin's energy hasn't been affected, he runs around the new house and tries to crawl up the stairway.

With it now feeling like winter, here's a good, hearty chili soup which goes good on days like these:

HOMEMADE CHILI SOUP
1-1/2 lb. sausage
2 medium onions
3 cups tomato juice
1 can kidney beans
1 Tablespoon chili powder
1/4 to 1/2 cup brown sugar
Salt to taste
2 to 3 tablespoons flour
Spaghetti

Brown sausage and onion in a deep pot. Add remaining ingredients, except spaghetti, stir well, and bring to a boil. Add some spaghetti to the soup. Cook until spaghetti is done, about 5 to 10 minutes over medium-high heat.

FEBRUARY 2007

The first of February has arrived and today we plan to move into our new house! The children are all so excited! On Saturday, Jacob, sister Emma and family, and sisters Verena and Susan helped us move most of our furniture, clothes, dishes, and other household belongings over. We still have two beds, a sofa, some chairs, and our stove left to move over. These are all big, heavy items. Verena and Susan and Jacob's plan to come help us move the rest in today. Some of the children have been sleeping in sleeping bags at the new house. But tonight we'll all be in our beds over there. So exciting!

I have a bad cold now. I think I am a little drained from the move and the walking back and forth between houses and this cold isn't helping. This past Monday, we finally got our final inspection and passed it, which was a relief. It has been a long 9 1/2 months but whenever I go over to the new house I think it'll be worth all the headaches.
Joe left to go to work around 30 minutes ago. So I decided with everything going on today I better stay up and get this written. I doubt that I'll be able to concentrate later on. The children are all so excited about sleeping in their new bedrooms tonight.

Seven-month-old Kevin loves when we turn him loose in the new house. He'll run around and try to see everything at once. We have to make sure we close all the bathroom doors and put a gate over the stairway. I've caught him running on top of the table a few times. He's full of energy and 2-year-old Lovina seems to enjoy helping him get into trouble. She never really got into my things like Kevin does. I think she's trying to get attention. Even though they are two years apart, they are almost the same height, as Lovina is very petite. They almost look like they could be twins. Such sweet little angels. What will life be like when they grow up? It helps to know God has His protecting hand over us.

Jacob's came over one night last week and hung our interior doors before the inspection. That is his job at work. It didn't take him long to have the doors hung.

We are finally having real winter weather. Quite a bit of snow and cold single digit temperatures. Hopefully this cold will put a stop to all the flu and colds going around.

Our thoughts and prayers are also with Joe's 93-year-old grandmother. She had surgery yesterday as she fell and shattered her upper thigh bone. Doctors don't have hopes that she'll be able to walk again. This will be hard on her as she was still active.

Try this good cookie, a cross between snickerdoodle and sugar cookie.

SUGARDOODLES
1 cup butter, softened
1 cup vegetable oil
1 cup white sugar
1 cup confectioners sugar
2 eggs
1 /2 teaspoon vanilla extract
4 1 /2 cups all-purpose flour
1 teaspoon baking soda
3 /4 cream of tartar

Preheat the oven to 375 degrees. Grease cookie sheets. In a large bowl, mix together the butter, oil, white sugar and confectioners' sugar until smooth. Beat in the eggs one at a time, then stir in the vanilla. Combine the flour, baking soda, and cream of tartar. Stir into the sugar mixture until just combined. Drop dough by teaspoonfuls onto the prepared cookie sheets. Bake for 8 to 10 minutes, or until bottoms are lightly browned. Remove from baking sheets to cool on wire racks

MARCH 2007

It has been three weeks now since we have moved into our new house. What a relief it was to finally be able to move in.

I didn't write this column for several weeks thanks to my editor and my daughter Elizabeth. Time has sped by so fast and we are gradually getting more and more adjusted. We'll continue to make small improvements and finishing touches to the new house as time goes by. For instance, Joe still wants to build a separate room in the basement for my canning jars. Since we heat from the basement, we need an insulated separate room so the home-canned food stays cool. We still didn't move all the canned food over from the old basement.

We have had some below-zero temperatures since we moved into the new house. We are learning how to adjust our coal stove to heat more when it's that cold. We had a few chilly mornings, but it really helped when we use our propane lights.

Church services will be conducted here next month on two separate Sundays, as we skipped our turn last summer. So, along with getting settled, we will start preparing for the services.

Four of our children have had the flu this week, so it was a bit hectic around here. But everyone is back to good health again, except Kevin. He was still feeling sick today. Following the doctor's advice, he has been making improvements, though. Tonight he acts back to normal, which means getting into mischief. He likes checking out my new cabinets. And, of course, we still need to keep our bathroom doors closed. We have an open stairway, so we use a gate to keep Kevin from climbing up. The minute he discovers the gate open, he climbs those stairs pretty fast. Kevin's OK going up, but I still don't trust him coming down.

With the weather warming up again into the 40s, the children have been busy making snowmen from the snow still left on the ground. This morning it was really foggy, so the school was on a delay. I'm hoping Joe and his driver make it to work OK traveling the long distance to work.

Joe and the boys are starting to work nights, cleaning manure out of the horse stalls here at home. Without gardening and mowing, it'll make a few less chores while preparing for church services. So, in some ways, it's easier to have them during winter - although, with the snow melting and the ground softening, we are having our share of mud. That is when I appreciate my new back entrance area. It's nice to leave their boots out there. Four-year-old Joseph came crying to me one day because he caught 7-year-old Benjamin walking across our new floor with his boots on. This was before we had moved in. I thought it was cute that he was so concerned about the new floors.

It is now 9:30 p.m. and everyone has gone to bed. So, I will sign off and call it a day, too. Good night and God's blessings to all.

MARCH 2007

It is 4 a.m. and Joe left for work a few minutes ago. It is very windy outside. Our thermometer shows 35 degrees. It is still dark, but I can hear tiny bits of ice clicking against the windows. I heard we are in for another ice storm. Only God can control the weather.

It is already March 1 and we have been in our new house for a month. I am still not organized. I probably won't be until the closets are all done. I also still need to sew new curtains for some of the windows. I'm just using the ones from the old house now. I would like to buy material and make new curtains for every window. Right now, though, I won't as material is so expensive and it'll take quite a few yards for 34 windows. Some of the curtains I'm using are still from our house in Indiana so they have had quite a bit of use.

I managed to get a little mending done this week. I'm so behind on that again. It seems that by the time I get laundry, cleaning and the daily work complete it's ready to start over on it.

I had my 12-year-old daughter Elizabeth's eyes checked this past week. She has been having headaches and has trouble seeing the chalkboard at school. She does need glasses and has to wear them all the time. I was around her age when I started wearing mine.

Strange weather. The temperature is still around 35, but it is thundering and lightning toward the east and still very windy. Nine-year-old Verena and 6-year-old Loretta came downstairs as they couldn't sleep because of the thunder and lightning. I told them just to go lay down in our bed and now it looks like they are dozing off to sleep again. They share a bed and awoke at the same time.

Saturday morning, Joe got up before the rest of us to tend to the stove. He decided to change a few mantles on our lights as they had a hole in them. It makes a little bit of smoke when you burn through the mantle (a cloth/mesh covering to the gas lights). It made enough to start the smoke alarm beeping. I think that was the quickest everyone has been out of bed. Some of the children were very scared and came running down the stairs yelling "Fire! fire!" At least now we know that they all know what to do in case of a real fire, although I hope we never have to experience that, but you never know. Only God knows the future.

Try this popular recipe which makes for a good late winter supper.
POOR MAN'S STEAK

1 ½ lbs. lean hamburger
1 can (10 ¾ oz.) cream of mushroom soup
1 small can drained mushrooms
1 t. salt
Pepper
¼ t. garlic powder
1 c. bread crumbs, dry
2 eggs
1 small onion, chopped

Mix together all of the above ingredients, except soup and mushrooms.
In large skillet, fry all meat together in some oil, keeping pieces intact. Drain on paper towels. Grease a square baking dish, form meat mixture into baking dish. Cut into nine pieces. Mix mushroom soup with 1/2 can water and 1/2 can milk or evaporated milk. Pour soup over meat in baking dish. Add drained mushrooms, spread around. Bake, uncovered, in 350-degree oven for 30-40 minutes. Makes 6 servings.

MARCH 2007

We are getting a lot of rain on this 60-degree morning, which should help thaw the ground from the cold winter. I am glad it wasn't like this on Sunday morning, as it would have made for a muddy mess around our new home when we held church services here. Sunday, the ground was still frozen, but we laid down cardboard on the bare ground, in case it warmed up during the day.

We had quite a bit of action on Sunday morning before church. Around 6 a.m., Joe decided to turn out our horses to the pasture field. We use the barnyard to park our church guests' buggies. Just as Joe turned out the horses, he thought of the one gate in the barnyard that was left open when they hauled manure the day before. It was too late. The horses had taken off out the drive already. It was pitch dark and hard to see where they went.

Finally, we heard them by our neighbor's woods. Joe walked back there and chased them home. We thought we had them all in when our pony, Stormy, decided to turn around and take off again. We finally caught the pony and hurried to get ready before the first people arrived for church. Joe was still bathing when the first buggy pulled in before 9 a.m. It was so much harder to put horses in while it was so dark outside.

Church services began at 9 a.m. We had everyone down in our 32-by-56-foot basement. It was a lot nicer than walking back and forth to our pole building -- like we had to do before our new house was finished.

After the services, we served lunch to everyone. Our menu consisted of homemade wheat and white sourdough bread, bologna, cheese, zucchini relish, Amish peanut butter spread, both sweet and dill pickles, red beets, jelly, butter, coffee, pepper and spearmint tears, pumpkin cookies, chocolate chip and sugar cookies. My sisters Emma, Susan and Verena really pitched in to help with everything, which was much appreciated. After all the dishes were washed and put away, popcorn was served to everyone. It was a pleasant day of worship and fellowship.

Fortunately, almost everyone in the house was healthy by the time services started. The week before we had our share of flu hit this household. Elizabeth is still home today from school. I had the flu Friday and Saturday, which made it rough preparing for church. I think we've all had it except Joe, and I hope it misses him. This week, six of our children had it. I spent that week tending the sick, doing laundry and mopping the floors to get the house ready for church services.

Last night, it was 70 outside, so Joe made supper on the grill. That gave me a break, and supper always tastes so much better when someone else cooks!

Spring has arrived, and we are all ready to see it come. It makes me hungry just to think about the fresh dandelions coming out soon, plus the rhubarb, winter onions, and all those early things from the garden. (Dandelion greens are a spring-tonic salad in many Amish households; they're served with a tangy sour cream dressing and chopped hard-cooked eggs for the Eichers' menus.)

I'll share my recipe for the Pumpkin Cookies. We served them after church this past Sunday. We love them with frosting on top.

PUMPKIN COOKIES
1 cup shortening or margarine
2 cups granulated white sugar

2 cups fresh pumpkin puree (or canned)
2 teaspoons baking soda
2 teaspoons baking powder
2 teaspoons cinnamon
4 cups all-purpose flour
Yield: About 4 dozen cookies

In a large mixing bowl, beat together the shortening, pumpkin and sugar. Stir together in a another bowl the baking soda, baking powder, cinnamon and flour. Add a half-teaspoon of salt, if desired. Stir together well and then add to the shortening/sugar mixture and blend to make a stiff cookie dough. Drop onto lightly greased baking sheets, spaced apart. Bake at 350 degrees (preheated oven) for 8 to 10 minutes.

APRIL 2007

The children are washing the breakfast dishes and sweeping the floors while I write this letter and ready it for today's mail. I almost neglected the column with the week seeming to go by extra-fast because the children were on spring break from school. So with five more children at home, there hasn't been much quiet time to concentrate and write. I had hoped to get the yard raked, but Michigan weather isn't permitting it. Right now, it is really blowing snow, and we have a thin layer of snow on the ground. The temperature was 25 degrees this morning. Is it April or January? My husband, Joe, started up our coal stove again last night. We hadn't used it for about two weeks. I had also washed, folded and put away the children's extra coats and snow pants, as I was thinking spring was here to stay. Obviously, I was wrong.

We had been enjoying dandelion greens that last week before winter decided to return. Now, with the snow, it would be hard to go out and pick some. We like tender, young dandelion greens fixed in a salad with hard-boiled eggs and a "sour cream" dressing made of mayonnaise, vinegar, salt and milk.

I don't make my dressing as sour as Mom did; I add less vinegar to the milk. The children seem to eat it better that way. Although some of the children do not care for dandelion greens, now I think they will come to like them. I remember not liking them until I was a little older, but now I love them.

Along with the dandelion salad, we like steamed potatoes and bacon. Horseradish is also a favorite at this time of year. I am still waiting for Joe's Uncle Soloman's homemade horseradish recipe from Holmes County, Ohio, that I would like to share with you readers when I get it. We like to eat horseradish with our hard-boiled eggs that the children color for Easter.

The children want to color eggs today, as Sunday is Easter. We want to do laundry, mop floors, and then I'll let them color around eight dozen eggs this evening.

Tomorrow, Joe will be home from work, as we don't work on Good Friday in this community (most Amish don't in other communities either). We use Good Friday as a day to honor our Lord Jesus for all the holy suffering he did as he was slain on the holy cross. We always honor "Him" at Easter, and always. Good Friday will be a nice family day to rest and read the Bible together. So often, our lives get too busy, so it's nice to have a day like this together. Our turn at hosting church services in our home is over with; we took two turns in a row on recent Sundays. There is a lot of work to prepare for services, but now everything has been thoroughly cleaned, which is a good feeling. Next on our list of things to do is clean up the yard and plant grass around our new house. But we will accept the weather God sends us and take one day at a time.

Also, to some who had written and asked about the pumpkin cookie recipe a couple of weeks ago, the recipe was printed correctly. The cookie dough does not require eggs. Meanwhile, here is a good recipe to use up any leftover ham from Easter.

HAM LOAF
1 pound baked ham, ground
1 pound raw bulk pork or lean ground beef
2 eggs, beaten to blend
2/3 cup cracker crumbs or uncooked oats
1/3 cup Minute tapioca
1/4 cup milk

Dressing:
1/4 cup cider vinegar

1/2 cup water
1/2 cup brown sugar
1 tablespoon wet mustard
Yield: 8 servings

Have oven heating to 350 degrees. In a large mixing bowl, blend the ground ham with the ground pork or beef, both eggs, crumbs or oats, quick-cooking tapioca and milk. Blend thoroughly. Shape into a loaf and place in a shallow baking pan to hold it with a snug fit.

In a small saucepan, boil the dressing ingredients a few minutes, uncovered --the vinegar, water, brown sugar and mustard. Pour over the unbaked ham loaf and bake at 350 degrees for about 2 hours, basting occasionally. Dressing should become thick and syrupy.
(Post note: The ham loaf may be well done after an hour of baking, so a cook might consider boiling the "dressing" in the saucepan longer to make it syrupy, then pouring it on the loaf the last 15 to 20 minutes of baking time.)

APRIL 2007

With some warm weather finally, we planted some garden goodies this week. Now the last few days it has been rainy and cool. Still, we planted 20 pounds of seed potatoes and want to plant more. We also planted lettuce, radishes, peas and yellow and sweet onions and some flowers.

Once it dries off again outside, I'd like to plant some corn, green beans, red beets, cucumbers and zucchini squash. It's enjoyable to have the whole family working outside in the garden. The younger ones enjoy planting their own little garden in the soil at the opposite end of the where we're working. We also mowed our grass for the first time this spring. It had grown quite a bit already.

Friday evening we were surprised to see Joe's Uncle Solomon and Jake and his wife from Ohio come to visit. They brought Joe's Dad and brother, Noah, along also. Solomon brought us a big root of home-grown horseradish. We planted a few starts and then made horseradish with the rest.

It turned out really good, and we are enjoying it. Solomon gave us his recipe and I'll share it with you at the end of this column. We appreciated Solomon bringing us some horseradish, as I always wanted a start of it to plant.
On Saturday we had more relatives come visit us. My uncle from Mississippi and uncles from Geneva, Ind., came to visit. So we've seen a lot of family in the past few days. Nice to be able to get caught up with visiting.

With the spring weather, we are still enjoying dandelion greens. Rhubarb looks like it's ready to use and the asparagus is peeping through, so we'll have more springtime goodies to enjoy. I do miss my winter onions, though, and hope to get a start again soon on those.

I have been working on my mending, which accumulates so fast with eight growing children in this house. Rainy days like today give me a chance to mend. I have a button here and there that needs to be sewed on also.
Joe bought me a sewing machine about four or five years ago that will sew on buttons. That really makes it a lot faster to sew than doing it just by hand.

Kevin is so fussy right now. I think he needs a nap, so take care until next time.

UNCLE SOLOMON'S HOMEMADE HORSERADISH
horseradish root
½ c. white vinegar
½ c. water
1 t. sugar
Pinch of salt

Clean and chop horseradish root very fine. Combine vinegar, water, sugar and pinch of salt, adding only enough horseradish to make it the thickness you like. Store in sealed container and refrigerate or use immediately. Optional: Add more sugar or salt to your taste if you want to.

MAY 2007

Here's a diary of a day in this Amish household:

5:45 a.m. It's Monday morning and my husband, Joe, has the day off from work, so we slept later than usual. Joe helps me prepare breakfast while our five oldest children get ready for school.

6:30 a.m. We eat a meal of eggs, fried potatoes, bacon, cheese, toast, juice and milk. I fixed a bigger breakfast because Joe is home to eat with us.

7 a.m. Our five school-age children leave for school. We sat out on the front porch before they left while they ran around outside. Now that they are off to school, the three youngest are playing nicely with their toys. Joe helps me with the dishes. Then I gather laundry while Joe fills the washing machine and the rinse-tub with water. Joe puts the laundry through while I hang it up outside. It is a very nice day, and all three children are out, playing in the sand.

10:15 a.m. Had a big laundry, and the lines are filled. I sure was glad to have Joe's help. It goes much faster than when I do it alone. Now I'm helping Joe fix up a warm place for our 70 chicks that arrive tomorrow. They are only 1-day-old. Forty are butchering chicks and 30 are laying hens. They need 90-degree temperatures, and with the cooler mornings and evenings we've been having, we decide to make room for them in the back entrance of our old house.

11 a.m. While Joe finishes getting the feeders and water troughs ready, I check the laundry and take down about half of it from the clotheslines. It's windy and sunny, and the laundry is drying fast.

Noon: I make salad and sandwiches for our lunch. After lunch, we look at the newspaper while rocking Kevin and Lovina. Kevin falls asleep, but Lovina doesn't. She goes outside again with Joe and Joseph.

1:30 p.m. We discover that our dog, Frisco, is having her little pups. She has three, but the first is stillborn. Joseph and Lovina are excited to see the little pups.

2 p.m. Joe comes in to let me know the sky looks dark and it could rain. Just then, it starts raining and he helps me get the rest of the laundry in. We manage to get it in before it has more than sprinkles of rain on the clothes. I'm folding laundry while Joe does some work in the barn.

3:25 p.m. The children come home from school and are excited about the puppies. They come in to have a snack of cookies and milk. I help them get their homework done.

4:30 p.m. We all go help Joe tear down a little building beside our old house that we have wanted down. We had someone come level the yard, so it's almost ready for us to plant grass.

7:30 p.m. We have a late supper of leftovers from last night that sisters Verena and Susan sent over. It makes for an easy supper since we all need to be outside working as soon as possible. We had potato casserole, barbecued hamburgers, pork steaks and corn. Then we enjoyed the brownies that my daughter Susan made when she came home from school.

9 p.m. It's later than usual for the children to be going to bed. By the time they all have a bath, brush their teeth, and we have our prayers, it will be past their bedtime. It's been a long day but an enjoyable one as we worked together. Good night and God bless everyone.

Here is a good brownie recipe. Enjoy!

CHOCOLATE CHIP OATMEAL BROWNIES
1 cup butter, at room temperature
2/3 cup white sugar
2/3 cup brown sugar
1/2 teaspoon vanilla
2 eggs
1 cup flour
1 teaspoon cinnamon
1 teaspoon baking powder
1/4 teaspoon ground nutmeg
2 cups semi-sweet chocolate chips
2 cups uncooked oats, quick or old-fashioned
Yield: About 2 dozen

Have oven heating to 350 degrees. In a large mixing bowl, beat together the butter, both sugars and eggs until fluffy. In a smaller container, stir together the flour, cinnamon, baking powder, nutmeg and a pinch of salt, if you like. Blend all the dry ingredients and 1 cup of the chocolate chips into the butter mixture. Stir in the uncooked oats. Spread batter into a greased 9-by-13-inch baking pan. Sprinkle with the remaining cupful of chocolate chips (chopping them into smaller pieces first). Bake at 350 degrees for about 25 minutes. Cool brownies in the pan before cutting.

MAY 2007

We had a much-needed rain a few nights ago. It was our first rain since we had planted grass over a week ago. The garden was getting really dry also, so the rain was welcome.

To beat the dry weather, my husband, Joe, had been watering the garden and the lawn. We see little patches of green grass starting to peep through now. It'll be nice once we have grass around the house. The garden has had a boost, too, since the rain. Our corn, green beans, and potatoes are up now. We sure were thankful for that rain. After it dries off I'd like to put out more of my vegetable plants. I also would like to plant more corn and potatoes.

My daughter Lovina had her third birthday. It's hard to believe she's three already. I'll never forget how sick I was when she was born. I had pancreatitis and had to have an emergency C-section. When she was seven-weeks-old I had gall bladder surgery. I do not miss getting those gall stone attacks. I am thankful to have good health again. We will bake Lovina a little cake and put three candles on it. Over the past few weeks, she has kept asking how many times we'll have to sleep before her birthday. We will give her a little Amish-dressed doll and blanket for her birthday. It has crocheted booties and a bib. I know she will love it.

I had my 36th birthday. When I was a child I couldn't wait for another birthday. But as an adult it is different, and dread comes with turning another year older. And speaking of years, the children only have 2 1/2 weeks of school left and then the doors will close for another term. It sure will be nice to have the children home for the summer.

Little Kevin's asthma seems better this morning and we hardly give him any more breathing treatments. His pneumonia has cleared up. I think the cooler, rainy days have helped. Of course with him feeling better he is back into mischief again. But I am glad to see him feeling better.

For a special way to end the day, I have a roast in the oven for supper. It sure makes for an easy supper. I put a roast in and then potatoes, onions, and carrots. Then I put cream of mushroom soup on top. The children and Joe like roasts like that and I think it's easy to make. I will have salad and cake also. Susan is helping Loretta bake a cake to serve to her class. She is celebrating her summer birthday at school with her class before the term ends.

With school ending, this is a recipe that the children like over the summer and one that many readers request through the years, so try it and enjoy!

HOMEMADE SNICKERDOODLES
1/2 cup margarine
1/2 cup Crisco solid shortening
2 eggs
1 1/2 cup sugar
2 3/4 cups flour
2 teaspoons cream of tarter
1 teaspoon baking soda
1/4 teaspoon salt
2 tablespoons sugar
2 teaspoons cinnamon

Mix first four ingredients thoroughly. Presift the next 4 ingredients together. Add to the first mixture. Form balls (walnut size). Roll into mixture of sugar and cinnamon. Place about 2 inches apart on ungreased cookie sheet. Bake 8 to 10 minutes at 375 degrees. Cookies will flatten into circles as they cook. Store well in sealed container. Makes 3 dozen.

MAY 2007

We are enjoying green onions, lettuce and radishes out of the garden. Rhubarb and asparagus fixed in different ways remain on the menu, also. Those early vegetables are always a treat. Even 4-year-old Joseph and 3-year-old Lovina are eating radishes and onions. They ask for water, though, to wash the garden goodies down. They take a bite and then a drink of water. We have a few children who don't care for either onions or radishes, so I am happy to see Joseph and Lovina giving them a try.

We now have most of our garden planted. I still would like to put out some more corn, onions, radishes and cabbage. We are still watering the grass and gardens every chance we get. It is still very dry here, and we are in need of rain. Last night, Joe and brother-in-law Jacob put in 165 bales of first-cutting hay out of our field. It was a hot, 90-degree day, so it was hard work.

Last night was also the fifth-grade orientation at the school for my daughter Susan and for Jacob and Emma's oldest child, Elizabeth. Since Joe and Jacob were baling hay, Emma and I took our daughters to the school with us. The boys stayed with Joe and Jacob. We dropped Lovina and Kevin off at my sisters, Verena and Susan's house. Our second daughter is now ready for middle school. And our oldest daughter, Elizabeth, has two more years of school left. She wants me to home-school her for her last two years. I'm not sure yet what we're going to do, but if I end up teaching her at home, I could teach her German along with the other subjects. She has good grades, so I don't think it would be too hard to teach her.   (Editor's note: Amish children traditionally attend school until just the eighth grade. The United States Supreme Court upheld the practice in a landmark 1972 case, Yoder vs. Wisconsin. Where Amish kids attend school varies. Some attend public schools, others parochial, and home-schooling is becoming more popular.)

I had a nice 36th birthday on Tuesday. Joe grilled hamburgers, and the girls baked me a cake. They even put candles on it.
On Friday evening, we gathered with Jacob and family, and sisters Susan and Verena for my birthday with the extended family. Joe went to get one of those big ice cream cakes. And we had fried chicken, mashed potatoes, gravy, corn, salad, cheese, pickles, hot peppers, watermelon, rhubarb pie, oatmeal pie and chocolate brownies. After supper, we played games. The children also played a lot of jump rope.

A couple of reader questions. A reader in California, Ky., wrote in about cookbooks:
The: "Best of The Amish Cook, Vol. 1," "Best of The Amish Cook, Vol. 2," "The Amish Cook Treasury" and "The Amish Cook's Family Favorites" are each about 200 pages with plenty of recipes and stories. The set of four can be purchased for $65 (regularly $100); additional sets for $50. Special offer ends Sept. 1; all past and current orders will be filled by Sept. 15. Send order to: Oasis Newsfeatures, P.O. Box 2144, Middletown, Ohio 45042, or call toll-free, (877) 583-2059.
Anyone who orders a full set of cookbooks will receive a free copy of "The Amish Cook Family," a colorful, photo-filled coffeetable cookbook, when it is released in late fall 2007. Anyone with questions can contact Amish Cook editor Kevin Williams directly at kwilliams@oasisnewsfeatures.com.

A reader in Lyons, Kan., requested an asparagus casserole recipe. Enjoy!

ASPARAGUS CASSEROLE
1 tablespoon grated onion
1/4 cup chopped red bell pepper
3 tablespoons butter
3 tablespoons flour
1 cup milk
1-1/2 teaspoons salt
1/4 teaspoon pepper
3 cups cooked asparagus cuts
3 sliced hard-cooked eggs
1 cup shredded mild Cheddar cheese
1/2 cup buttered bread crumbs
Yield: 4 to 6 servings

Saute onion and bell pepper in butter until soft. Blend in flour then gradually stir in milk. Add salt and pepper; continue to cook, stirring, until thickened.
In a greased baking dish, alternate layers of asparagus with the hard-cooked eggs. Pour sauce over all, then top with the shredded cheese and buttered bread crumbs. Bake at 350 degrees for 25 minutes.

JUNE 2007

The children and I just had a light lunch of cold meat sandwiches. We had "Egg Dutch" for breakfast, which is pretty filling, so I decided that sandwiches would be good enough.

The temperatures are in the 80s now, but the wind makes it feel cooler. The sky looks like a rain could blow up, which we could really use.

My eldest daughter Elizabeth, who turns 13 on Thursday, and I did the laundry this morning while the rest of the children did dishes and swept floors. We have most of the clothes inside already folded. The wind makes the clothes dry fast.

We also did some hoeing and weeding in the garden and transplanted some wave petunias into hanging pots. Whenever my husband Joe gets around to putting more hooks on my porch I like to hang the petunias there. Meanwhile, a finch is sitting on five eggs in my hanging fuchsia plant. We try to be careful when we water it and not get any in her nest of eggs.

The older girls are rocking baby Kevin and Lovina to sleep for their afternoon naps. They are singing which sounds nice. They harmonize well together already at their young ages.

School doors have closed for another term. I can already feel that I have more help here at home. The girls did a good job in helping around the house this forenoon so I told them they can have the afternoon off.
We sold Frisco's (our rat terrier's) puppies this week. Joseph hated to see them go. He spent a lot of time with them while the other children were in school.

The recent rains have really helped our hayfield grow also, along with the grass and garden. Of course, rains also bring weeds out of the ground. Joe plans to run the tiller through wherever he can tonight, then we'll hoe the rest of the garden. I wish I had a small tiller that I could handle and would fit between the narrower rows. It would go a lot faster than hoeing. I still want to plant my third batch of corn, so that'll be more plants to tend to.

This past Sunday, we attended a sad funeral in Indiana for a 32-year-old Amish man that drowned in his pond. Our thoughts and prayers are with his wife and four small children. She will have many lonely days ahead.

Along with the sad event we also go to see a lot of family. We stopped to see where niece Elizabeth and her husband Paul live. It makes me feel older to know I have nieces married and starting their life together. We also stopped to say "hi" to sister Leah, Paul and family since they weren't at the funeral. Leah treated us with all kinds of snacks and sandwiches before we started for home.

I also got to visit with a good friend of mine while visiting in Indiana. She gave me this recipe, which goes good if you want something a little different, but simple, for supper.

JUNE 2007

Before the school doors shut for the summer, there were some fun activities. Six-year-old Loretta went with her class to the zoo, which was enjoyable for her. And Elizabeth received an award at the academic awards ceremony that marked the end of the year. So now the whole summer is ahead and I enjoy having their help around the house. Meanwhile, we still are all in shock over the drowning of a 32-year-old Amish man from the community where we used to live. As I wrote last week, we attended the funeral for him. We still don't have many details yet, but he left behind a wife and four children ranging in age from 4 weeks to 5 years.

Such a tragedy, but once again our Heavenly Father is warning us all that there is no certain age to die. Again we ask why, but we know he makes no mistakes so we need to leave it all in his hands. The deceased was a brother to two of our brother-in-laws on Joe's side of the family.

So just try to live every day fully. That is what we try to do in this household and our days have been full lately. Yesterday I processed 21 quarts of homemade rhubarb juice concentrate. This will make for a good homemade punch. All you have to do is add your favorite juices, soda or whatever you want. My sister, Emma, gave me the recipe, which I really appreciate.

I am not using mine this year yet as I just planted rhubarb last fall. Meanwhile, though, our horseradish is coming along good. As is our asparagus, which we transplanted last year.

We were blessed with quite a bit of rain, which has done wonders to our newly planted grass. The grass is looking better already. It seems a person can water it, but it's not the same as when it gets rain. The garden is almost dried off and needs hoeing and wedding. We sure are enjoying the homegrown lettuce, radishes and green onions.
Our hanging plant on the front porch is still providing a home for a finch. The children are excited and can't wait to see when the eggs hatch. I remember a finch making a nest in one of my mother's flowers one year. How exciting it was for the grandchildren to see the little birdies.

The children still are enjoying the first days of their summer vacation.

JUNE 2007

Before the school doors shut for the summer, there were some fun activities. Six-year-old Loretta went with her class to the zoo, which was enjoyable for her. And Elizabeth received an award at the academic awards ceremony that marked the end of the year. So now the whole summer is ahead and I enjoy having their help around the house. Meanwhile, we still are all in shock over the drowning of a 32-year-old Amish man from the community where we used to live. As I wrote last week, we attended the funeral for him. We still don't have many details yet, but he left behind a wife and four children ranging in age from 4 weeks to 5 years.

Such a tragedy, but once again our Heavenly Father is warning us all that there is no certain age to die. Again we ask why, but we know he makes no mistakes so we need to leave it all in his hands. The deceased was a brother to two of our brother-in-laws on Joe's side of the family.

So just try to live every day fully. That is what we try to do in this household and our days have been full lately. Yesterday I processed 21 quarts of homemade rhubarb juice concentrate. This will make for a good homemade punch. All you have to do is add your favorite juices, soda or whatever you want. My sister, Emma, gave me the recipe, which I really appreciate.

I am not using mine this year yet as I just planted rhubarb last fall. Meanwhile, though, our horseradish is coming along good. As is our asparagus, which we transplanted last year.

We were blessed with quite a bit of rain, which has done wonders to our newly planted grass. The grass is looking better already. It seems a person can water it, but it's not the same as when it gets rain. The garden is almost dried off and needs hoeing and wedding. We sure are enjoying the homegrown lettuce, radishes and green onions.

Our hanging plant on the front porch is still providing a home for a finch. The children are excited and can't wait to see when the eggs hatch. I remember a finch making a nest in one of my mother's flowers one year. How exciting it was for the grandchildren to see the little birdies.

The children still are enjoying the first days of their summer vacation.
(Editor's note: The recipe that was submitted with this week's Amish Cook was the same as last week.)

RHUBARB JUICE
8 pounds rhubarb, washed and cut up
8 quarts water
2 12 oz. cans frozen orange juice
3 cups pineapple juice
4 cups sugar
3 oz. box strawberry gelatin

Combine the rhubarb and water and cook until soft. Drain and add the orange juice, pineapple, gelatin and sugar. Stir until sugar is dissolved. Put into jars and process.

JULY 2007

I am writing this column while daughters Elizabeth and Susan are making us a breakfast of scrambled eggs and toast. I need to get this in today's mail so they are taking up the task of preparing the morning meal. It is nice to have them home from school during the summer. We plan to do a lot of laundry and general weekly cleaning today. We'd also like to go over to the old house and do some clean up.

We were blessed with a very welcome rain last night. Everything was really dry but now looks so refreshed this morning. It has cooled off a little giving us a break from the upper 90 degree temperatures. The high humidity has caused 22-month-old Kevin's asthma to fire up. We are giving him treatments and it seems to give him relief. Kevin slept good through the night now but had a very miserable day yesterday.

Tomorrow my husband Joe starts an eight-day vacation from his job. We are all glad to have him home and no schedule to follow will be a nice change.

Saturday we plan to attend the Coblentz reunion in Indiana. We haven't been to the annual reunion for three years. It will be enjoyable to see my uncles, aunts, and cousins again. Dad came from a family of 13 and he was the second oldest so there are always lots to visit with. Dad and Mom will be greatly missed as will two of our aunts. Life goes on and we must accept the changes that our "Heavenly Father" sends, although it's hard at times.

July is a month of birthdays in this household. On Sunday, daughter Loretta turned age 7. She and our son, Benjamin, will both be age 7 until he turns 8 on July 14. Then on July 24, Joseph turns 5.

Our garden seems to be doing well despite the dry season so far. We are now enjoying potatoes, peas, zucchinis, hot peppers and a few cucumbers. Radishes are pretty well over with for the year and red beets are nice sized already.

The five oldest children plan to take two weeks of swimming lessons in July. I am glad if they learn how to swim, especially after the death of the Amish man by drowning a few weeks ago in our old Indiana community. (Editor's Note: It is not uncommon for the Amish church to hold swimming lessons or hunting safety classes for their children)

We heard that sister Leah and Paul's oldest son, Ben, age 24, is in the hospital with pancreatitis. Haven't heard if he could come home yet or not. Sure hope he has a speedy recovery. On a more exciting note, we also heard the news of brother Amos and Nancy's oldest daughter Susan's wedding that will be held on July 26. So July will be a busy month.

JULY 2007

We are enjoying my husband Joe's vacation week. We have no schedule to follow, no certain time to get up in the morning. It's really nice for a change.

On Saturday, we spent the day in Indiana attending the Coblentz reunion. It had been three years since we attended and a lot of changes can take place in a family in that time. Everyone was tired from the long day when we arrived back home around 11:30 p.m.

On Sunday we mostly rested and celebrated Loretta's birthday with a cake and candles. She and Benjamin will now both be 7 for two weeks until he turns 8. Benjamin is always glad to jump up to the next year so he feels older than Loretta again.

We went to Jacob and Emma's for a barbecued chicken supper last Monday. The chicken was from what they had raised and butchered themselves, so everything tasted so fresh.

On Tuesday evening, Jacob and Emma and family and sisters Verena and Susan came for a haystack supper. The nearby town was setting off fireworks for the 4th of July holiday, which we can see in the distance from our house. We enjoyed sitting on our front porch watching the fireworks. They seemed really close by so we had a nice view of them. Also on Tuesday, July 3, Joe and Jacob and some of the children took our boat out on the nearby lake for fishing. They caught some nice bluegills and cleaned them when they got back here.

Everyone stayed here for the holiday night and then Joe and Jacob went fishing again early the next morning. When the men got back from fishing, we all had a big brunch of eggs, potatoes, biscuits, sausage, gravy, cheese, hot peppers, cookies, applesauce, milk, tea and juice. In the afternoon, we played kickball with the children, which was enjoyable. Even 3-year-old Lovina liked to kick the ball and be included in the game. We didn't count her points but she loved running the bases.

We made an early supper with a lot of garden goodies. Fresh potatoes, green beans, cucumbers, onions, lettuce and hot peppers were on the menu. Joe also grilled pork steak and we had cake and strawberries. All in all it was a well-spent Fourth of July.

This morning we slept a little later than usual. Now we have the wash lines filled with laundry while Joe is working in the old house tearing out the cabinets. We'd like to set them up in our basement. We are gradually getting the old house emptied as we'd like to start tearing it down.

The finch's little birdies have now flown from the nest in my fuschia plant. It was interesting to see them hatch and grow.

I have another zucchini recipe to share this week. My zucchinis are really producing right now.

ZUCCHINI PINEAPPLE BREAD
4 eggs
2 c. sugar
1 T. cinnamon
2 t. baking powder
1 t. salt

1/4 t. baking soda
2 t. vanilla
1&1/4 c. oil
3 c. fresh grated zucchini (I peel mine first)
3 c. flour
1 c. chopped nuts (pecans)
1 small can crushed pineapple in its own juice

Mix dry ingredients except sugar together and set aside. Beat eggs until light, then gradually add sugar. Add oil, vanilla and pineapple, then dry ingredients. Fold in zucchini and nuts. Bake in loaf pans at 350° for one hour depending on loaf pan size.

JULY 2007

Life is back in full swing again after my husband Joe recently went back to work after vacation. Plus, our five oldest children leave everyday for 2 1/2 to 3 hours of swimming lessons. Elizabeth is catching on fast and can swim short distances. I know even a good swimmer can drown but I feel safer knowing they can swim.
I never learned to swim and that makes me more scared of deep water. Joe sometimes takes the children fishing on his boat. Even though they wear life jackets, I'll be more relaxed knowing they can swim.

We continue to celebrate birthdays this month. On Saturday, July 14, we marked Benjamin's 8th birthday and on July 24 it was Joseph's turn. Joe and I celebrated our 14th anniversary on July 29. The years fly by and it is hard to believe we already have been married that long.

I finally got a card out to sister Leah and Paul's son Ben, age 24. He had spent a few days in the hospital for pancreatitis. I haven't heard too much about how he is getting along, but I hope he is improving.

We were invited to Brother Amos and Nancy's daughter Susan's wedding on Thursday, July 26. This is the third of Dad and Mom's grandchildren to get married. I've tried to answer some recent reader mail in today's column. A reader asked what kind of sewing machine I use. It is a treadle sewing machine, which has a variety of stitches. I can also make button holes or sew buttons.

A reader also asked if the Amish are allowed to have buttons on their clothes. Yes, depending on which community a person lives. In the one we moved from, the men and boys had snaps or hooks and eyes on their shirts, but not buttons.

Here in this community and all the surrounding Amish communities, the men and boys have buttons on their shirts. We don't have zippers in this community. Instead, we put buttons on the men's and boys' pants so there are always plenty of buttons that need sewed on. A reader was puzzled about why her dandelion green salad tastes bitter. Always use dandelion greens that do not have the flowers yet, otherwise they will taste bitter. The best dandelion greens are the first ones you see coming through the soil. Hopefully, next spring, this tip will solve your problem and you will enjoy them as much as we do. I also wanted to clarify for those readers who asked about my strawberry freezer jam recipe. The jam can be stored in the freezer for up to a year. You also can use the fruit of your choice with the same recipe for a different flavor of jam.

As I wind up this letter I would like to once again thank you readers for your encouraging letters and also the birthday cards. They were all greatly appreciated. It is your encouragement that gives me the strength to take time out of my busy life to write this letter each week. May God bless you dearly.

Here is another great way to use up your zucchinis if your gardens are producing as much as ours are. It is also something easy to make and our family loves them.

ZUCCHINI PATTIES
3 cups peeled and shredded zucchini
3 eggs
salt to taste

Just before you're ready to start frying, mix together the above three ingredients. Drop by tablespoon onto a preheated, buttered frying pan. Mash and shape into patties and fry until golden brown on each side. Top with a slice of cheese and serve. We like to eat these like this or also on a sandwich with lettuce, tomato and onions.

JULY 2007

All is still quiet and peaceful here at the Eichers this morning. I decided to write this column before waking the children. My husband, Joe, left for work a few hours ago, so there's not much activity in the household right now, which is a perfect time for writing. I'll start in on the laundry right after fixing the children's breakfast. There's always a lot of laundry to be done in this household, but today should be a good day for clothes to dry on the line.
Last night, we had pizza, cupcakes and root beer floats for son Joseph's 5th birthday. He was proud to get all the extra attention and to be allowed to choose the menu for supper.

Joe and I had our 14th anniversary on July 15th. How could these years slip by so fast? Mother's 71st birthday would have been on July 18th. Although she's not here with us anymore, we will always remember that day. Sister Emma had her 34th birthday on July 19th. We enjoyed barbecued pork chops for supper that evening.

My cousin William and his wife, Cathy, recently gave us a surprise visit. They live about 90 minutes from here.
On Friday evening, quite a few people from the community gathered to make 3,000 pizzas for a fund-raiser. The funds were to benefit a family in our church district because they need help with their hospital bills.

At the pizza event, four assembly lines with about 15 people on each line were kept busy. The "pizza assembly line" fund-raiser was held at the home of a church member. A lot more people were required to keep those of us on a line well supplied with ingredients.

I was helping on the "supreme" pizza line, and we also had a "meat-lovers" pizza line. The lines operated for nearly six hours, and there was work involved before and after, such as assembling the pizza boxes and cleanup.
It was interesting to see how all that worked, and it showed how many hands make lighter work. It is even nicer to go help when you know it's for a good cause.

Saturday was delivery day for all those pizzas. Fifteen drivers were hired to go deliver pizzas in this Amish church district and in other nearby Amish church districts. The task was beyond horses and buggies.

Daughter Elizabeth, age 13, went with sister Verena on Saturday to help deliver pizzas. Each van was loaded with 200 pizzas we'd assembled. Verena and Elizabeth left around 6 a.m. and came home around 5:30 p.m. It was after Elizabeth was home that she badly sprained her ankle. She has been getting around on crutches since Saturday evening. We were relieved when X-rays didn't show a break. This is so hard on her, as she is used to being active. Also on the injured list: My sister Susan was off work for a week after she hurt her hand at work. It became infected and swollen. She's still under a doctor's care, but has gone back to work.

We felt sorry that she had to go through pain after being gone all day doing a good deed, but such is life. It could have been worse, and I am thankful it was not a break.

Yesterday, the girls and I put up around 20 quarts of pickles. We are enjoying our first garden tomatoes and sweet corn. We were disappointed to see the raccoons had raided some of our patch already.

Tomorrow morning at 5 a.m., we start out to attend the wedding of niece Susan. More on that next week. God's blessings to all.

Meanwhile, try this strawberry recipe. (Post note: To avoid the risk of salmonella contamination -- a slight risk even in constantly refrigerated eggs in clean, uncracked shells -- substitute a pasteurized egg-white product for fresh egg whites.)

FROSTY STRAWBERRY SQUARES
2 egg whites
1 cup sugar
2 cups crushed fresh strawberries
1 cup whipping cream

Beat together egg whites, berries, and sugar for 10 minutes in a large bowl. Make sure the bowl is very large because the mixture will triple in size (if there's not a trace of fat or yolk from the eggs, beater or bowls).
Whip the chilled cream in a separate mixing bowl and fold the cream into the berry mixture. When well-blended, turn the berry mixture into molds or a pan and freeze at least six hours. Cut into squares and serve. Delicious!

AUGUST 2007

We have had an extra full house here the last two evenings because Jacob and Emma's four children have been staying with us. We are all excited to announce the arrival of a 5 pound, 7 ounce boy named Steven Jay to Jacob and Emma. He was born by c-section on July 30. He joins siblings Elizabeth, 10; Emma, 9; Jacob, 8; and Benjamin, 5. After five years this is such a welcome addition to the family!

We drove to the hospital with horse and buggy tonight to meet our new nephew and cousin. He is such a cutie! Our little Kevin hesitated about welcoming Steven since this is "his" Aunt Emma. Our 3-year-old Lovina was really proud and I think she's thinking of the baby as another doll to play with.

I am glad mother and baby seem to be doing fine and plan to be dismissed tomorrow evening. My daughter Elizabeth, 13, will help Emma with household duties for a few days. I know she'll do a good job as she is a big help to me.

On Saturday, we spent the day helping Jacob and Emma on some various jobs. Kevin fell asleep on the way home after playing hard all day. Daughter Susan carried him and rocked him and I changed his diaper and gave him back to Susan as he was still sleeping good. Shortly after that, Susan came running to me saying "something is really wrong with Kevin!" After not knowing what to do, we had a neighbor to call EMS and they arrived quickly. After doing blood tests and X-rays at the hospital they decided it was a seizure from a fever that had jumped to 106 in a hurry. The fever was caused from a viral infection. Kevin hadn't acted sick at all so it caught us by surprise. On Monday I took Kevin back to the doctor for a check up and he got a clean bill of health.

We were so scared as we never experienced anything like this. How small we felt. We know God was with us but would I have been strong enough in faith if things wouldn't have went the way our prayers went? We need to remember that our Heavenly Father cares for us and will never lay a heavier burden on us than we can carry. My children seem extra special this week.

Thursday we left at 5 a.m. to attend niece Susan's wedding. I was one of the cooks, so it was a busy job. They had two delicious meals with fried chicken on the menu.

We ended up back home shortly after 10 p.m. I didn't stay to help wash all the dishes. Joe needed to leave for work at 3:45 a.m. Friday morning so we hurried right after the wedding. We missed not having Jacob and Emma at the wedding.

I need to wrap up my writing today as I would like to can some hot peppers and pickles. My red beets are also ready. Meanwhile, here's a good recipe to use your peaches with this time of year. I made this the other night and the children really liked it!

AUGUST 2007

Our thoughts are in Holmes County, Ohio, as today the funeral is being held for Joe's 58-year-old Aunt Ruth. We regret that we were unable to attend. Our thoughts and sympathy, though, are directed that way this morning. Again, such an event is a reminder to us that God is in control. We do not know what lies ahead in the unknown future, but with God as our guide it is easier to go on. (Post note: Holmes County, northeast of Columbus, is home to the world's largest concentration of Amish population.)

Daughter Elizabeth is at Jacob and Emma's -- still helping out. She plans to come home tonight, and we are all excited about that. We miss her here at home, although I was glad to let her help my sister Emma after the birth of her new baby boy. Our children love to go visit the new baby, Steven, and would love to be there with him all the time. (Update from Oasis Newsfeatures: After Lovina wrote and mailed in this column, her 9-year-old daughter, Verena, took a nasty fall while playing outside at Emma's. She spent a night in the hospital and was diagnosed with a concussion and fractured sinus.)

Daughter Susan and I made a big batch of homemade salsa this afternoon, using our garden tomatoes. We also made some hot sauce because this family likes hot peppers, and we always plant those. Then we made a batch of peach jam. Susan also made a peach cobbler to go along with our supper tonight.

The "Quik Chef" from Tupperware really helped in chopping all the vegetables for our salsa. We had run out of our home-canned salsa, so this family will be glad to have some more. I would like to make quite a few more batches this month.

I also need to process some more homemade "V-8 juice." We enjoy that for breakfast. I put in jalapenos to make the blended vegetable cocktail juice more hot and spicy-tasting.

We have had rain every day this week in lower Michigan. We are so thankful for it because it is much needed. Everything was looking so dry. Now our grass looks greener. Also, our hay field looks more promising for a third cutting. Garden plants are doing better now, too. They had been withering in the hot sun and from the dryness. Another finch has a nest in one of my hanging Wave petunia plants on my porch. The four little birdies hatched a couple of days ago. The finches must think my porch flowers are a good, safe place for their nests.

With the canning season starting, I need to make a trip into town for canning supplies. I did 11 quarts of dill pickles and some hot peppers yesterday. Now I'd like to do red beets, once the garden dries up.
Meanwhile, try this recipe to use up some of those fresh peaches this time of year.

CREAMY PEACH PIE
1 cup sugar
1/2 cup flour
1/2 teaspoon salt
1/2 teaspoon cinnamon
2 cups half and half
6 to 8 cups fresh, sliced peaches or 1 (29-oz. can) sliced peaches, drained
1 unbaked pastry pie shell, 9-inch deep dish or a shallow 10-inch shell
Yield: 8 servings

Combine sugar, flour, salt and cinnamon in a small bowl and blend well. Add to the sliced peaches in a large mixing bowl. Toss to coat. (Post note: California fresh peaches are mechanically defuzzed before they go to markets, so you may wish not to peel the fruit for a rustic pie, or partially to peel them. If peeling the fruit completely, an easy way to slip off the skins is to dip them in boiling water for 20 seconds, as for tomatoes.)

To the peach mixture in the mixing bowl, add the half-and-half cream and blend well. Turn the peach filling into the unbaked pie shell with a standing rim. Protect that rim with crimped foil strips. Bake pie at 400 degrees in a preheated oven with rack in the lower part of the oven. Remove the foil strips the last 10 minutes of baking time. Total baking time may be 45 to 55 minutes or until the filling is set. Cool before cutting. Completely peeled apple slices can be substituted for peaches

AUGUST 2007

As I write this, we are halfway through the middle of August already. In a few weeks school will be back in session. Where did the summer go?

Nine-year-old daughter Verena is still recovering this week from a concussion she suffered after a bad fall last week. Ê I had to bring her to the doctor yesterday for her follow-up check-up. Since she was still getting dizzy spells he sent her to the hospital for a second CAT scan. It showed nothing worse so the dizziness must still be after-effects from the brain concussion she had. The doctor put her on antibiotics as she was also having a fever which he thought came from an infection in her sinus.

This morning Verena's fever is gone and she's able to stay up longer. I am so thankful that this wasn't worse. Verena will have to stay quiet for a week or so yet. No running or buggy rides which can really bump a person around.

Sister Liz, Levi and their four children were spending the day out here in Michigan when Verena fell. We had all gathered at Jacob and Emma's for a delicious barbecued chicken dinner. Levi's came out to meet baby Steven.

Joe and I stayed with Verena at the hospital on Saturday evening until Sunday afternoon. Sisters Verena ad Susan and Jacob and Emma took care of our other 7 children. Levi and Liz and family headed for home later in the evening. Ê They waited to start home until we had the results for Verena, which we appreciated.

It was nice to all be back home again as a family on Sunday evening.Ê Joe and I were tired from losing sleep at the hospital. Verena had to be woken up every hour to make sure she is OK. Sometimes she was sleeping really good and it was hard to get her awake. Once again God's protecting hand was over us.Ê

I made "hot wings" for supper last night. But I wasn't too pleased with the recipe I used.Ê The children, though, thought they were good. We have so many wings since we butchered the chickens. I am wondering if someone would have a really good hot wing recipe that they'd share with me?

Last night we also stuffed banana peppers with cream cheese and Velveeta. We then wrapped a piece of uncooked bacon around the outside and used toothpicks to hold it in place. Joe put them on the grill. They were delicious.

AUGUST 2007

It is a nice, sunny day after a thunderstorm during the night. We haven't had many sunny days in the past week, so this was a nice chance for things to dry out.

I had hung my clothes outside to dry on Tuesday morning, but then it started to rain so we had to quickly bring them in. Most of the clothes were still damp round the edges when we took them off the line. We hung a lot of the wash in the basement and Joe put a line on our covered porch to hang dresses, shirts and clothes that needed to be on hangers.

Then, on Wednesday, some of the children and I went to sister Emma's to help do her laundry. It was a nicer day and everything dried by evening.
Emma's baby, Steven, is three weeks old. We sure are enjoying him. Our little Kevin seems to be accepting his newest cousin and wanted to kiss him. We just make sure we give Kevin a lot of attention also. It is hard to believe that a week from Sunday Kevin will be two years old already.

Tomorrow evening we will go to sisters Verena and Susan's for a pizza supper in honor of Verena's birthday, which was Aug. 22.

On Saturday, Joe's family will get together to sell most of his Dad's furniture. He moved in with Joe's oldest sister and husband recently. It's so much nicer for him to be living with someone else instead of alone. His skin cancer seems to be healed so far. He treated it with a natural remedy. (Editor's Note: Embracing herbal and natural remedies are a big part of Amish culture. The mention does not denote an endorsement or opinion about the pros or cons of such treatment, but is merely a cultural insight. Kevin Williams, editor)

Last Saturday, we spent the day at Jacob and Emma's. Joe helped Jacob build a pump house for their pump and motor before the cold weather sets in. They still have a few finishing touches to do on it. Meanwhile, the girls and I helped Emma do laundry and some canning. Sisters Verena and Susan also were there.

Along with everything else, we are gradually working on getting the siding off our old house. We want to recycle it and hopefully it'll help a little with the cost of demolishing our old house.

I've had quite a few readers request a repeat of the homemade sauerkraut recipe I had in last year. Since this is "sauerkraut season" we are heading into, with cabbage ready in gardens, I will share the recipe again here.

SAUERKRAUT
Cabbage
Vinegar
Salt
Cold water

Shred cabbage and put in jars. Add 1 teaspoon salt and 1 tablespoon vinegar to every quart of cabbage. Fill jars with cold water. Put lids on and turn tight. Put in cellar for two months and then it's ready to eat. If you don't have a basement or cellar, store in a cool place.
(Editor's note: Lovina provided this recipe as an illustration of how they've made homemade sauerkraut in their family for generations. Only experienced canners should attempt home-canning recipes. USDA canning guidelines should be followed.)

SEPTEMBER 2007

t has been another busy day here at the Eichers. Besides working outside we processed 25 quarts of pickled red beets. These are the red beets we serve for the church meal when services are held at our place. I had a small dish of beets left that wasn't worth filling another quart jar. So the children soon emptied it enjoying the beets for a snack. They also thought it was fun helping skin the beets.

Children Susan, Benjamin, and Loretta pulled all the beets from the garden. We had some that were baseball sized. I only had one and one half short rows of beets planted so I was surprised to get 25 quarts.

Daughter Elizabeth mowed the grass while the other children hitched Stormy (our pony) to the wagon. They then used him to haul weeds and cornstalks from the garden out to the field. Doing the work with the pony helped make their work easier and more fun. Even our youngest, Lovina and Kevin, enjoyed the rides out to the barnyard and back.

This was the children's last week at home, so they were eager to get in as much fun as they could. Where has the summer gone to?

On Sept. 4, our school opened their doors for another term. Five of our children are in school this fall. Susan is in the fifth grade, entering middle school. Verena is in third grade, with Benjamin in second and Loretta in first. Then Joseph, age five, goes 1/2 day to a pre-kindergarten. This is to get them used to school and to learn the basics so they will be ready for kindergarten next year. It will also help Joseph get used to the English language as he mostly talks in German at home

My oldest daughter Elizabeth is a seventh grader and I will home school her. She wanted to, so I thought I'd give it a try. I will be able to give her German lessons this way. She'd also like to learn to use the sewing machine. She is a good student and has great grades so I'm not worried about teaching her. It'll probably help me renew a lot of the academic skills myself. I look forward to having her here at home with me.

My husband Joe will have a four day weekend coming up. He will keep working on preparing to tear down our old house. We also have our third cutting of hay to cut so if it doesn't get rained on it should be ready to put in by Saturday.

On Sept. 2 our "baby", Kevin, had his second birthday. He is sure a big boy, weighing 30 pounds, one pound more than 3-year-old Lovina. They keep each other entertained, playing and fighting for the same toys. After a "fight", though, they will always hug one another again. Such darling angels are a good example for us grown ups!
With carrots being ready in the garden, try this carrot pie recipe. God bless you all!

CARROT PIE
1 9 inch unbaked pie shell
3/ 4 cup sugar
2 cups chopped carrots
2 eggs
1 teaspoon ground cinnamon
1 teaspoon vanilla extract
3 /4 cup milk

Preheat the oven to 400 degrees F. Press the pie crust into the bottom and up the sides of a 9 inch pie plate. Bake the pie shell for 3 to 5 minutes, just to firm it up, then remove from the oven, and set aside. Place carrots in a saucepan with enough water to cover. Bring to a boil, and cook until tender, about 10 minutes. Drain water, and mash carrots until smooth. In a medium bowl, mix together the carrot puree, sugar and eggs. Mix in the cinnamon and vanilla. Gradually stir in the milk. Pour the mixture into the partially baked pie shell. Bake for 10 minutes in the preheated oven, then reduce heat to 350 degrees. Bake for an additional 40 to 45 minutes at the lower temperature, or until firm. Can be served as a dinner or dessert.

SEPTEMBER 2007

It is a dreary-looking morning. The sky is cloudy and I am wondering if I should do my laundry. We planned to wash curtains and windows today, but I will wait another hour and see what the weather will be. No sense in hanging things outside to dry if they are going to get wet again!

Susan, Verena, Benjamin, Loretta and Joseph left a few minutes ago at 7 a.m. to begin their school day. Lovina is still sleeping, Elizabeth is doing some writing and Kevin is playing with little toy horses. He tries to make them all stand in a row. Usually they keep falling down, but he keeps standing them back up. This keeps him entertained for quite a while. His asthma has been firing up with the humidity, so he had a bad day yesterday. We started giving him breathing treatments, and this morning he seems a lot better.

Joseph comes home from school around noon. He seems to like school but is a tired boy by evening.
Elizabeth and I prepared 13 quarts of V-8 juice on Saturday and managed to do a big laundry. Joe and the other children were working on cleaning up some of the mess around the old house.

Labor Day ended up being a busy one around here. Jacob, Emma and family and sisters Susan and Verena came to help us around here. We worked on clearing out the basement in the old house. We still didn't have everything moved over here yet.

Also, most of my canning jars were still over there. Joe and Jacob tore off some more siding while we moved the jars. The children had our pony, Stormy, hitched up to the pony wagon to help haul things away. Then in the afternoon, we put out 188 bales of hay in our hay field. This was a hot job. We put in a long day, but quit earlier to get the children all cleaned up before they started their first day of school on Tuesday.

Yesterday Elizabeth, Lovina, Kevin and I went to Jacob and Emma's to help them with some work. Elizabeth and I helped Emma do her laundry and processed 22&1/2 quarts of homemade V-8 juice.

Emma's baby Steven is 7 pounds and 4 ounces and is an active little boy. It's a change for Emma to take time to care for a little one after five years but she's enjoying it. We are sure enjoying helping to spoil him.

Kevin enjoyed his second birthday and is saying two and tries to put up two fingers. Such sweet blessings sent from our great God.
With all the tomatoes still available from the garden, try this quick recipe to use some of them up.

TOMATO PANCAKES
4 eggs, lightly beaten
2 c. diced home-grown tomatoes in their juice
40 Saltines
Salt to taste
Butter for frying

Combine the eggs, tomatoes, Saltines and salt. Shape into 4-inch pancakes and fry on medium heat in buttered skillet. Fry for about 2 minutes on each side.

SEPTEMBER 2007

This week finds a lot of the women in our area making homemade grape juice. A van-load from our church went to a "u-pick" farm to pick grapes and apples. We had a trailer along to put all our fruits in after we picked them.

It is a relief to be done processing the grapes, but I am so glad to have our own grape juice again. We got around 200 quarts of juice. Joe and the children helped take the grapes off the stems and wash them on Tuesday evening. The next day Elizabeth, 13, helped me put the grapes into juice. Now, today, Elizabeth will do two days worth of schoolwork. It sure helped to have her help me. She is enjoying her home-schooling, and I like having her home. She is also learning a lot of about food processing. The learning will come in handy as we have also apples here that need to be made into sauce soon. This winter, I'd like to teach her how to use the sewing machine and let her try to sew some clothes.

Next Friday is the upcoming wedding of niece Carol in Berne, Indiana. We plan to attend. It's nice that it's on a Friday and Joe won't have to go to work the next day. I am a cook at the wedding, and Elizabeth has to help serve the children's table.

On Saturday, our neighbors are having a "doughnut drive" to help a family in our church with hospital bills. Then the following Saturday, a family is doing a "sub drive" to help another family. For the sub drive, a lot of women will go the day before and help cut up vegetables. At 3:30 a.m. the next morning, people will gather to help put the sub sandwiches together. They will then have drivers to go deliver them in nearby Amish communities. With going to the wedding it looks like we won't be able to help out, but it is nice the way everyone helps one another out around here. Our new hens are starting to lay eggs. Twenty out of 30 are laying already and with the older hens we are getting well over 20 eggs a day. We'd like to butcher our older ones now so I can make and can homemade chicken broth. That's another thing waiting to be done on our "to do" list.

I took 5-year-old Joseph to the eye doctor for his first eye exam and he needs glasses. With myself included we now have seven pairs of glasses around here. All of us need to wear them all the time. I tried to get everyone a different frame or color so it's not so confusing.

Autumn begins this weekend. I noticed some of the leaves are changing color already. Gardens are also getting that autumn look.

Try this recipe as a good way to use some homegrown grapes.

GRAPE PIE

2 1/2 c stemmed blue concord grapes
Water
1 c sugar
1 tsp lemon juice
2 1/2 T clear jel (thickener available in stores)
1/2 c water
1 double pie crust, prepared

Stir grapes vigorously. For those who have electric blenders, you can put grapes in blender, adding enough water until 1" over grapes. Blend. Put through sieve to remove seeds and skins. Measure juice and add enough water to make 2 3/4 cup. Add sugar, lemon juice, and the clear gel mixed with water. Cook until thick, stirring constantly. Bake in a double pie crust at 425 for 25 minutes.

OCTOBER 2007

After a few 90-degree days, unusual for fall, we have had a cool morning of 50 degrees. Autumn has arrived and its evident with the leaves starting to change colors; some are falling.

We plan to do laundry today. Then I need to gather our clothes that we will wear to the wedding tomorrow of our niece, Carol, in Berne, Ind. It's nice to have all the clothes set out the day before. It makes getting ready early in the morning go a lot faster.

The five scholars (editor's note: a common term the Amish use when referring to school students) left a few minutes ago at 7 a.m. Five-year-old Joseph went to school for the first time with his glasses. I hope he will be careful with them.

On Saturday, we butchered our 21 older laying hens. This week I canned them into chicken broth. This will make good chicken noodle soup which the children and Joe love. Older laying hens are so different to butcher than broilers. It's easy to see why they say older hens make better broth.

Joe has been cleaning and tilling one of our gardens. I have green peppers and cabbage and flowers left in that garden. The other garden needs to be done yet. The only vegetables left in there are tomatoes and hot peppers. That's another reminder of autumn and the upcoming frosts.

The factory where Joe works is slowing down to four days a week. While he'd rather be working five days, it'll be nice for Joe to have time to get caught up here at home.

We have someone interested again in moving our old one-story house. They'd take it down the road and add it to their place for a garage. The siding has already been taken off, but they'd redo everything anyway. Hopefully in the next month things will start taking shape one way or another. We're glad to get done before the snows start flying. A reader has asked what a haystack supper is so I will run the recipe again. The ingredients are listed, but amounts not given because it just varies according to how many people you have coming. This meal is popular at the young people's gatherings because it's easy and you can adapt it to how many are coming.

HAYSTACK SUPPER

Soda crackers, crushed
Hamburger, browned, drained and taco seasoning added
Lettuce, chopped
Tomatoes, chopped
Green peppers, chopped
Onions, chopped
Spaghetti or rice or both (cooked until soft)

Put some of each on your plate, one layer at a time. Top with shredded cheese or a homemade cheese sauce. Also good to add is salsa or ranch dressing if you want to.

OCTOBER 2007

It is enjoyable to take a break from all the work around here to write this column. Right now, I am working at defrosting and cleaning my gas freezer/refrigerator. I also have bread and cinnamon roll dough rising. My husband, Joe, asked me the other day when I'm going to make another batch of cinnamon rolls, so that was a hint that I best make a batch. They never last long around here after I fix them.

Today looks like it's going to be another beautiful day. We had rainy and cooler weather the first part of the week. I treasure these nice days to get things done outside before cold weather sets in.

Last night, the girls picked about eight quarts of hot peppers from the garden. I canned some of them. I hope to make another batch of "V-8" juice yet before the frost.

Early Friday morning, we traveled to Berne, Ind., for niece Carol's wedding. They had a beautiful day. Afterwards, we stopped in to visit with my sister Liz, Levi and children. Then we also saw brothers Amos and Albert and their families at the wedding. Most of Joe's family were there, including his 93-year-old grandmother. She recovered quite well from the bone break she had. She keeps going and doesn't give up, which helps a lot.

While at the wedding, we heard the sad news of cousin Emma's husband's death. His name was Andy. Early this year, their 14-year-old boy was killed from getting kicked by a horse. Our sympathy goes out their way, and may God be with them as they go through this time of trial. They live in Salem, Ind., so we couldn't make it to the funeral. Our thoughts and prayers were with her and her family even though we weren't there.

Meanwhile, in this household, we've been battling illness. Three of the children were home from school one or two days, as they were running a fever. They are all back to school now, so I don't know if it was a short flu or something else. Yesterday, they had "Walk to School" day, which is a safety-training activity about walking safely, and 5-year-old Joseph missed out on it. He's ready to go back to school and excited to see his cousin, Benjamin, again, who is in his grade.

Now, I must get back to my work. I have laundry yet to do. It looks to be a nice day to dry clothes. Tomorrow, Joe will be home, so I imagine he'll work on the old house again. There is always plenty to do.

OCTOBER 2007

It is a cold, rainy October morning with the temperature down to 47. A brisk wind is blowing making it feel colder than that, though.

Last night the girls and I picked the last of the tomatoes, green peppers and jalapenos from the garden as I was afraid it might frost. It didn't yet but I'm afraid it won't be too long now before it does. We wore our coats and that wind still felt so cold. Joe and our son Benjamin were over at my sisters doing some repair work for them. It was such a rainy night. It was good to all be back together again at the end of the evening.

Now we have tomatoes to work up today. I will probably end up making more homemade vegetable juice as I have plenty of jalapenos and green peppers to still use up. I'll also can some of the jalapenos.

On Saturday, we spent the day at sister Emma and Jacob's house helping them with some chores. Joe helped Jacob put in a new hitching rack. It wasn't long before the little boys were tying their bikes up at the hitching rack pretending they were horses.

We also butchered 23 of their old chickens and cooked the meat off. We then processed 35 quarts of chicken broth. Emma also put some chicken meat in the freezer to use in casseroles. I think Emma was glad to have that big, greasy job done. Sisters Verena and Susan also helped.

Emma's baby Steven is such a sweetheart and doesn't lack attention when we're all there. He's 2 1/2 months old now. He really smiles and enjoys the attention.

Farmers were busy in the fields earlier this week getting their beans harvested. The corn looks like it is not too far off from being harvested.

Another thing that we need to do soon is order our hard coal for the winter months. We have some left from last year but it'll go fast once we start the coal stove. Our propane lights help a lot for a little heat on cool mornings like this.

Our stove is the basement and we heat our whole house with that stove. There's a big vent in the floor where the heat comes up. Then we have the cold air returns along the outside walls.

Joe hopes to get my canning room completed this winter and the shelves built for my canning jars. Everything, though, takes time.

I'll share my egg-in-a-nest recipe. My children enjoy this before leaving for school in the morning. Its fast, easy and I have a big skillet that can do four at a time. Enjoy!

EGG-IN-A-NEST
1 slice of bread, buttered on each side
1 egg
salt and pepper to taste

Take a glass and make a hole in the slice of bread. Then put bread in a medium hot skillet. Put the eggs into the hole. When the bread is toasted, flip over and lightly toast until the egg is cooked to your liking. Toast the cut out circle from the bread on each side also.

OCTOBER 2007

Today is Oct. 17, which would be my parents 50th wedding anniversary if they were still living. Sometimes I let my mind wander and wonder how life would be if they were still here with us. Then I think of our Great Heavenly Father and how He makes no mistakes. Why do I question His plans when I know "He" knows our future and has a reason for everything? Once again it reminds me of our human nature and how quickly we tend to question His ways. We need faith and prayers.

Joe's Dad had his 69th birthday on Oct. 8. We couldn't go for his birthday as a few of the children were sick that day. Hopefully we can still do something for his birthday soon. He went bear hunting recently with Joe's sister Mary Ann's husband, Jake, in Michigan's Upper Peninsula. We didn't find out how it went yet but know he was looking forward to it.

Nephew Ben Shetler, age 24, was published to be married on Nov. 15 to a girl from Wisconsin. Ben would be my parents oldest grandchild. He is my sister Leah and Paul's oldest child. Ben and Rose Marie plan to live in Wisconsin so this will make for an empty spot in the shelter home.

I was baking this afternoon which puts a nice smell into the air.. I put a roast and all the trimmings in the oven while I was baking so I'd have an easy supper. I baked bread, cinnamon rolls, apple pie and sugar cream pie.

We now have a big dumpster out beside the old house so things should start taking shape in the next week or so with tearing down our old house. Some neighbors are going to cart away half of the house for use as a shed. Joe still wants to take the chimney down in the part that the neighbors will move. Next we'll get all the windows out in the part that gets torn down. What a relief it will be to have the old house gone!

We've been mowing the yard and cleaning up for the winter the past few evenings. The children are already enjoying the leaves and work hard to gather them all up in a pile. They have fun covering each other up. It makes the job of raking leaves a little more interesting. We still haven't had a frost yet this fall.

As I write this it is evening and the rest of the family is sleeping, I think I will join them now. Good night!

HOMEMADE SUGAR CREAM PIE
1 c. water
1 1/2 c. sugar
1/2 c. flour
1/2 tsp. salt
1/2 c. butter
1 c. heavy cream
1 tsp. vanilla

Boil water with butter. Remove from heat. Mix sugar, flour, salt and stir into above mixture. Add cream and vanilla. Sprinkle with nuts. Bake at 450 degrees for 10 minutes, then 350 degrees for 40 minutes.

N OVEMBER 2007

We are now well into November. Today is brother-in-law Jacob's 35th birthday. We plan to go there tonight in honor of his birthday. His wife Emma will have pizza and ice cream and cake on the menu. We'll also bring along some food but I'm not sure yet what to make. I'll think of something.

My nephew Ben's wedding in Wisconsin is only two weeks away. We are making plans to go. I need to get some sewing done before then and make sure everyone's clothes are in order.

On Friday, Joe and Jacob are both off work so they plan to start taking the windows out of the old house. Also the chimney in the part of the house that will be moved needs to be taken down. Joe and Jacob then need to begin working on cutting apart the roof so we can start tearing down the section of the house that won't be moved. Our goal is to have it down by the end of next week. But we also have all sorts of other fall chores which need to be done around here. For instance, leaves need to be raked, firewood has to be carried and stacked, and plenty of laundry needs done. So far this week we've had nice sunshiny days. We did laundry two times already and would like to do more tomorrow if weather holds out.

Five year old Joseph just came home from school. He only goes until lunch time. It was an exciting day at school for Joseph. He had to furnish the snack today for his class, which was fun for him. He also had to take something for "show and tell" which excited him. The children take turns bringing the snack for everyone. I should have had this column done before he came home but time did not allow it.

Now Joseph is sitting beside me asking one question after another. His first question he asked before he had even closed the door: "Mom are we ready to go to Jacob and Emma's house?" I explained to him that we need to wait until the other children and Dad come home. This didn't make him too happy. Then he asked: "which horse we will take?" I told him we plan to take the 3-year-old colt, Ginger. He was even more unhappy at that answer as he doesn't trust her yet since she has had a few stubborn spells. He said 13-year-old Diamond is his favorite and he wants to take him. I tried to explain that Diamond used to be like Ginger, too, when he was her age.

A typical 5 year old but God grant me the patience to always take time to answer their hundreds of questions. After all my mind was churning on what I could write next when he came home. Well he just helped me finish the column. My world would seem empty without the children.

Let us pray that we will bring them up to always follow our Dear God.

With Thanksgiving now just a few weeks away, try this recipe for homemade stuffing which would go good with turkey!

AMISH POTATO-BREAD STUFFING
5 or 6 medium potatoes, cooked in their skins
1 cup milk
4 slices whole-grain bread
1 ½ tablespoons canola oil
1 cup chopped onion
1 cup chopped celery
¼ cup finely chopped fresh parsley
2 teaspoons seasoning
Salt and ground black pepper

Preheat the oven to 350 degrees. Peel cooked potatoes and place in a large mixing bowl. Mash the potatoes with 1/2 cup of the milk. Cut bread into half-inch cubes. Place these in a small mixing bowl and pour the remaining milk over them. Soak for several minutes.

While bread is soaking, heat the oil in a medium-sized skillet. Add the onion and celery and sauté over low heat until the onion is lightly browned and the celery is tender.

Combine the onion and celery mixture with the mashed potatoes in the large mixing bowl. Stir in the soaked bread, parsley, and seasoning mix. Season to taste with salt and lots of pepper.

Pour the mixture into a well-oiled, 2-quart baking dish. Bake for 50 to 60 minutes, or until the top is a crusty golden brown.

NOVEMBER 2007

Part of our old house is now torn down. Last Friday Joe and my brother-in-law Jacob worked hard to get the windows out, the chimney down and whatever else needed to be done. Our old house was a split-level, so there were two floors to work on getting taken down.

The one-story part is all that is left now and that should probably get moved next week by a local Amish couple that wants to convert that portion into a shed. With the house down I will have a lot better view of the road and surrounding fields. It will be really nice once the basement is filled in and everything is leveled out.

My garden frosted last Friday and now it's history for this year. I need to go out and pick and dry the marigolds and zinnia flowers. These make for cheap but pretty flowers from year to year.

The first really cold mornings also meant that Joe started the coal-stove in the house on Tuesday evening. The coal-stove, which is in our basement, heats the whole house by moving the warm air upward through ducts into all the rooms. On that cold Tuesday we had some snow flurries and it was windy. But the house was cozy and it felt good to have the warmth come through the vents from our basement.

We might miss out on seeing the last of our old house being moved as we plan to leave on Wednesday morning for Wisconsin. This will be a short trip. We'll return home on Friday evening. On Thursday, we will attend nephew Ben and Rose Marie's wedding all day. I will be a cook at the wedding, it'll be a busy day.

(Editor's note: For long-distance journeys like this one, it's common for the Amish to hire non-Amish van drivers. This is what the Eichers will do for the wedding trip.)

I don't know what job I'll be assigned until I get there. Usually at weddings, a paper will be hanging up on the wall telling the cooks what their assignments are. I always like it when they assign all us sisters to the same job. It's more time spent together. It seems like I get a different job at each wedding I go to. One time I got the mashed potatoes, another time the gravy. Other times I've been in charge of the pudding or the salad. Probably the hardest job is frying chicken!

We plan to start out Wednesday morning at 7:30 a.m. Our three other older children will come later in the day in a separate vehicle with my sisters Verena and Susan and Jacob and Emma and family. This will give the children another half day at school. We plan to all meet back together in Wisconsin Wednesday evening. We hope and pray we'll all make it safe and sound.

We won't start heading back for home until Friday morning. This will give the driver's a good night's rest before starting for home. As far as I know the rest of my family have plans to go too. I wish everyone safe travels.

I need to get started packing this weekend. Packing clothes for 10 people can be quite a chore but I enjoy traveling. It's always good to come back to "home sweet home" though.

Meanwhile, I've had readers ask for my sweet potato recipe. Try this one for your Thanksgiving meal!

CANDIED SWEET POTATOES
6 sweet potatoes, washed and pared
2 tablespoons butter
1 cup firmly packed brown sugar
1 ¼ cups water
½ teaspoon salt

Preheat oven to 350 degrees. Cut potatoes into cross-wise slices 1/2 inch thick. Arrange in a 2 quart casserole and mix in remaining ingredients. In a small bowl mix butter, brown sugar, water and salt until well-blended. Pour over sweet potatoes. Cover and bake at 350 for 40 minutes. Uncover and continue baking for 30 minutes or until potatoes are tender.

NOVEMBER 2007

We arrived home safe and sound from our Wisconsin trip around 6:30 p.m. Friday evening. We went to Wisconsin to attend the wedding of my nephew, Ben Shetler, and his bride, Rose Marie. The trip was long, but enjoyable. We started out on Wednesday around 8:30 a.m. It took a long time to get the van loaded and the little ones in their car seats. Between Albert's and us we had seven children ages 1 to 6 in car or booster seats. I thought the little ones did really well to travel that far. We only stopped three times on the way there and two times on the way back home. We had a good driver who knew the way there.

The wedding day was sunny, but cold and windy. The wedding was held in a "bank barn," which is built into a hillside for protection against wind and cold. A back entrance is at the second-floor level. Kerosene heaters also provided some warmth.

My job was the help make the salad for the wedding meal. Two other women were assigned to do that job with me. The salad was a tossed lettuce salad. We used maybe 12 to 13 big heads of lettuce and diced up a big bowl of tomatoes and had a large kettle of dressing. Other food served at the meal included fried chicken, mashed potatoes, gravy, noodles, dressing, cheese, homemade bread and vegetables. For dessert, it was pies, puddings, cakes, fruit and "nothings," which is a popular deep-fried pastry served at weddings back in Indiana.

It was good to return to the warmth of the motel that night. The younger children were tired and fell asleep right away. The next morning we took them to the indoor pool and they enjoyed the water. It was interesting to see how much more advanced they were in the water after taking swimming lessons this past summer.

Two-year-old Kevin acts afraid of the water, though. Jacob took 3-month-old Stephen in the water and he looked like he was enjoying it.

After eating breakfast at the motel, we started loading up for the long trip back home. Our 5-year- old, Joseph, and Albert's 4-year-old, Andrew, kept us entertained. One minute they were arguing with each other and the next minute they were saying "sorry" and that they liked each other again. If only grownups could be like this and forget so soon.

This is now Monday morning and Joe is back at the neighbor's woods trying his luck with deer hunting. He doesn't have any work this week. We will be glad when things pick up at work.

It will be the holidays soon and homemade fudge and other candies begin to find their way onto our menu.
Try this one for a delicious fudge!

CHOCOLATE FUDGE RECIPE
1 ¼ cups margarine or butter
3 (1 ounce) squares unsweetened chocolate
½ cup Karo light or dark corn syrup
1 tablespoon water
1 teaspoon vanilla extract
1 pound confectioners sugar
1 cup chopped nuts
Grease an 8-inch square baking pan.

Melt margarine or butter and chocolate over low heat. Stir in corn syrup, water and vanilla extract. Remove from heat. Stir in remaining ingredients until smooth.
Turn into pan. Cool and cut into squares. Makes 1 3/4 pounds.

NOVEMBER 2007

It snowed enough last evening that we have a nice layer of white on the ground. The children were excited to see it snow. Eight-year-old Benjamin and 5-year-old Joseph were outside after dark rolling a big ball of snow. They wanted to make a snowman but the snow was mixed with leaves making a dirty-looking snowman. Two-year-old Kevin just stood by the window watching the snowflakes falling. The boys were going through my storage totes digging out their snow-pants, mittens and other winter wear. We still don't have enough hooks to hang up all these extra coats. With all the children's coats, we have quite a big collection.

We had a nice Thanksgiving at my sister Susan and Verena's house. They prepared a big turkey stuffed with dressing, mashed potatoes, mixed vegetables, salad, cheese, pickles, tomatoes, sourdough bread roll, cheese ball and crackers, pumpkin roll, pumpkin pie, cake and ice cream.

After our meal, we spent the afternoon playing games. Jacob, Emma and family were there also. We had an enjoyable day there together. Let us remember to thank our Heavenly Father for all he does for us, not only on Thanksgiving Day but every day!

Joe has been trying his luck at deer hunting lately. On Saturday morning when Joe was back in the neighbor's woods hunting, we saw 14 deer running out of the trees and into our hayfield. We were wondering if Joe had seen them. But it wasn't long before Joe came out and said he shot a deer. We had some pretty excited children. The girls hitched our pony Stormy to the two-wheel cart and Joe and Elizabeth drove to the woods to bring the deer back. Now this afternoon when Joe gets home from work, we want to cut up the meat.

We are guessing that we'll be able to get around 65–75 pounds of meat from the deer. We need to have about 20 pounds ready for tonight for a man who will make deer sausage out of it for us. Sometime soon, we are going to go over to an Amish friend's house to see how she cans deer meat and makes deer bologna out of it. It sounds like you can just shake it out of the can and heat it and slice it. If I have enough meat left over, I'd like to have some steaks and then try my luck making deer jerky. I'll let you know how it all turns out!

Benjamin likes to go back in the woods with Joe to help watch for deer. He told Joe not to shoot the little "Bambis" though.

The men are here working on getting the house ready to move again. It might be able to be moved today yet. It is interesting to see how they go about moving it. It is sitting on skids in our yard.

DECEMBER 2007

Joe is still trying his luck at deer hunting. He has two more days left to hunt with shotgun here in Michigan. The snow we had is mostly all gone, but it's a cool 27 and windy. The snow made it a little easier to track deer.

Joe's successful deer hunt last week has given us some good meat. We cut up all the deer meat this week and now we have the tenderloin and some steaks in the freezer. The rest we chunked to have made into deer sausage. Are there any readers that would have a deer recipe to share? I'd like to try different ways to prepare the meat. One thing I want to try is making "deer jerky," as it sounds good.

We are invited to Joe's grandmother's birthday who on Sunday is will turn 94. We would love to go but she lives in Berne, Indiana and the trip back and forth gets expensive due to rising gas prices. The drivers have to charge more to make up for the expense. So we decided not to go. We do wish her God's blessings on her birthday and good health in the future.

It is hard to believe that we are already well into December. The holidays are approaching fast and all the family gatherings are being planned. Joe's family will get together at his sister's house where his Dad also lives on December 15 for brunch at 10 a.m. On the evening of December 14 we are invited to a Christmas gift exchange in our community. This is for all the Amish children in this area that are home-schooled. Our pre-schoolers also exchanged names as well. This gives the home-schooled children and the younger ones still at home something to look forward to.

On December 29 sister Liz and Levi have plans to have the Coblentz family Christmas gathering. Next year it will be our turn to have it here at our house. We are going in order of oldest to youngest as to who takes a turn to have it each year. The family has increased to a total of 63 now. My parents have four married grandchildren and two great grandchildren.

Three year old Lovina and two year old Kevin are playing with their rocking horse as I write this. They both get on it at the same time They can really entertain each other but they have their times when they both want the same toy at the same time. Then later on you'll see the same toy laying there and nobody wants it. Kevin comes to tattle to me but I can only understand some of his words. Lovina can entertain herself sitting at her little table writing with a pencil and paper. Although one day she decided to write on my wall which didn't make me too happy. It will be helpful to her when she starts school that she likes to write and color.

Elizabeth is outside doing the morning chores in the barn. I want to go add coal to the coal stove and then give Elizabeth her spelling test when she comes in. She's doing a great job in home-school although she misses her friends and teachers at school.

Readers have asked for my pumpkin pie recipe. This is good to fix during the holidays, or you can cut it out of the paper and save it for next Thanksgiving!

PUMPKIN PIE
1 cup sugar
1 tablespoons flour
1 teaspoon cinnamon
1 /2 teaspoon pumpkin pie spice

1 teaspoon salt
2 eggs, separated
1 cup pumpkin
1 cup milk

Combine dry ingredients. Add egg olks, milk, and pumpkin. Fold in beaten egg whites. Bake at 400 for 35-45 minutes or until toothpick comes out clean. Makes 1 9-inch pie

DECEMBER 2007

Monday was daughter Verena's birthday. She was excited because she made cupcakes to take to school and treat her classmates. But then school was cancelled due to slick roads and she was disappointed that she couldn't go. I told her that she could still take them the next day.

The younger children are all bundled up except 2-year-old Kevin and are having fun sliding down the nearby hill with their sleds. The sleds really slide nicely on this ice and snow.

Last Sunday, brother Amos, Nancy and children and their two married daughters came for the day. Also along with them were brother Albert, Sarah Irene and family and our sisters Susan, Verena, Emma and Jacob's and family. We ended up with about 50 people here for dinner. Joe grilled chicken for everyone and we also made mashed potatoes, gravy, corn and peas. Everyone also brought a dish to share, so we had salads and quite a few desserts.

It turned out to be a rainy day so we stayed indoors and played games in the afternoon. During the visit, I got to meet my new great-niece Lisa. This is brother Amos's first grandchild. This would be Amos's daughter Elizabeth's baby who was born Sept. 18.

We celebrated Verena's birthday on Saturday because we thought she'd be in school today. We fried some deer steak for her birthday. She is the one out of all our children that likes deer meat the best. I fried it like a "poor man's steak," which means I fried it down a little and added cream of mushroom soup and baked it. We also had French fries and ice cream and cake to celebrate.

My condolences go out to the three Amish widows who lost their husbands in a van crash last week here in Michigan. They will go through some trying times raising their young children by themselves. May God give them the strength to go on. A person wonders why so many young husbands were taken but it helps to know that God makes no mistakes and that he has a plan for each of us in life. Our sympathy also goes to the family of Joe's great-uncle Solomon Schwartz. We could not make it to the funeral but our thoughts were with them just the same.

Our rat terrier dog, Frisco, had four puppies on Friday. Joe fixed a place for her in the pole barn where there is some heat. Joe was afraid in would be too cold for the little puppies without a special spot fixed up for them.

Yesterday we had church services at our neighbor's house. And we all planned for the annual Christmas potluck supper in two weeks. This is something our church does each year. They pass around a tablet while us women are at the table and we all write what we will bring. Then they make sure we have enough of everything. I am bringing an "overnight salad." As the name suggests, you should make the salad the night before. Here is the recipe:

OVERNIGHT SALAD
6 to 8 cups shredded head of lettuce
1 to 2 cups of crumbled cauliflower
8 ounce frozen peas (quantity to your taste)
1/4 cup onion
1/4 cup carrots to your taste
8 ounces cheese to your taste
8 crumbled strips of crispy bacon
1 cup salad dressing (Editor Note: Miracle Whip would work well here)
1 /2 cup sugar

In a large bowl, cut and mix together the lettuce, cauliflower, peas, onions, and carrots. Stir together salad dressing and sugar and put on top. Add bacon bits and cheese last.

DECEMBER 2007

It is shortly after 9 a.m. as I write this. The school had a two-hour delay this morning because of the snow. We have drifts of snow everywhere, some up to four feet, from a storm that started Saturday evening. Daughter Elizabeth, 13, shoveled a pass to the road for the schoolchildren. They all went this morning except for Joseph, 5, who didn't have school today since he only goes in the a.m. He acted disappointed not to be able to go with them. Now he is singing "Jingle Bells" and his ABCs at the kitchen table. He is watching me write this column and wondering how I can write so fast.

With all the snow over the weekend it put us in the mood to start a 1,000-piece puzzle. It is a gift from my sisters, Susan and Verena, and daughter, Elizabeth. Elizabeth would like to glue it together and hang it in her room when it is done. It is an "Amish country" puzzle named "Flying Hammers," which shows a barn-raising scene near Mount Hope, Ohio. The workers are building a new barn to replace one that was destroyed by a lightning strike. We have completed three-fourths of the puzzle already with mostly my husband, Joe, Elizabeth and me working on it. This morning 2-year-old Kevin got upset and grabbed the puzzle, ruining about 12 pieces. We were lucky he didn't grab more of it. So far, he has done pretty well to not touch it.

Some friends gave us a "stow and go" puzzle wrap-up, so if you need to put it away for a while, you can do so without losing your work. While we were working on the barn-raising scene, the younger children had fun putting together 100 piece-puzzles yesterday. Putting together puzzles keeps them quiet for a while, and they have fun.
Today is deer opening season again to hunt for doe with a shotgun. I'm not sure if Joe will get too much time to go, but I'm sure he'll try to find time.

Friday evening we enjoyed the homeschool Christmas party at a church member's house. Since our daughter, Elizabeth, is homeschooled, we were invited to attend. Also, preschool-age children were invited. It was a carry-in supper, and there was plenty of food. After we ate, the children all exchanged their gifts. I am guessing there were 25 or more children to exchange gifts, including the preschoolers, who also exchanged together. Lovina, 3, and Kevin, 2, were both unable to go because they were recuperating from being sick. But Elizabeth had fun at the event, and it was nice to hear ideas from the other mothers on tips about homeschooling.

My sisters, Verena and Susan, came to stay with our other children while we were gone, which we appreciated. On Saturday, we missed out on the Eicher Christmas gathering because of the little ones being sick. I guess that is life with children, but they should always come first to us parents.

Everyone seems back to good health now, and I hope it will stay that way over the holidays. Benjamin, 8, was so excited to see the snow Sunday morning that he was out playing in it before it was quite daylight. He just loves the snow. Next Saturday on the 22nd, my husband, Joe, will have his 39th birthday. Only another year before he reaches the big 40!

THOUGHTS AND A RECIPE FROM JOE EICHER

It is hard for me to pick out a single favorite recipe, but I always think it is a treat to have cinnamon rolls or chocolate chip cookies. They both taste best right warm from the oven. Reading through Volume III I am sure everyone will know what my favorite breakfast is: eggs, fried potatoes, bacon, cheese, toast, and sometimes a glass of homemade V8 juice. I prefer side pork over bacon if we have some. My favorite pies are pecan and rhubarb. And I choose macaroni salad over potato salad. Here is Lovina's recipe for homemade macaroni salad:

MACARONI SALAD

3 cups cooked macaroni

1/2 cup diced carrots

1/2 cup diced celery

1/2 cup diced onion

In separate bowl, mix:

2 tablespoons mustard

1 cup miracle whip

2 tablespoons apple cider

1 1/2 teaspoons salt

1/2 cup sugar

2 tablespoons milk

Mix to rest and add more seasoning if preferred.

CHILDREN'S CHAPTER

Stories, artwork, and remembrances from the Eicher children. As of this writing, they are:

Elizabeth: 16

Susan: 14

Verena: 12

Benjamin: 10

Loretta: 9

Joseph: 7

Lovina: 5

Kevin: 4

-Thank-you Mother-

1.

Somebody so dear is praying each night
For wisdom to show us the way that is right
It must be our Mother, her love is so true
And her prayers waft to Jesus like a Rose's perfume

-Chorus-

Thank-you Mother, for praying for me...
For pleading for futures that we cannot see,
They call you old-fashioned, but your love is so true
And your prayers waft to Jesus like a Rose's perfume

2.

Please hold to the alter, don't ever give in...
'Til all of us children have been born again...
Then keep right on praying, so we will stay true,
We love you dear Mother, we're thankful
for you!

-With love,
daughter,
Elizabeth

-2009-

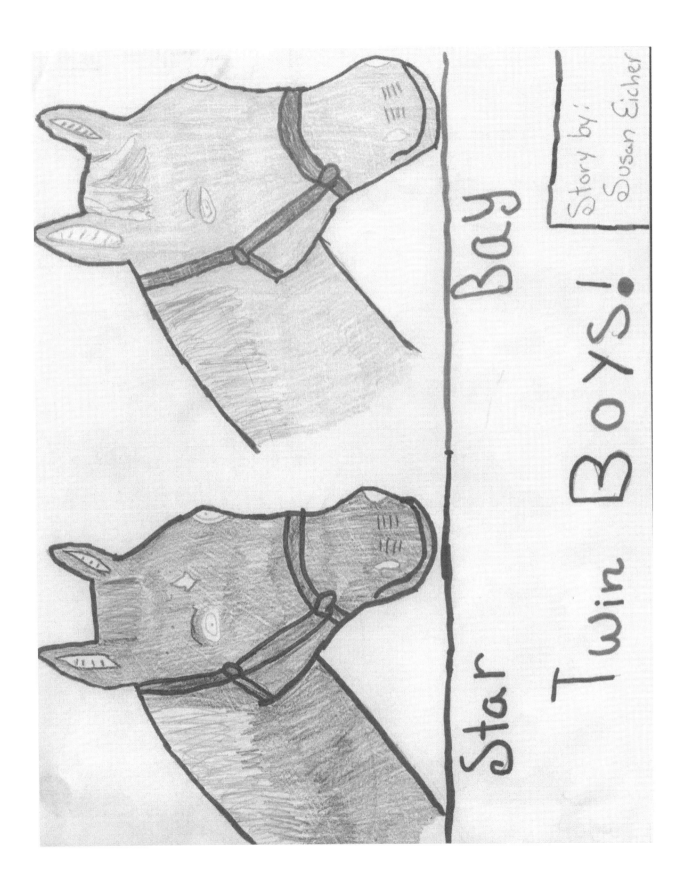

Twin Boys   by Susan Eicher
age

Twelve year old twins Joshua and Joseph were preparing for a race. They loved horses. Joshua's horse was named Star. He thought that was a great name for the horse because she was black with a white star on her forehead.

Joseph had a horse named Bay. Bay was a bay colored horse with a white tail and mane. Both boys wondered which horse was faster, Star or Bay.

"I think Bay is faster" Joseph said as they walked to the barn one day.

"Huh? You really think so? Joshua said with a grin.

"Yup" replied Joseph

"Well I don't think so" Joshua said and took off running for the barn. Joseph ran to catch up. The boys were close brothers but often argued which horse would win a race.

A big race was planned and a notice was put in the local newspaper. Both boys were getting more sure their horse would win.

One morning Star whinnied as Joshua came in the barn door. "How are you?" he asked her patting her back. Joshua grabbed a scoop of grain and poured it in the grain box in Star's stall just as Joseph walked in.

"What took you so long?" Joshua said smiling.

"Oh I was just taking my time" replied Joseph laughing as he got a scoop of grain for his horse too.

"You were just being slow Joe again" Joshua chuckled, "Just like your horse."

"Oh I think you better watch what you say. My horse will outdo yours by far. Joe teased back.

The next day the boys took their horses out for a practice run. Each were having their own thoughts about the race.

If Joseph thinks Bay will win

I think he's wrong. I'll show him Joshua thought to himself. I think Star runs so much faster than Bay when I ride her. It's like we're flying in the wind. We're a pair! She's the perfect horse he was thinking as he led her out to the track.

Joseph was also having thoughts of his own. Joshua is so convinced that Star will outdo my Bay. I'll just let him think that he's going to win the race. After running her around the track he brought Bay back in the barn, to put her back in her stall. What a beautiful horse Bay was. She ran with her head held high & took high steps with those long legs. Joseph loved watching Bay run when she pulled a wagon. Star was a pretty horse too and ran somewhat like Bay. But she didn't bring her hooves up as high as Bay. They were both attractive horses, but the question remained. Which could run faster?

4.

It was early Friday morning, the day of the race. Joseph and Joshua were ready for the race and could hardly wait. Jumping out of bed they ate their breakfast and ran outside. They wanted some time to spend with their horses before they had to leave for school.

With blonde hair flying and blue eyes twinkling they dashed out of the barn. "The bus!" Joseph yelled dashing after Joshua

"How long were was the bus waitig asked Joshua

"I have no idea, but I wish he would honk his horn. answered answered Joseph

After they arrived home from school they brushed their horses until they were all shiny. They brushed the horses tails and manes until it felt like silk.

"I'm finished! Are you?" Joshua whooped
"Yes!" Joseph answered.
"Let's go! I'll go tell Dad and Mom we're ready." Joshua yelled as he raced to the house.

Joseph grabbed Bay's halter and started towards the horse trailer. Bay snorted as Joseph patted her on the neck. He talked softly to her as he tugged on the rope and she walked onto the trailer. "See you could do it!" Joseph grinned. He loved that horse and she always made him feel proud. He closed the door as Joshua came walking.

"What in the world were you doing in there?" Joshua wondered.

"Putting Bay on the trailer," Joseph answered.

"So you really think Bay will win"

"I don't know."

"You think they might both win?"

"Yeah we'll go over the finish line at the same time. Joseph snickered

Dad came walking and lead Star into the trailer. "Jump in boys we're ready to go!" Dad said gleefully. Joshua and Joseph jumped into their friend's truck.

An hour later they arrived at the place where the race was being held. More and more people arrived as it came closer to the time for the race to start

"Five minutes until the race will begin." A man boomed over the intercom Joseph and Joshua got ~~settled easier~~ in their saddles. Joseph had a red saddle and a red saddle blanket. Joshua had a blue saddle and a blue blanket. The horses pricked their ears forward and nervously jumped at every sound. The saddles & blankets had been a birthday gift from their parents for their 12th birthdays. Star and Bay looked beautiful with the saddles on. Star stamped her foot and swung her head around impatiently. She was a little wilder than Bay. Riding to the starting line they waited for the man to say go.

At the sound of the man's voice saying "Go" the ~~horses~~ boys told their horses to go. They both started off at a full gallop side by side. Joseph leaned forward and urged Bay on. "Come on Bay Hee yah!"
Joshua leaned forward whispering in Star's ear "We can do it ~~Star~~
They stayed side by side until

Star tripped from running so fast. She stumbled but caught her footing before she fell and ran on.

Bay whinned when she saw Star pull up beside her again. Both horses ran for dear life, going faster than they ever went before. Dust flew, people cheered, but both horses didn't notice anything other than the race. Nearing the finish line both horses were side by side again. They galloped over the finish line at the same time. Joshua and Joseph slowed their horses down. Both weren't sure if one was over the finish line before the other.

Both boys were astonished when they annouced that it had been a tie and they had both won. Everyone was cheering.

Both boys were excited when they each received $150.00. As the man handed the money to them he told them to take the horses where everyone could see them.

They are so beautiful, yelled the crowd of people. Their parents came walking glad for the boys but also thankful they were both okay and that there had not been any accidents.

They loaded up the horses and headed for the hour drive home. That evening the boys gave both horses an extra portion of grain. They were both happy the race ended like it did.

Mommy I Love You

Mommy I love you
For all that you do.
I'll kiss you and hug you
'Cause you love me too.
You feed me and need me
To teach you to play,
So smile 'cause I love you
On this Mother's Day.

2007

Love — Loretta

Joseph 2010

You always clean the fingerprints
I leave upon the wall.
I seem to make a mess of things
Because I am so small.
The years will pass so quickly,
I'll soon be grown like you
And all my little fingerprints
Will surely fade from view.
So here's a special handprint
A memory that's true.
So you'll recall the very day
I made this just for you.

Lovina AGE-5

You always clean the fingerprints
I leave upon the wall.
I seem to make a mess of things
Because I am so small.
The years will pass so quickly,
I'll soon be grown like you
And all my little fingerprints
Will surely fade from view.
So here's a special handprint
A memory that's true.
So you'll recall the very day
I made this just for you.

Kevin Age 4

Made in the USA
Charleston, SC
21 February 2010